About the author: I live in Cumbria I have been writing for many years.

My novels are a mix of romance, drama & comedy.

My interests are music, writing, reading, theatre, films & travelling around the UK.

You can find me on Twitter AlexStone@glitter452

Also available by the same author

English Girl Irish Heart
Glamour Girl
Spotlight

Blurb UK Ltd
Highlands House, Basingstoke Road, Spencers Wood, Reading, Berkshire RG7 1NT

First published in Great Britain by Blurb 2022

Printed & bound in Great Britain

Life is a drag

*It would be the premiere of Polly's re-make of
Desperately Seeking Susan in New York in a month's time.
She couldn't wait she had worked hard on the film.
Polly knew she could never compete with Madonna's
performance in the original.
Which was a classic eighties movie but she'd tried her
best and loved doing the role.
Polly was now twenty seven even though she loved her
career family life was also important to her.
She wanted to have a baby she and wife Corey had a
daughter but they were thinking of having another child.
They had said they would wait a year or two Polly didn't
want to wait she loved her children.
Luke was now thirteen Marie was almost five a third child
would be perfect she also wanted to move to New York.
Ever since Polly had been coming to America for her
movie career she'd fallen in love with New York.
She seemed to spend more time in America than the UK
Polly knew she just had to convince Corey it was a good
idea to move there Polly was sure she'd say yes.
As Polly walked into their bedroom with a cup of tea
Corey was half asleep 'Cor it's me you're tired'.*

Corey had been working hard lately to promote the singles from her second solo album.

Which had done well in Europe 'I love you' Polly said.

'I love you too' Corey replied wearily that evening they were seeing a concert Polly was happy.

They would have a good time Christmas week was approaching Corey never looked forward to Christmas.

As long as her mother was around Polly wasn't happy either the dreaded Christmas visit from Marie.

The mother-in-law from hell Polly assumed since Corey had given her the ultimatum accept my partner.

Or stay out of my life Marie had to annoy her at any chance she could get try and ruin their lives.

Polly couldn't stand it anymore she loved Corey's biological mother Carol who was much nicer.

Polly thought Marie was a bad mother what person would leave her own child age seven.

To be brought up by a violent and alcoholic father she knew her own mother wasn't perfect.

That she'd spent years hooked on alcohol and drugs but at least she'd turned her life around was a decent person.

Marie was always trying to upset her split them up she'd never succeed their marriage was too strong.

They loved each other.

That Friday days before Christmas Marie paid a visit to their London apartment.

Another reason to move to New York she couldn't just come round if they lived on the other side of the world.

The idea sounded tempting to Polly 'so how's my favourite grandchild?' Marie asked 'fine' Corey said.

Looking over at her adorable four year old daughter.

'She's so pretty she's the spitting image of Corey I bet she'll be a model or something when she grows up'.

'Maybe a dancer' 'mam listen' 'yes Corey' 'I need to tell you something' 'what is it?' 'it's Marie she's autistic'.

'What?' 'I don't know why it's just something that happens it's no-one's fault' Polly said 'but she's so pretty'.

'So you're saying all kids with special needs are unattractive you know what did I expect from you!'.

Corey was angry at her mother 'I was just saying!'.

'Then don't! she has problems communicating showing emotion she doesn't like loud noises there's quite a lot'.

'I mean she'll have to go to a special school but there's no reason why she can't live a life like anyone else'.

'I do know about autism more than you do Polly!'.

'Everything will be ok' Corey assured her mother

'Got anymore film roles lined up? you were very good in that film' 'I Love Paris great actress' Marie asked.

'Not at the moment' Corey said 'can I have another cup of tea?' Marie asked 'we've run out of milk and sugar'.

Polly said hoping Marie would go soon 'I'll go get some'. Corey offered 'back soon' that was all Polly needed to be left alone in the house with Marie.

'I like this living room' Marie said 'I redesigned it to have a Moroccan feel' 'you like that sort of thing' 'yes'.

'About Marie having autism I'm sorry to hear that'.

'It's fine she'll be good with us' 'it is something you did?'.

'What do you mean?' 'did Corey drink take drugs?'.

'She doesn't do drugs not for years you know that'.

'Well you must have done something' 'are you implying this is Corey's fault?' 'no it's your fault'.

'Trouble always seems to follow you!' 'that's rubbish!'.

'I remember you at school going with men and women your teacher your step-mother's brother'.

'I was married to Andy! for five years it was a serious relationship'.

'If Corey hadn't met you she wouldn't have had a child with special needs' 'yes she would she carried the baby'.

'How dare you! so what if she's autistic it's not like years ago there's so much more help nowadays'.

'She still won't be normal!' 'you're such a bitch!'.

'I curse the day she ever met you!' 'why cause I'm a woman! or maybe cause I used to be a glamour model'.

'No because she can do so much better than you you believed your friend Romina'.

'When she showed you those photos of Corey with another girl' 'anyone could have fallen for those photos'.

'Maybe you were looking for an excuse to split up with her' 'as if! everyone knows how much I love Corey'.

'You believed your friend over your partner!' 'yeah well Romina was devious she wanted to split us up just like you! no-one will ever spilt us up whatever you say!'.

Corey soon returned Polly was angry Corey knew they didn't get on it was a bad idea.

Them even being in the same room together Corey couldn't stop her mum visiting even though she wanted to. If she said no she'd only leave messages begging to see her after she left Polly was glad 'I'm sorry ok' 'really'.

'Yes I never asked her round' 'course you didn't!'.

'Polly listen!' 'no I've had enough! the things she says'.

'I'm your wife and she doesn't care!' 'I know look she'll never accept us you know that'.

'Do you know what she said to me?' 'tell me' 'she said that it's my fault our daughter is autistic'.

'That it's something to do with me that I'm bad luck'.

'Like a curse' 'it's ok' 'no it's not!' ' maybe it's my fault
she's autistic' 'no Cor it's no-one's fault' 'but it might be'.
'I'm high functioning autism' 'what?'.
 'I was diagnosed as a child I don't tell many people'.
'Because I don't want to be treated differently'.
'Why did you never say even at school' 'I wanted to fit in'.
'I'm good at passing for normal it's just one of those
things' 'I'm glad you told me'
'It doesn't matter what she thinks ok just forget what she
said' 'how can I when she's always round here!'.
'I can't stand the woman even if she's your mum'.
'Oh god!' Polly sat down on the floor 'what's wrong?.
Corey asked Polly was struggling to breathe 'are you
having an asthma attack? I'll get your inhaler' 'help me'.
Polly was getting hysterical Corey was worried she
dialled 999 an ambulance arrived quickly.
As Polly was taken to hospital where she was given
oxygen to help her breathe.
Corey wished she'd never invited her mother round it was
probably her mother who had caused her asthma attack.
This was the final straw the next day Corey paid a visit to
the hotel where her mother was staying.
Where she filmed her BBC cookery show 'how are you?'
Marie asked as if nothing had happened 'fine no actually'.

'I'm not happy' 'why?' 'why do you think what you said to Polly!' 'I'm sorry I never meant it'.

'You said it was Polly's fault our daughter is autistic'.

'I know it came out it was a reaction I'm sorry she believed her friend thought you'd cheated on her'.

'When you didn't listen Corine you can do so much better than that tart you married!' 'Polly is not a tart'.

'So what if she was a glamour model it pays well and I can't do any better than Polly'.

'She is the woman I married my wife we love each other almost five years we've been together'.

'After you said those things to her she had a asthma attack' 'I know is she ok?' 'like you care!'.

'They gave her some oxygen she'll leave at the end of the day their putting her on medication so yes she'll be ok'.

Corey was angry there was no getting through to her mother she would always hate Polly.

She would just have to make sure she kept them apart.

Corey hoped she wouldn't have to see her mother so much in future as she always caused her stress.

Hopefully the next year would be better after the shock of finding out Douglas was her son not her step-brother.

Secretly adopted by her mother when she was thirteen.

He would be coming over the next day to see her Corey couldn't wait to see him.

Ever since she'd found out she was his mother she'd began to feel more maternal towards him.

Also because he was now fourteen they could have proper conversations she could give him advice.

They could have fun hanging out together going to the London Aquarium the London Eye go shopping.

Or they'd go to see a film Corey didn't see him very often.

Since he was at school but when she did she enjoyed spending time with him the next day Douglas arrived.

With Daniel her brother her mother was with them but at least she got to see Douglas.

Corey was pleased to see them and Polly as they all chilled out in the living room.

There was only a few days to go before Christmas.

Corey and Polly were happy they both loved to be surrounded by family.

'Douglas can't see Status Quo with you' Marie said.

'Why not?' Corey asked 'it's January school time'.

'It's just one night mam' 'I know but Douglas is hardly gonna go to London for one day'.

'I'm not having his education suffer' 'it's one night'.

'I don't care he's not going!' Corey ignored her mother.

As she chatted to Douglas 'don't worry ok we'll go to a concert in February' Marie gave her a look.

Polly knew why she didn't want him to go to the concert it was because she was jealous of Corey.

And her close relationship with him she really was vicious and bitter 'I think we should all go to a concert'.

'When Douglas has time off school' Corey smiled at Daniel grateful 'how are you?' Daniel asked Polly.

'Great you?' 'I'm grand' 'got a girlfriend?' 'no there was someone just dating' 'you'll find someone soon'.

'I hope so if only you weren't a lesbian' Daniel smiled at Polly she knew he'd always had a crush on her.

'Well I am' 'stop hitting on my wife' Corey said joking.

'I'll try not to' it would have been a perfect family evening if Marie hadn't been there to ruin things as usual.

Around 9pm they got ready to leave 'I've had a great time I'll see you Christmas Day' Marie said.

'You're not invited!' Polly said remembering how every time they had dinner with her she ruined the atmosphere.

The last time she had constantly complained about Polly's cooking 'what?' 'you heard Dan and Douglas can come'.

'But you're not invited' 'Corey might have something to say about that!' 'this is my apartment!'.

'And you're not welcome here!' 'Corey!' 'Polly's right'.

'It's her house sorry mam' 'fine have a good Christmas'.
'Oh we'll have a great Christmas' Polly said 'bye sis and you Polly' Daniel said 'thanks' 'bye Dougie'.
'Text me' Corey said 'bye' she said missing them already.
'Thank god! she's gone!' 'Polly!' 'your mother drives me up the wall I've just had a asthma attack'.
'I don't want another one she's not welcome here!'.
'No means no!' 'I agree with you' 'really' 'yes you've given her enough chances to make peace'.
'For us all to get along' 'I feel the same way this is your house you can invite who you like'.
'Actually it's our house' 'I know I can't stand her anymore I don't want her ruining our Christmas'.
'She won't anymore because she won't be here' Corey said 'do you still feel ill?' 'I've got my medication'.
'I'll look after you' 'I know I love you darling'.
'What would I do without you? Cor' 'yes' 'I can't wait for us to have another baby' 'me neither in a year or two'.
'I was hoping sooner' 'maybe the band's recording our third album' 'you don't have to get pregnant I will'.
'I'm taking time off work' 'we'll have a baby'.
'I've promised we will' 'great love you' 'love you too'.
They kissed Polly couldn't wait to have another baby.
She was happy with their family.

But a new baby would be perfect even better Marie
wouldn't be there to ruin their Christmas.

The next day she left messages on their phone pleading to
be invited for Christmas dinner Polly deleted them all.

As planned Christmas Day was perfect her mum and dad
all the family she loved it New Year's Eve soon came.

They were spending it in Dublin every year they changed
it London one year Dublin the next.

Polly, Corey & Daniel went out together with Douglas
and a friend to a pub Polly loved it there.

As an ex-alcoholic she stuck to coke.

She also thought that since they were supervising
teenagers that at least one person should be sober.

Corey decided to let Douglas and his friend have some
alcohol they were underage but it was New Year's Eve.

One drink wouldn't hurt Polly was having a great time
even without alcohol.

She signed autographs for some people and danced she
was having the best night of her life.

They danced the night away waited for the clock to strike
twelve Polly decided to go see how Douglas was.

She could see he was unsteady 'how much have you had to
drink?' 'two or three' 'alright'.

Polly watched as he collapsed 'Douglas!'.

She was worried 'Cor' Polly called as she came over.
'What's happened?' 'it's Douglas he's ill I think it's the
alcohol' 'oh god! it's my fault' 'no it's not'.
'You only gave him the one drink' 'I know but it's enough!'
'it's ok I'll take him to hospital'.
When Douglas arrived at hospital turned out he was ok
he's just had one too many to drink.
Corey felt guilty for allowing him to drink she knew her
mother wouldn't be happy if she found out.
Of course she did Douglas told her accidently she was
angry and gave her a telling off.
Polly suggested they go see Status Quo as planned in
Dublin on January 9th despite what Marie had said.
Corey thought it would be a good idea they were staying
at Corey's house they lied to Marie.
Saying they were seeing a show at the theatre they knew
she wouldn't like it if she found out.
That night they went and had a great time at the show
Corey spent so much time playing concerts herself.
That it was nice to see someone else for a change
everyone had a good time.
The next day Corey received threatening messages on her
answerphone from her mother.
They'd bumped into Corey's Aunt Matilda at the concert.

An annoying busybody at the best of times who couldn't wait to tell her mum Corey was angry.

So she couldn't even take her own step-brother/son to a concert to have fun her mother had gone too far.

Corey had enough she decided she would try not to let her get to her a few days later she decided to go see her.

Hoping they could sort it out Corey knocked on the door Douglas answered 'hey is mam in?' 'I'm here'.

A stern voice said as her mother appeared at the door.

'Can we talk?' 'Douglas get to your room!' 'why?' 'do as your told! let's talk then' 'I'm sorry about what happened'.

'You gave him alcohol he's underage I don't care if it's New Year's Eve!' 'I know it was wrong ok'.

'I promise it won't happen again' 'and you took him to a concert without my permission!' 'I'm sorry!'.

'Your always sorry! aren't you Corine' 'I thought we'd have a good time and we did' 'he's too young!'.

'To be going out to rock concerts!' 'he's fourteen isn't that what teenagers are supposed to do'.

'He's got studying to do you want him to get a good job'.

'We did nothing wrong he's allowed to go out and have some fun with us it's just me Polly and Dan'.

'That's the problem I don't want him being influenced by your lifestyle' 'our lifestyle!' 'oh I get it now!'.

'Because we're a lesbian couple we didn't choose to be gay no-one chooses it it's a preference not a lifestyle'.

'Despite what you think of us!' 'well he doesn't need to be influenced by either of you!' 'oh come on!'.

'What's that supposed to mean!' 'you used to be a cocaine addict! an escort girl and the rest of it!'.

'That was years ago I was a teenager! I'm twenty seven now!' 'I don't care and that little tart you married!'.

'She was a glamour model Polly's a great person!'.

'I love her your just an evil witch!' Douglas smiled as he overheard their conversation.

He thought the same as Corey 'I warned you remember!'.

'That if you can't accept Polly you can't accept me and you wouldn't listen! you know I feel sorry for Douglas'.

'If this is what he has to put up with!' 'this is the final straw!' 'oh really mam it was the final straw years ago!'.

'Just because you're his birth mother doesn't mean you have any right to tell me what to do!'.

'I'm his legal guardian! I raised him not you I'm his mother!' 'I can't even spend time with my own son!'.

'He's not your son he's your step-brother!'.

'I gave birth to him! I'm his mam!' 'your not his mother you never were!' Corey said angry.

'You only saw me in the holidays and left me with my alcoholic father! who beat me and Dan'.

'Look at the marks on my back he beat me so hard!'.

'That wasn't my problem! he promised me he wouldn't touch you this is about Douglas!'.

'And you always trying to undermine me!' 'I do not!'.

'You do! you went behind my back! not once twice!'.

'It won't happen again we were having fun' 'too late I've made up my mind!' 'about what?'.

'I don't want you or Polly seeing Douglas anymore'.

'What you can't?' 'I can and I will!' 'you can't stop me seeing him!' 'I can do as I please'.

'Now please leave my house!' 'you can't stop me from seeing him!' Marie slammed the door in Corey's face.

She was upset she was sure her mother was just jealous and didn't mean it and was sure she'd change her mind.

Corey wanted to see Douglas she couldn't stop him after all she was his real mother she looked up.

Douglas was at his bedroom window he opened it 'Corey'.

'Don't listen to mam' 'I'll text you ok see you soon'.

She waved he watched her walk home sad he wanted to see her he enjoyed hanging out with her.

The next day Corey flew home to London she couldn't believe it when she received a letter a week later.

*From a solicitor from her mother with a restraining order
she wasn't allowed anywhere near Douglas.*

*Else she would be arrested Corey panicked how could she
do that? maybe she could talk her mother round.*

*Get her to change her mind she didn't think it would work
they'd just end up having another row she called Daniel.*

*He always gave her good advice 'what can I do?'
she asked 'she is his legal guardian' 'I know'.*

*'She brought him up' 'I know that I didn't know he was my
son till a few months ago she never told me'.*

*'It makes no difference the fact that you were only thirteen
when you had him'.*

*'They'd just look at you as his step-sister also if she can be
this devious just think how she'd be in court'.*

*'Oh I can just imagine' 'the things she'd say about you the
things she'd use against you in court'.*

*'Drugs the fact you used to be an escort girl that you're in
a same sex relationship'.*

'And even the fact that you have high functioning autism'.

*'I don't do drugs anymore that's all in the past me and
Polly we're as stable as any married couple' 'I know that'.*

*'But in court everything would be magnified exaggerated
everything'. 'you're right but I love Dougie'.*

'He's my step-brother my son he gets on well with Polly'.

'I know I'm sorry I don't know how she can be so cruel'.

'I'll have a word with her see what I can do' 'thanks'.

As Corey put down the phone she hoped Daniel would be able to sort everything out.

She decided to concentrate on her career Polly felt sorry for her after she told her everything.

How could her mother do that try and stop her seeing her son days later Dan phoned her back.

To say their mother wouldn't change her mind Corey was so upset she tried not to let it affect her but it was so hard.

She was angry and couldn't believe her mother would ban her from seeing Douglas Corey loved being with him.

They'd become close when Polly was out she lay on the bed thinking how could she stop her seeing her own son?.

It was so unfair life could be cruel Corey continued as if everything was ok Polly knew she wasn't herself.

She knew why Marie had stopped her seeing Douglas because she was jealous of their relationship.

Polly chatted to Corey that evening trying to make her feel better 'Cor listen there's only one reason she's doing this'.

'Because she's jealous' 'I know that it doesn't make me feel any better' 'you can't let her get to you darling'.

'Yeah well she already has' 'this is what she wants'.

'how would you feel if someone said you couldn't see Luke anymore' *'I'd be heartbroken'* *'now you know how I feel'*.

'She's ruined everything' *'then don't let her'* *'it's too late'*.

'She already has mam's banned me from seeing Douglas my own son and there's nothing I can do about it'.

'There must be something' *'there isn't ok'* *'but she hasn't got a good reason to ban you she's just jealous that's all'.*

'She has plenty of reasons she can use I used to do drugs I'm a lesbian' *'so you don't do drugs now'.*

'They'll make me out to be some kind of out of control ex drug addict who's not stable enough to look after a child'.

'That's not true anyone could come round check on us see we're a happy family stable normal like anyone else'.

'Not in the eyes of the Irish law' *'what do you mean?'*.

'Us we're like second class citizens it's hard to even adopt a child as a gay couple' *'so we don't need to adopt'.*

'We've got our own kids' *'they don't respect us lesbians'.*

'They think it's not right I mean they have civil partnerships but it's not like in the UK'.

'They'd use it against me in court' *'so what does your sexuality have to do with anything he's your son'.*

'It doesn't matter but she's his legal guardian his mother'.

'I'm just his sister that's how it is' *'you can't let her win'.*

'I've got no chance against her'.

'But you have she's a sour old witch!' 'I haven't and you know it ok I love him so much!' 'I know darling'.

'We've always had a special bond I can't see him anymore I tried to text him I got a text back'.

'It was from mam she says he won't be texting me from now on she's given him a new phone' 'it's ok she's a bitch'.

'And she's gonna be sorry' 'thanks for making me feel better you know whatever she did I always loved her'.

'Not anymore I just can't she's ruined my life how can she be so mean?' 'you don't need her darling you've got me'.

'Daniel, Carol we all care about you I promise things will be ok' 'I hope so' 'it will trust me darling'.

Corey didn't see the point of fighting against her mother. She would never win that evening Polly made Corey a hot chocolate to make her feel better.

Polly however was happy her career was going better than ever her TV series Taste had been recommissioned. For a second series where she played a restaurant critic in the first series she'd let herself go a bit.

With all the food she'd been eating to prepare for the role. This time she was making the effort to lose weight and look good Polly was happy.

She was also doing a remake of Educating Rita for ITV. Polly couldn't wait and knew she was perfect for the role.

She'd been approached for the part before but had been busy Polly felt bad things weren't going so well for Corey.

She hoped by some miracle Marie would change her mind about the restraining order.

Maybe if they had a baby it might take Corey's mind off things she'd taken a break from movies.

And was just doing TV stuff Polly knew she and Corey made good parents they loved their children.

And decided she was going to have a child with her friend George.

Polly wanted their child to know who the father was and he wanted to have children with Jay his partner.

She decided to pay a visit to Blackpool to visit them George was happy to see her 'you're looking good have you lost weight?' 'I might have I feel better'.

'well you look great about you know is Corey ok about it?' 'George we've done nothing but discuss having a baby'.

It was a slight exaggeration but once she got pregnant she knew Corey would be happy.

'And obviously we don't have to have sex' 'thank god for that darling! you know I love you and you're gorgeous'.

'But it's only cock for me' 'I understand besides if I ever have to see another man's you know what'.

'I mean it was great between me and Andy'.

'But I never felt comfortable you know what I mean'.

'I understand so how does it work then?' 'my eggs your sperm easy' 'we go to a clinic?' 'yes'.

'I mean I got pregnant when I was eighteen it wasn't that long ago I know I had an abortion but it should be fine'.

'Well we can't wait to be parents can we Jay? and to have a mother as gorgeous as you' 'I can't wait to help you'.

'It might take a few tries oh and you can't tell anyone not even your best friends you know if the press find out'.

'Darling our lips are sealed but what's gonna happen when you do get pregnant and the press find out?'.

'I don't care the press always write about me anyway let's give them something to write about' 'Polly you're a doll'.

'It's fine really you're my friends anyone can see how in love you are' 'well let's do it then' George said.

'I'll make all the enquires oh I wouldn't ring Corey up right now 'I'm sorry to hear about her son'

'And what happened the other night' 'she'll be alright'.

'Well send her our love' 'I will' 'cup of tea?' Jay offered 'oh I'd love one' 'coming right up'.

Polly was happy it was all systems go she and George were having a baby she couldn't wait.

She was sure Corey would be happy about it it might even cheer her up days later she had an appointment.

At the clinic they gave her some fertility drugs to take the next day a story appeared in the media.

Saying she'd been spotted outside a fertility clinic Polly lied to Corey saying she'd gone with a friend.

Corey was busy in the studio and had to stay in a hotel for a few days because she finished so late in the morning.

A few weeks later nothing had happened Polly told herself it might take some time.

One day she turned up at the clinic for an appointment her consultant wanted to meet with her she was excited.

Maybe she could be pregnant he called her into his office 'Polly' 'yeah what is it? tell me I know it might take some time to ger pregnant I'm prepared to wait a few weeks'.

'Or months'' 'I have to be honest with you I don't think this is going to work' 'why not?'.

'I don't think you can have anymore children' 'but I had a baby at thirteen I got pregnant again at eighteen'.

'I was barely an adult' 'maybe it was luck your eggs well the chances of carrying a baby are quite small'.

'And if you did get pregnant there's a high chance you'd probably mis-carry'.

'If you wanted to have a baby you probably should have done it three years ago I'm sorry Polly'.

'I just wanted to help George and Jay start a family'.

'I know' 'I suppose I should be grateful I've got two children and don't be sorry it's just life'.

'Thanks for everything you did for me' 'ok well goodbye Polly' 'bye' she felt slightly upset as if she was a failure.

She hadn't felt that way for years Polly knew it wasn't her fault that it was just one of those things.

She remembered what she'd been told by a psychic once that she would have fertility problems.

Polly didn't believe her at the time she wanted another baby so badly she felt it would complete their family.

As she took a walk along the Themes river as she sat on a bench she felt sad was it the situation

Or the drugs she was on? she couldn't get pregnant and there was nothing she could do about it.

Polly phoned the next day to tell George and Jay the bad news she knew they'd understand.

They were lovely about it maybe things would be ok after all she opened the door happy to be home.

'Cor hi darling how's things?' 'what have you done?' 'going behind my back!'.

'I don't know what you mean!' 'maybe this will help refresh your memory!'.

Corey threw her fertility drugs on the sofa 'I'm sorry'.

'Really when were you planning to tell me you were planning a baby with your gay best friend!'.

'You know about George and Jay' 'we've discussed it before' 'no we haven't I said in two years time'.

'Not now I can't believe you lied to me!' 'I didn't lie about anything!' 'yes you did!' 'you know I wanted a baby'.

'I thought we both did' 'how can you be so devious!'.

'I wasn't!' 'yes you were and you know it!' 'alright I know I should have discussed it with you' 'well are you?'.

'Am I what?' 'pregnant' 'no' 'why not? I know it takes some time! good luck!' 'Cor! don't be like that!'.

'Like what Polly! my son is being taken away from me'. 'I have no visitation rights! and all you do is go on about having another baby!" 'it wasn't just for me'.

'It was for George and Jay' 'no you were being selfish'. 'Thinking about what you wanted I don't want another baby!' 'Cor listen please! if that's how you feel!'.

'I do how can you!' 'how did you find out?' 'George left a message on the answerphone'.

'What you did was wrong' 'why is it wrong? isn't it natural to want a family' 'we have a family'.

'You've only just found out he's your son he was your step-brother' Corey looked angry 'I'm sorry alright'. 'I know how much you love Douglas how close you are'.

'It's mam I never want to see her again the way she acts towards me the things she says' "it'll be ok'.

'I'm here for you 'what would I do without you' 'I'll make you a cup of tea' a cup of tea always made things better.

If only for a while that afternoon Polly felt guilty that maybe it was her fault for going on about having a baby.

She hadn't put Corey's feelings first and hadn't realised how upset she was about Douglas.

Polly vowed in future they would talk through their problems she would make sure she looked after Corey

Days later Corey felt better things would be ok Polly thought she wanted to help her

They chatted in the living room 'I'm sorry about everything I feel like it's my fault'.

'Going on about having a baby' 'it's ok we can have a baby I mean if it's what you want' 'no darling listen'.

'We can wait a year or two' 'so what happened when you went there? to the clinic?' Corey asked curious.

'I can't have anymore children' 'why? I mean you had Luke' 'I was only thirteen I had more eggs'.

'They've diminished over the years it's alright just one of those things I'm sorry about Douglas you know'.

'Your mother is a sly, evil, conniving bitch' 'I know'.

'It doesn't matter I can't see him I have no rights'.

'Says who?' 'she's his legal guardian I only found out a few months ago I'm his mother' 'so what darling'.

'You've always been close couldn't you see about getting visitation rights' 'I don't know' 'Cor he's your son'.

'I know your right and Dan's right but what's the point in going to court you know exactly what they'd say'.

'You can try can't you' 'yes' 'well then I'm sure Dan agrees with me' 'he said I shouldn't go to court'.

'Because they'd only use stuff against me' 'listen'.

'You can't let her win you've got to see your son'.

'You're right I have' 'well then' 'ok I'll do it I'll make enquires' Corey decided Polly was right.

Why shouldn't she fight to have access to Douglas after all he was her son she talked to Dan.

Who agreed she should try and get access Corey knew it would be hard almost impossible.

But she was determined to fight her cause she found out from Daniel he was just as keen to see her.

Corey waited till the beginning of March before taking action.

Polly was preparing for the release of her new film she was excited about the premiere.

Of her re-make of Desperately Seeking Susan in New York and another in London she felt like a proper movie star.

Polly felt on top of the world her career was going better than ever the film had got surprisingly good reviews

She knew Corey was angry about the situation with her mother Polly hoped Corey would get custody.

Or at least visitation rights that would teach her mother not to meddle in their lives anymore.

Daniel had been researching Irish law in preparation for the upcoming court case they chatted in his flat.

Corey hoped it would turn out ok 'usually the mother gets automatic guardianship but in your case it's different'.

'Since you only found out about six months ago'.

'I still love him he's still my son' 'I know but she's his legal guardian it's going to be harder than we thought'.

'If the father isn't married to the mother he's not considered but that's not an issue in this case'.

'If I brought Colin into this it would only confuse things even more besides Douglas doesn't know about him'.

'It says children have a right to visit with a non-parent'.

'What does that mean?' 'I'm not sure are you sure you wanna do this?' Daniel asked 'yes read on'

'Grandparents may apply' 'she's not his biological grandmother Carol is'.

'I don't think we should bring Carol into this it would only confuse things even more unless we have to'.

'I've just thought of another problem same sex marriages aren't legal in the republic of Ireland' 'I know'.

'They'll take into account your relationship with Polly .

'We're married we've been together five years'.

'She could use it against you you know it says the parent the child lives with usually gets custody'.

'And the other visitation rights' 'that's what I want'.

'Visitation rights I know my relationship our relationship with Polly and Douglas will be assessed in court'.

'I don't care she has no rights to take him away from me'.

'I know let's hope you get to see him' 'me too thanks for helping me doing all this research' 'it's fine'.

'You should have been a lawyer' 'anything I can do to help you your my sister' 'thanks'.

Two weeks later Corey was in court in Dublin her lawyer told her there was no chance of her getting custody.

And to go for visitation rights she agreed she didn't want to cause problems for Douglas.

After all she'd grown up with Marie as his mother she had to respect their relationship.

She just wanted to be able to see him as Corey entered the courtroom she tried not to be nervous.

Trying not to show any weakness to her mother she decided she would try and keep calm if possible.

'Right let's begin' the judge said 'please tell the court your
real name' the judge asked.
'Corine Carol Marie O'Hanlon' 'thankyou' her mother
was asked the same question they were ready to begin.
'So Mrs O'Hanlon tell me what is your relationship with
your son like?' 'we have a great relationship'.
'I've raised him since he was a baby six weeks old he's my
son I love him we're never apart we get along very well'.
'He tells me everything he also gets on well with his
step-father Clive' Corey knew it was a lie.
Douglas had told her before that he was scared of him she
knew she'd get her chance 'Corine...Corey'.
'Tell me what your relationship with Douglas is like?'.
Her mother's lawyer asked 'I always assumed I was his
step-sister then last year I found out he was my son'.
'I was only thirteen when I had him' 'how did you feel
when you found out?' 'I was shocked I'd been lied to'.
'How did you find out you were his mother?' 'uncle
Tommy told me at the pub before Christmas'.
'And how did Douglas react?' 'he was surprised like me'.
'But it didn't affect our relationship it made us closer'.
'You must have felt a maternal bond' 'yes I did I love him
as my brother and my son' her mother's lawyer stood up.
'Is it true your only asking for visitation rights'.

'Because you found out that he's your son' 'that's exactly why I'm asking I've always been close to my brother'.
'I thought you just said he's your son' 'he's both my mam over there is not my real mother'.
'But growing up she was the only mother I ever knew when she was around so Dougie's my step-brother'.
'Mrs O'Hanlon' Corey's lawyer asked 'why did you lie to your daughter biological or not?' 'she was only thirteen'.
'Her father my ex-husband was violent there was no way a child could have been raised in a house like that'.
'Were you together long?' 'seven years'.
'From the age of seven Corey and her brother were raised in a violent house regularly beaten'.
'And subjected to a drunken father of which she was aware of' 'no I was not'.
'He promised me he wouldn't harm the children and I believed him Corey told me a few years ago'.
'The truth of course I was upset' Corey knew she her mother was lying she'd never shown any emotion.
When she had told her at her wedding to Polly.
'Anyway what's this got to do with Douglas?'.
Soon the court was adjourned Corey was sad at her mother's lack of emotion towards her.
Had she ever loved her? Corey didn't think so.

She wasn't sure which side the jury was on 'you did well'
her lawyer Greg said 'really I was shaking inside'.
'You kept your cool' 'thanks' 'you can do it you know'.
Corey hoped so she wasn't sure the next day she was back
in court feeling more confident.
About getting access to Douglas she knew what to expect.
'Mrs O'Hanlon tell me what Douglas's relationship with
his step-father is like?' Greg asked her mother.
'They have a wonderful relationship they go fishing,
bowling, to the movies'.
'He's the only father he's ever known I'm the only mother
he's even known we're a solid family'.
'Tell me why your relationship with Corey broke down'.
'It was because of Polly' 'actress Polly Patterson'.
'Who Corey has been in a relationship with for five years'
'yes' 'tell me what happened?' 'I never could stand her'.
'Even at school she slept around men and women'.
'What's that got to do with anything!' Corey said angry.
'You'll get your chance in a minute continue' the judge
said.
'I never liked her but I was prepared to give her the
benefit of the doubt because she was with Corey'.
'Polly had an unfortunate childhood she grew up in care'.
'She used to be an alcoholic she went to rehab'.

'I saw her drunk so many times the amount of times I had to stop her New Year's Eve Christmas Day'.

'Any excuse for drinking and when there were children around' 'did they ever see her drunk?'.

Her mother's lawyer asked 'I saw her tipsy I saw her drunk her favourite was pink champagne'.

Corey was angry Polly had never been drunk in front of the children only once.

She only drank on special occasions 'so you weren't comfortable with her being around Douglas'.

'Or other children?' 'no I wasn't' 'does Corey drink?'.

'Only occasionally she has more restraint'.

'And she has to supervise Polly' 'Corey is Polly still an alcoholic?' 'she used to be she's been sober for ages'.

'In all the times we've been together I've rarely seen her drunk' 'so she's no risk to the children?'.

'No she's a great mother' 'is it true she regularly flies to America for her film career?' 'yes'.

Her mother's lawyer gave her a smug look.

'She's a successful actress that money will go to the children's education' 'but is she often away?'.

'From the children' 'sometimes' 'end of questions'.

It had been a more testing day Corey thought 'did you hear the things they said about Polly being a drunk?'.

'Saying she's an alcoholic she never drinks'.
'Corey listen don't worry' Greg said trying to reassure her
'she's trying to ruin everything'.
'She's trying to wind you up use anything to stop you
seeing Douglas whatever you do don't let her get to you'.
'I'll try not to' the next day was the final day of the case.
Corey had no idea which way it would go she was glad
that it would soon be over.
Polly and Douglas were present in court Corey had
confidence the judge would listen to them properly.
And take into account what they said and the wishes of a
fourteen year old boy Polly was called first to the stand.
'Please state your full name' 'Susan-Marie O'Malley'.
'Do you swear to tell the truth the whole truth and nothing
but the truth?' 'yes I do'
'Polly tell me what kind of a mother Corey is?'.
'She's a great mum she always puts the kids first she's
great with my son Luke our son'.
'She's great with Marie our daughter she's autistic she's
always on the internet researching the condition'.
'Seeing how she can make things better' 'how did you
react when you found out?' 'we didn't care life's a lottery'.
'Sounds like you have a nice family' 'we do we're really
stable and happy'.

'What about Mrs O'Hanlon's claims that you drink regularly?' 'it's not true I did used to be an alcoholic'.

'But since I've been with Corey since I was twenty one'.

'I've hardly touched a drink for five years'.

'Except on special occasions Corey or my mum supervise me I never have more than two glasses of wine or a pint'.

'I'm really strict I went to rehab a few years ago to sort myself out'.

'Now Mrs O'Hanlon aside from the drinking issue it seems these two have a very stable family'.

'So tell the court why you don't think your daughter shouldn't see you're her son?' the judge asked her

'I don't think Polly or her friends would be a very good influence on Douglas' 'in what way?'.

'Apart from the obvious situation of two women living together I don't approve of her friends' 'tell us more'.

'Her uncle Sam is gay very gay effeminate man I don't have a problem with gay men' 'could've fooled me'.

Polly said 'also her friend George another gay man a drag queen transvestite'.

'I would rather if Douglas turned out to be gay it was because he is not because he's been influenced'.

'By a certain lifestyle' 'I understand' 'are these men threatening or a danger to children in any way?'.

'I don't know them I just don't want my fourteen year old son around them at that age I'm very protective of him'.

'I understand your reasons apart from that are there any other reasons you want to tell us about?'.

'Polly or Corey shouldn't have custody of my son because I offer a stable home which I have done'.

'Since he was born' 'right now I would like to call to the stand the defendants son' Greg said

'Please state to the court your full name'.

'Douglas Michael O'Hanlon' 'now I just need to ask you a few questions it won't take long just tell the truth'.

'Tell me what your relationship with your mother Marie is like?' 'it's great she's the only mam I've ever known'.

'She nags me but I love her we're really close'.

Corey couldn't believe what she was hearing.

'Your step-father what about him?' 'we get on well'

'We go fishing together watch films' Corey knew Douglas hated his step-father he would never say those things.

Clearly he'd been made to say those things by his mother her heart sank she had no chance now.

'Tell me what your relationship with Corey your step-sister is like?' 'it's great we get on well'.

'What happened when you found out she was your real mother?' 'I didn't care I still love her it wasn't her fault'.

'She was only thirteen when she had me' 'Douglas are you happy with your mother and step-father?' 'yes'.

'Thankyou Douglas that will be all this jury will return on an hour with their verdict court adjourned' 'Cor'.

Polly said she looked upset 'I need to be on my own' 'alright I'll meet you in ten minutes' Corey walked away.

As she was angry and upset 'what's going on?'.

Polly asked Daniel 'I don't know' 'those things Douglas said about Corey' 'I know'.

'He's been put up to it by mam he would never say those things I know my own brother he hates Clive'.

'What can we do?' 'not a lot to be honest she won't get visitation rights now not all those things mam said'.

'Just goes to show some people will do anything to get what they want no matter what'.

'I'm ashamed to call her my mother' Corey returned a glum expression on her face 'don't worry sis'.

'She's out to get you' 'I know that and she's succeeded' 'she hasn't' 'she has she's taken my son away from me'.

'Turned him against me' Daniel put his arm around Corey 'I know Dougie and I know he wouldn't say those things'.

'She put him up to it you know that' 'that's what makes it worse using a fourteen year old child against me why?'.

'It's me she hates' Polly said 'if you were with someone else she wouldn't be doing this'.

'She'd hate whoever I was with that's what she's like'.

They all felt bad for her as they made their way back to court they knew what the verdict would be.

'A verdict has been reached by the jury after hearing all the evidence'.

'Mrs O'Hanlon Marie you've brought Douglas up all his life you appear to be a good mother'.

'Looking out for his best interests' Corey disagreed.

'The fact that you are not his biological mother makes no difference he also has a step-father who loves him'.

'Corey and Polly have a stable relationship but same sex marriages are not legal in the republic of Ireland'.

'Douglas is fourteen an important age in any child's life'.

'Any upheaval for no good reason would not be a good idea Douglas has also spoken to the court'.

'Said that he is happy where he is however Corey clearly cares for him so I am going to allow supervised access'.

'Supervised!' Corey said angry 'once a month for two hours the verdict is final court adjourned'.

Corey looked upset Polly thought it was all her mother's fault as they left she had a satisfied look on her face.

'Happy are you!' Polly said angry at Marie.

'Polly nice to see you' 'bitch! we all know you put Douglas up to it! he wouldn't say those things'.

'How do you know what he'd say I'm his mother'

'You're a cruel conniving bitch!' 'Polly leave it!' 'no Cor'.

'If you had any decency this would never have gone to court! she's his real mother she loves him!'.

'You've ruined their relationship!' 'she's his step-sister'.

'You only did this because you hate me and using a fourteen year old kid against us' 'have you finished now?'.

'I'm going to get my son mine not yours not her's!'.

'Your such a bitch!' Douglas was whisked away by Marie Corey was upset at what had happened.

'I hope he's satisfied all the money I spent on lawyers'.

'So I could get custody! for him to turn around and lie in court say what great parents they are!'.

'How he doesn't love me!' 'he does!' Daniel said trying to calm Corey down 'listen he was put up to it'.

'I knew I couldn't win with her!' 'don't be defeated Douglas told me he loved you'.

'That he wants to live with you he doesn't feel he can live with mam or Clive anymore he's not happy'.

'He never said' 'he's not allowed to talk to you she took his phone away'.

Corey couldn't believe what she was hearing.

'Anyway I told him the truth how you love him he loves you' 'I love him too' 'Cor don't worry it's ok'.

'It's her she gets to me' 'don't let her this is what she wants ok Clive threatened him told him'.

'He said if he said he wanted to live with you he'd beat him up' 'bastard! how can she use him against me Dan!'.

'You'll see him at the end of the month' 'I know thanks for everything'.

Days later Polly and Corey were back in London trying to forget about the court case.

Corey wished she'd never applied for visitation rights.

Two hours a month wasn't enough one day when Corey was out Rita Polly's best friend came to visit.

She hadn't seen her for a while 'cup of tea?' Polly offered.

'Go on stick us on a brew' Polly went to get the tea offering Rita biscuits 'how's things?' Polly asked.

'Not bad' 'tell me about the adoption?' Rita and Terry were planning to adopt a child 'we've been refused'.

'Why?' 'I don't know maybe because we're a lesbian couple' 'it can't be loads of gay couples do'.

'I don't understand' 'neither do I Sue we'd make good parents we don't smoke or do drugs what do you think?'.

'You helped bring up your severely disabled sister'.

'There must be a reason' 'now I know why everyone goes abroad easier' 'don't worry it'll happen' 'I hope so'.

'You and Terry will make great parents' 'thanks I know we will I'm twenty seven now I'm ready for it' 'it'll happen'.

'I know I've got it! the reason why they won't let you adopt maybe because you're HIV positive'.

'I never thought of that' 'it makes no difference' 'I know'. 'But some people don't know all the facts and they judge people you know'.

'I've known I've had it since I was eighteen I'm still here I'm not dead' 'I know but you know how hard adoption is'. 'In this country they'll use anything' 'but I'm fine I'm not going anywhere' 'I know darling don't give up'.

'You could try again London instead of Leeds'.

'Probably just the same' 'you can still try' 'alright I won't give up' 'good' 'so what happened?'.

'With the court case?' 'don't ask the bitch ruined it like we knew she would' 'I thought she would'.

'But isn't she out the picture' 'she's never out the picture'.

'You should have seen her smug as anything they slated Cor tried to make out I was an alcoholic'.

'Unable to look after kids course it was all rubbish don't you think social services would have called round'.

'Well I'm glad she's not my mother-in-law'.

'She sounds like a right bitch' 'she is she didn't like
Douglas being so close to Corey she was jealous'.
'Marie doesn't care what it does to Corey how much it
upsets her' 'can't you appeal?' 'maybe there's no point'.
'You know what it is' 'what?' Polly asked 'they view Corey
as his step-sister who's found out she's his mother'
'And has decided she wants custody' 'that's not how it is'.
'I know but that's how they view it they see Marie as his
mother who raised him add to that his step-father'.
'The perfect family then they look at you two a lesbian
couple even if you are married they view it as illegal'.
'So for Corey to get custody you'd have to prove she's an
unfit mother or he's a terrible father'.
'That he's so unhappy he can't live with them so unless you
can prove that you've got no chance'.
'You know you're right I never thought of it like that Cor
only wanted visitation rights'.
'She's only allowed to see him two hours a month
supervised he used to visit we'd take him out in London'.
'To the aquarium and the London Eye Douglas loved it he
can't visit us anymore Corey's house in Dublin'.
'It's really nice a great place' 'don't worry bad people
always get their comeuppance in the end'.
'I know you're right' 'trust me I am' 'what you up to?'.

Fighting spirit

'I'm going to church to light a candle for dad' 'I'm sorry'.
'I don't know what I'd do if my dad died' 'I miss him so
much' Rita looked as though she would cry 'it's ok'.
'I shouldn't cry it's a beautiful day' 'I think you cope with
it well' 'thanks I miss him so much our chats'.
'I've thought about seeing a psychic people say
I shouldn't' 'if you want to you should I'd come with you'.
'Really' 'yeah' 'alright I'll look into it I'll let you know'.
Polly enjoyed seeing Rita she was her best friend chatting
to her always made her feel better.
She couldn't imagine never having a dad although as a
child her dad hadn't been around.
Due to her growing up in care now they had a close
relationship she had her mum and sister Kaleigh.
And her half-sister Emily and step-mum Wendy Polly
loved her family.
That evening she decided to go to a lesbian club with
Corey and Rita.
Corey was promoting her latest single from her solo album
as well as working on a new album with the band.
Polly was concentrating on her business venture with her
uncle Sam re-inventing a closed down famous gay club.

In London she was loving it getting it ready to open to the public she was popular with the gay audience.

And now she wanted to give something back by making the club look as good as possible.

Sam had been a club promoter and knew what he was doing but Polly wanted to be able to put her ideas in.

For years she'd just done films now she was doing other things a clothing line, perfumes and she loved it.

That evening Polly was visiting the club they were doing it up as she sat in the bar area.

She couldn't wait to see what it would be like as she sipped a coke relaxing 'Polly' she looked over.

She couldn't believe it was Adrian her ex-manager who had ripped her off during her glamour modelling days.

By making her sign a dodgy contract then later tried to sue her after she became a successful actress.

What was he doing there? why couldn't he leave her alone to get on with her life 'what are you doing here?'.

'I read all about your plans you and your uncle Sam'.

'I read it in Attitude magazine' 'don't tell me you've come to offer business advice' 'maybe' 'then don't!'.

'Uncle Sam's been a club promoter for years and I think I have a pretty good eye for design'.

'You've done well for yourself' 'I know I have'.

'And everything I've done since my first film has been my hard work so don't you dare say you made me'.

'I won that Oscar BAFTA and golden globe that was all me' 'I know what can I say I underestimated your talent'.

'Is that your way of saying sorry?' 'ok I'm sorry for everything can't we just be friends'.

'Are you forgetting what you did to me making me sign a faulty contract you stole my credit card'.

'You ripped me off thousands millions of pounds you stole from me!' 'alright I admit it I needed the money'.

'I'll never forgive you for stealing my money I worked hard for that!' 'I'm sorry I was short of cash'.

'What about what you did to all those other glamour models? stole their money!' 'I'll pay you back one day'.

'How?' 'I've got a bar in Spain' 'you'll never pay me back and you know it! it'll take years why are you here?'.

'I came to see how you're getting on' 'just fine! I don't need your help!' 'do you still see George?' 'yes why?'.

'I'm opening up a drag club in London' 'he's happy in Blackpool why don't you do it yourself?' 'me in a dress'.

'You must be kidding! I do actually want to make money'.

'How's Corey?' 'you hate Corey' 'actually I've warmed to her I loved I Love Paris she's a good actress and singer'.

'I'm so proud of you all you've achieved and your sexuality you never wanted me to talk about it'.

'I thought it might affect your career and I was wrong you make a terrific lesbian' 'thanks'.

'So do you have an open marriage?' 'no I do not!'.

'I love Corey! it's not an open marriage she's the love of my life' 'ok calm down' 'what about you?' 'dating single'.

'It's hard now you know' 'why?' 'apart from the fact I'm an old queen I've got two kids to look after'.

'You are joking! you with kids don't make me laugh'.

'My sister died of cancer their eleven and twelve it's not like I'll be changing nappies I'm their favourite uncle'.

'You're sister's kids' 'yes' 'I'm surprised' 'well I had no choice it was either me or them go into care'.

'So that's the situation I'm not bad looking after them but it ruins my life I mean I can't bring boyfriends round'.

'Well that's a shame' Polly didn't feel sorry for Adrian.

'So can we be friends?' he asked 'are you forgetting you spiked my drink' 'it won't happen again' he assured her.

'You look good' he said 'thanks' 'you've lost weight'.

'I know I have I've taken up cycling' Polly informed him.

'Well it's been good seeing you again maybe one day we can be friends again'.

'Until then I'll admire your career from afar bye darling'.

Polly wasn't happy Adrian was hovering around the nightclub she wanted to forget about him.

Corey went home to visit Daniel in Dublin she always missed her brother.

As she arrived at her home she was happy she thought about Douglas how he couldn't come round anymore.

How if he did come to the house he had to be supervised two hours one day a month which had now been changed.

To every six weeks her mother could even appeal to get her banned from seeing him completely.

Corey had finally realised what her mother was really like cruel, mean, heartless a nasty piece of work.

It was too late she had what she wanted and had stopped her seeing her own son.

And there was nothing she could do Polly was right she knew she'd done it out of jealousy.

She couldn't bare to see her having a relationship with her own son Daniel knocked on the door.

As she let him in they hugged 'how's things?' he asked .

'Not too bad' 'glass of lemonade?' 'why not' Corey made poured them lemonade as they sat down 'what's up?'.

'I just miss Douglas our chats going out with Polly'.

'Like a family I know we've never had the perfect family but that's how I feel'.

'Like she's taken away our relationship she doesn't care'.

'Her lawyer destroyed me in that court room told Douglas what to say I hope she's happy'.

'She'll never stop till she's ruined my life split me and Polly up I hate her so much she's not my mother anymore'.

'To think I loved her for so many years she was so mean to Polly I guess there's nothing I can do' 'actually...'.

'What?' 'it's about Douglas he isn't living with mam'.

'Where is he?' 'living at his mate's Michael' 'what?' 'he couldn't stand to live with mam' 'why isn't he with you?'.

'I've got a new girlfriend she hates kids' 'he's fourteen'.

'It'll be fine' 'how is it fine! if social services find out he'll be taken into care did you think of that?'.

'I mean he's your nephew do you want him to be taken away so we'll never see him again!' 'course not'.

'Listen Cor I tried to talk to him his mind's made up he hates mam because she nags him tells him what to do'.

'He hates Clive you know that' 'do the courts know?'.

'Course they don't I haven't told anyone' 'this whole situation is wrong all because of mam'.

'Not wanting me to see him now look what she's done!'.

'Tell me about it' 'what can we do?'.

'Maybe you can talk to him I've tried' after tea they decided to go to Michael's house.

It seemed a nice enough district 'what if they find out I've been here?' Corey asked 'trust me they won't'.

As they walked up the drive knocking on the front door his dad answered he seemed nice Corey thought.

She'd met him once before 'Corey hi I wondered when you might come to visit' 'I'm not supposed to be here'.

'Don't worry I won't tell anyone' 'thanks can I come in?'.

'Come in the house is a bit of a mess' 'it looks fine really'.

Corey walked inside she thought it wasn't too bad except for too much brown and green.

And a golden and red Arabian style carpet.

She drank some tea as they chatted it turned out he was separated from his wife for a few years.

She was now with a younger man and he was bringing up his son on his own.

It was clear the house needed a woman's touch 'where's Douglas?' 'upstairs their playing on the Wii'.

'Go on up' she walked upstairs she heard shouting .

'Just another level!' 'Douglas' 'in a minute' 'answer me'.

'No just let me finish the level' Corey was upset Douglas was more interested in playing a computer game.

Than speaking to her she decided to leave it as she walked downstairs 'I'm going now' 'are you sure?' 'thanks'.

'For letting me visit' 'anytime'.

As they left Corey got into the car he looked up she saw Douglas peering out the window she gave him a look.

As they pulled away in the car he felt guilty he'd wanted to see her he hadn't realised it was Corey.

He loved her so much the next day Corey decided to meet Douglas in town with Daniel.

She would get to see him properly 'Dougie' she hugged him 'how are you?' she asked 'good' 'I've missed you'.

'And I'm pissed angry that you were too busy playing computer games to even speak to me' 'I'm sorry'.

'I didn't know it was you' 'who did you think it was?'.

'Michael's sister' 'it was me and do you know I was taking a risk coming to see you'.

'Mam's got a restraining order out on me and what the hell were you playing at in court!'.

'Do you know how much I spent on lawyers what happened?' 'I don't know' 'I thought you hated Clive'.

'I do' 'then why did you say all that stuff? how you like to go with him to the movies fishing' 'I'm sorry'.

'They made me say all that stuff I didn't want to'.

'They made me say that I loved Clive he said he'd beat me up if I didn't mam threatened me'.

'They made me promise to say those things that I loved mam' 'alright it's not your fault'.

'I didn't mean to have a go at you I am really happy to see you' Corey said as Douglas smiled 'let's go shopping'.

Corey said she loved spending time with him she had missed him they had a great time shopping.

Only half way through the afternoon Corey found herself hiding behind an ice-cream van.

After spying one of her mum's friends she wished she could see Douglas whenever she wanted like it used to be.

At the end of the day she felt sad 'I suppose you'll be going back to Michael's house' 'yeah' 'ok then'.

'I don't have a home' 'don't say that' 'it's true' 'so tell me you really couldn't live there anymore' 'no'.

'Clive's always angry shouting at me' 'did he ever hit you?' 'sometimes' 'the bastard! why didn't you tell me?'.

'I couldn't see you anymore I was scared mam would have a go at me' 'so you've had enough' 'yeah'.

'What did mam say when you left?' 'I sneaked out the house' 'what happened?' 'she went mad she came round'.

'Michael's house I was so scared she comes round shouting she said she's going to make me go home'.

'I feel safer at Michael's house' 'but their not your family'.

'It's ok Michael's dad says I can stay as long as I want'.

'Is it what you really want?' 'I'm not going back to mam's' 'what if she forces you to?' 'she can't' 'she can'.

'She's your legal guardian' 'I don't care I don't want to live with her'. 'If the courts find out they might put you into care' 'they wouldn't' 'they might what about Dan'.

'Can't you stay with him' 'he's got a girlfriend'.

'I'll try and sort something out' 'thanks' Corey thought about what Douglas had said and what she could do.

'Why can't Douglas live with you?' she said to Daniel.

'Lizzie doesn't like kids' 'Douglas is fourteen' 'you're his step-brother nephew he can't stay with a friend's dad'.

'It's fine if he's happy there' 'listen if social services turn up if the courts find out about this'.

'It's only a matter of time before he'll be taken into care'.

'I won't will I?' 'maybe' 'no-one will find out' Daniel said.

'How do you know all it takes is a teacher finding out someone rings up then that's it all over'.

'We won't be able to see you' Corey said 'listen Dougie's fine where he is' 'Dougie you won't tell anyone'.

'Where you are' Corey said 'course not' 'you need a stable family' 'he's got us' Daniel said 'we visit him'.

'We don't look after him Dougie I know your fourteen but you need someone to look out for you'.

'Make sure you go to bed on time that you've done your homework the courts gave mam and Clive access'.

'But their not doing their job' 'this is the next best thing'.

'I know he'd be happy with you and Polly but you couldn't get access' 'that was before'.

'The fact that he's living somewhere else' 'what if you got refused again then Dougie did end up in care' 'maybe'.

'I want to make sure he's brought up properly I'm sure Michael's dad is a nice man but he needs us'.

'To care for him as well' 'if you're sure you want to go to court again' 'I am Greg was a good laywer'.

'Does that mean I'll be able to live with you?' Douglas asked 'I'll try my best' 'you shouldn't make promises'.

'You can't keep' 'Dan I never make any promises I can't keep' 'you think you can get custody' 'I can try my best'.

That afternoon Corey said goodbye to Douglas as she returned home thinking about things.

Whether or not she could try again for custody would she win if she did try again? surely she had a chance.

After all clearly Douglas wasn't happy the fact that he was living at a friend's house the next day she visited again.

'So what do you think about me getting custody again trying living with me' 'would I have to leave Dublin?'.

'Course not I have my house here I thought you could spend the holidays in London'.

'Or I could get Dan to look after you joint custody' 'his girlfriend hates me' 'if she hates you she must be a bitch'.

They heard a knock at the door 'is Douglas here?'.
'No he's not!' 'don't lie I know he is!' Corey quickly
recognised the voice 'it's mam hide get under the bed'.
'I'll go in the wardrobe' Corey found a satin sheet just in
case 'where is he?' 'I told you he's not here!'.
'I'm gonna find him! take him home with me right now!'
Douglas lay under the bed hoping he wouldn't be found.
'Mam do you have to do this!' 'shut up Daniel! this is all
your fault!' 'mine how?' 'it just is!'.
'I know Corey's been round my friend saw you all in town
together very cosy! well you can tell her from me'.
'She's breaking the law!' 'tell her yourself!' 'is she here
then? Corine! I want words with you!'.
'Where are you then?' Marie went round the house
checking every room behind the sofa under chairs.
She headed upstairs as she checked under the bed luckily
she couldn't see Douglas she hadn't found him.
As she opened a wardrobe Corey was hiding behind a
long coat 'well wherever they are'.
'You can tell them they won't be able to hide from the law
for much longer! when the courts find out about this!'.
'What about when the courts find out your own son hates
you so much he's living with his friend!'.
'Why don't you keep out of this!'.

'If you weren't so jealous of Corey! none of this would
have happened in the first place!' 'he's my son!'.
'Grandson actually Corey's his biological mother'.
'I'm his legal guardian! her claim for custody was
laughed out of court remember' 'really'.
'Yes and you know it!' 'well I don't want anything to do
with you anymore your an evil bitch!'.
'Corey gave you so much more love than you deserve'.
'And you never cared you do everything you can to upset
her do you know what she went through'.
'That's not my problem!' 'well mam that's it then I can see
it's no good talking to you since you never listen!'.
'I will get Douglas back even if I have to camp out here
every night!' 'then you'll be arrested for trespassing!'.
'Don't you dare threaten me! I'm going!' Corey and
Douglas listened to the conversation as they watched from
the window as she drove away 'she's gone that was close'.
'Will she really keep watch on the house?' 'Dougie if she
does I'll be calling the police'.
'To escort her off my property' Michael's father said.
'It's all clear the witch is gone' Daniel said Corey was
relieved she was gone 'not long she'll be back'.
'She's determined to take Dougie away from us
I'm definitely re-applying for access'.

'I mean if I explain the situation they've got to listen to me Douglas needs a stable family life' 'your right'.

'I think you should try again for custody' Daniel said.

'Really' 'yes' 'ok then I will' Corey knew it wouldn't be easy she'd been turned down once before.

This time Corey knew had a better case so she consulted her lawyer about making a new case.

She wasn't looking forward to another court case but she had no choice she was doing it for Douglas.

So he could have a stable life on May 3rd Corey arrived in court in Dublin.

She didn't enjoy having to face her mother again as she gave her a look from across the court room.

Clive sat next to her Corey gave her full name as Greg presented her case and why she wanted custody.

'My client believes her son step-brother is not happy where he is with his mother and step-father'.

'She wants to give him a more stable life and she believes she and Polly can do that' 'thankyou'.

Her mother's lawyer stood up 'my client believes in her son's best interests to keep being a good mother'.

'As his legal guardian provide a stable family life with her husband as she has done over the past fourteen years'.

'She believes it is not in his best interests to live with her daughter who's partner could be a bad influence'.

'With her lifestyle' Corey couldn't believe yet again she was bringing Polly into it 'right let the case proceed'.

'Corey tell the court why do you think you should have custody of your son?' Greg asked.

'I don't feel Douglas is happy with the situation' 'why is that?' 'he doesn't get on with mam hasn't for a while'.

'He doesn't get on with Clive never has I want him to be happy I feel he could be happy living with me'.

'Has he told you he's unhappy?' 'yes I spoke to him I know I'm not supposed to be seeing him'.

'More than two hours every six weeks but when my brother Daniel told me about the situation' 'what is the situation?'.

'Douglas living with his friend Michael and his dad he's a nice man but I just don't think is right'.

'For a fourteen year old boy not to live with his family'.

'I agree your mother was awarded custody why do you think he has chosen to move out?' 'he wasn't happy there'.

'Can you explain more?' 'he told me he's scared of Clive'.

'That he's hit him a few times when he felt he didn't deserve it' 'has he always been violent?'.

'I wouldn't know' 'Mrs O'Hanlon is this true?'.

The judge turned to Marie 'no it's not true'.

'Are you aware lying under oath is a criminal offence'.

'He hit him once when he felt he deserved it we don't have a violent house my ex-husband was violent'.

'Douglas is probably lying' 'why would he do that?'

'Why not he lives with two parents why wouldn't he want to live with a young couple'.

'The freedom to do whatever he likes what child wouldn't want that' 'why has your relationship broken down?'.

'It hasn't' 'then why is he living with a friend's father?'

'he's at that age he's fine with us not a gay couple'.

'Sexuality is not the issue here' 'I'm sorry it's an issue for me I don't want my son being gay because of them!'.

'Corey let me ask you something have you ever acted in a sexual way in front of your children?' 'no'.

'We never kiss not with tongues anyway' 'good thankyou'.

Douglas was called to the stand as he gave his name Corey hoped he wouldn't say the wrong thing

'Just a few questions if won't take long tell me why you left home to move in with your friend?' Greg asked.

'I wasn't happy living with mam' 'why not?' 'I don't get on with them' 'why did you leave the house?'.

'We were rowing' 'with your parents?' 'yeah' 'what about?' 'she wouldn't let me out the house' 'why not?'.

'Because she controls me she doesn't like me going out anywhere except Judo practice'.

'Has she always been controlling?' 'most of the time especially the last two years' 'why is that?' 'I don't know'. 'She's always angry with me' 'do you feel unhappy living there?' 'yes' 'that's why you moved out'.

'To your friend's house' 'yeah' 'what about your step-father?' 'we don't get on he doesn't like me'.

'You've never liked him?' 'never' 'has he ever hit you?'.

'Yes sometimes I'm scared of him I try and avoid him but I can't that's why I left home'.

'You told the court last time you were here that you got on well that you did things together went fishing'.

'To the cinema' 'I'm sorry I lied he said he'd batter me if I told the truth' 'how did you feel when he said this?'.

'I was upset because I wanted to be with Corey'.

'You get on well?' 'yes' 'that will be all thankyou for answering my questions'.

The first day of the court case had ended Corey was happy Douglas had finally told the truth.

What Marie and Clive were really like the court had to listen to him the next day the trial resumed.

Corey was in court for 10am it was Marie's turn if it was anything like the last time she would be just as spiteful.

'My client wishes to continue being a good mother to her son' her lawyer spoke.

'Mrs O'Hanlon please tell me why you wish to resume custody of your son?' Greg asked.

'I don't think it's suitable for a fourteen year old to live with a gay couple'.

'You think they might be a bad influence on him' 'yes'.

'In what way?' 'I don't agree with it and I don't like Polly he doesn't know her they've only met a few times'.

'I don't agree with their lifestyle a child will always be better off with a heterosexual couple in my opinion'.

'Listen I've raised him since he was a baby I'm his legal guardian not her! he belongs with me!'.

'Is it true your controlling?' 'no I just look out for him'.

'Like any other parent would' 'he says you stop him leaving the house' 'he's a fourteen year old boy'.

'He needs discipline' 'what about your husband'.

'Has he been violent?' 'not when I've been around he hasn't' 'so your saying your son is lying'.

Her lawyer stood up 'may I just say Marie is Douglas's legal guardian she raised him'.

'It would not be in the child's best interests to come from a broken home when he's only got two years of school left'.

'Corey tell me about your relationship with Polly'.

'We've been together five years since we were twenty one we married not long after we love each other'.

'Would you describe your relationship as stable?' 'solid'.

'I never want to be with anyone else' 'is it true Polly still struggles with alcohol addiction?.

'Her mother's lawyer stood up Corey wondered what else they would say use against her.

'This is a serious addiction is this the kind of person you want looking after your child?'.

'What if Polly couldn't look after your son what would happen?' 'we have two children we are good parents'.

'Do you think I wouldn't be able to look after them'.

'What if you weren't there or relatives?' 'I can manage'.

'I'm a good mother' 'your too young to know the needs of a teenager!' her lawyer said Corey was so angry.

'I'm twenty seven! not sixteen I'm an adult' 'you enjoy being a mother?' the judge asked 'very much so'.

'That's all I needed to know we'll call it a day'.

'Court dismissed' Corey knew they couldn't get to her she hadn't touched drugs since she was twenty one.

So they were using Polly's alcohol problem ad the fact they were a gay couple against them,

The next day would be the last day of the court case Corey was dreading it.

As Corey entered court she tried to be confident it was hard Daniel had been called as character witness.

'Daniel tell the court about your relationship with your sister' 'she's my sister my best friend'.

'What is she like as a person?' 'she's a nice girl kind caring funny we've always been close our father beat us'.

'We've always been close whatever happened we always had each other' 'what is she like as a mother?'.

'She's great very loving she takes the kids on days out keeps them occupied Marie's autistic'.

'She's almost five now she has special needs she takes care of her she and Polly are inspiring as a couple'.

'In what way?' 'their love for each other their great with the kids just like any other heterosexual couple'.

'Do you believe Corey should have custody of Douglas?'.

'Yes' 'why?' 'I don't believe mam is a good person to be around' 'why?' 'she's cruel nasty homophobic bitter'.

'She said it was Polly's fault Marie is autistic because of them being gay like she deserves bad things to happen'.

'She hates Polly for no reason other than the fact Corey married a woman Polly isn't an alcoholic anymore'.

'She never drinks except on special occasions I could write you a list of things my mother has accused people of'.

'In fact I'm ashamed to call her my mother'.

'What about Clive? your step-father you know him well'.

'I don't like him he's not nice Douglas is scared of him'.

'Tell me' 'he told me he hides in his room when he's around they don't get on' 'and he has been violent?' 'yes'.

'He's my nephew I care about him he tells me things Clive is a nasty man he shouldn't be looking after Douglas'.

'You don't think he should be with your mother?' 'no he'd been even more unhappy I'm scared he might run away'.

'End up in care we don't want that I want to look after him so does Corey she's twenty seven not a child'.

'She's a good mam' 'thankyou Daniel' Greg said 'if Corey lives in London how is she going to look after him'.

'He'll have to change schools'?' Marie's lawyer said angry at Daniel's revelations to the court.

'She has a house in Dublin she spends as much time here as she does in London we want what's best for him'.

'How often do you see him?' 'as much as I can I'm his older brother I look out for him'.

'Especially the situation the way it is I want to make sure he's happy settled which he isn't at the moment'.

'Why haven't you gone for custody yourself?'.

'Because Corey is his mother she's a good parent she'd be good for Douglas but I also want to be there'.

Douglas was called to the stand 'please tell me who you want to live with' Greg asked 'Corey' 'not your mam' 'no'. 'Why?' 'she makes me unhappy I feel sad and I don't like my step-dad I never have'.

'Do you have a problem with the fact she's part of a lesbian couple?' 'no I love her I don't care'.

'So you want to live with her?' 'yes' 'do you like Polly?'. 'She seems nice' 'and your brother you like spending time with him?' 'yes he looks out for me'.

'We're really good friends' 'good thankyou the jury will take an hour's break before returning with the verdict' Corey hoped they wouldn't award her mother custody. Or worse put Douglas in care two hours later they returned for the verdict.

Corey was convinced she would lose 'well having looked at the evidence the jury has come to a decision'.

'I think in this case it would be wrong for Douglas to go back with his mother and step-father'.

'It's pretty obvious this man is not a good influence apart from the fact he is obviously a violent man'.

'Even if it is occasionally any violence is wrong when children are involved'.

'And the fact that Mrs O'Hanlon and her husband forced their son to lie under oath'.

'Because he was scared of being beaten add to that her controlling nature' 'this is wrong! I'm his mother'.

'Please be quiet! the fact that Corey is in a same sex relationship should have no influence'.

'In this case Corey has been in a civil partnership for five years her relationship with Polly is built on stability'.

'And love for each other together they have built a stable family with their children'.

'Mrs O'Hanlon's house is not stable or loving'.

'This is wrong!' 'be quiet please! under Irish law same-sex partnerships are illegal'.

'However since Corey divides her time between Dublin and London where they are legal'.

'She wouldn't be breaking the law usually I would award custody to the parent the child lives with'.

'But not in this case' 'you are joking!' Corey smiled to herself as her mother became angrier.

'Douglas is fourteen a young adult capable of making a decision on who he wants to live with'.

'He has decided he wants to live with his biological mother however taking into account work commitments'.

'I wouldn't want school to be interrupted and since Corey divides her time between here and London'.

'I've decided to award you and your brother Daniel joint custody Mrs O'Hanlon you may have visitation rights'.
'If you decide to apply two hours every month if Douglas wishes' 'he doesn't' Corey said she couldn't believe it. She'd been awarded joint custody with Daniel she was so happy the judge had seen what her mother was like.
Corey knew Douglas would be better off with her and Daniel she wanted to do the best she could for Douglas. It wasn't right for a fourteen year old to be living with a friend's father now he'd be able to have a stable family. Corey smiled as Douglas came over she hugged him.
'Happy' 'yeah' 'you know what joint custody means'.
'I get to be with you and Dan' 'yes when I'm working in London you'll be here are you happy about it?'.
'I'm really happy' 'I can't believe we got custody'.
'I know neither can I Dan this is the best news!'.
'Happy now are you! you won't get away with this!'.
Marie said angry 'get away with what?' 'I can't believe a court awarded you and Daniel custody'.
'Don't be surprised if he turns out gay!' 'your just bitter sexuality has nothing to do with it!' Corey said,
'This is about what's right he doesn't want to live with you' 'he's my son!' 'no he's my son!'.
'You took him away from me you could have told me!'.

'I would have let you bring him up I wasn't gonna have a child with dad around I'm a good mother and so is Polly'
'I don't care about you or that tart! I'll appeal!'.
'His needs come first not yours I'm going home now with Douglas!'.
That evening Corey cooked for him and Daniel she was happy nothing could ruin the moment.
As she stuck a photo of her mother on a dartboard in the kitchen throwing darts as she collected them off the board. Corey smiled she would never let her mother ruin her life ever again Polly was happy for her.

Happy family

That afternoon Corey returned home to her London house with Polly 'how's the night club going? Corey asked.

'Good' 'I can't wait to see it when it's finished'.

'You have to come to the opening night when I was with Andy we were always hanging out with drag queens'.

Polly said 'sounds like a great business venture' 'oh it is'.

'How come your friends with Adrian again?' 'I saw him in a pub in London he says your friends again'.

'I wouldn't say that we got chatting that's all' 'don't get too friendly he's not to be trusted remember' 'yeah I know'.

'Have you heard his sister died of cancer he's raising her kids' 'your joking! how old are they?' 'eleven and twelve'.

'I think they'd be better off in care can you seriously see that man looking after anyone except himself'.

'Well their almost teenagers I'm sure he's doing an alright job' 'I hope so' 'anyway let's not talk about Adrian'.

'How's Stace?' Polly asked 'great in the studio recording'.

'She's just come back from New York lots of shopping'.

'And going to restaurants she went with Marcee for a trip jazz clubs she said she wants to chill for a while'.

'I don't blame her she's been working since she was sixteen like me' Polly said.

Stacey was their closest friend they had all gone to school
together in Ireland as teenagers.

She was also Polly's cousin by marriage her aunt Wendy
was Polly's step-mum married to her dad.

They had also recently become step-sisters when her mum
had married Stacey's dad Paul 'Douglas is here'.

'He came over with Dan and his new fiancée' Corey said
'he's engaged' 'yeah she couldn't wait to get her claws
into him' 'she's not very nice' 'no she's awful'.

'What's she like?' 'she got done for benefit fraud' 'what
happened?' 'she said she couldn't walk'.

'When she was working at a jewellery shop' 'how do you
know?' 'a friend of a friend in Dublin'.

'It's not that she's not very nice you'll see what I mean
when you meet her' 'where's Douglas?' 'upstairs'.

Polly went upstairs taking her things 'hey' she said.

'Hi' he said 'I hope you've made yourself at home' 'yeah'
'good I got you some clothes I hope you don't mind'.

'Thanks' 'so what do you think of Dan's new girlfriend?'.

Polly asked 'she's ok what's for tea?' 'beans and waffles'.

'Great I'll see you in a minute' Polly changed into
something more comfortable as she went downstairs.

'Can't go wrong with beans and waffles' Polly said as she
sat down at the kitchen table 'I know'.

Corey joined her with Douglas 'glad to be home?'.
Corey asked 'course darling I've missed you' 'I missed you
too' Corey smiled 'you've not heard from Marie'.
'Mam no but she's left messages threatening me how she's
gonna get Douglas back so I've changed our number'.
'Good don't worry she'll get the message' Polly assured
her 'what have you two been up to?' Polly asked.
'We went to the London Aquarium' Douglas said 'must be
nice now you're on school holidays' 'yeah I like London'.
'This is your second home now' 'third Dan has joint
custody remember' 'I think it's a good arrangement'.
'Split your time between here and Dublin I think
everything's worked out for the best'.
They heard a knock at the door 'who's that?' Polly
wondered as Corey opened the door 'hi' she said.
'Not a bad time is it?' Daniel asked he'd arrived with his
girlfriend Lizzie 'we were just having tea' Corey said.
Slightly angry they'd been interrupted 'it's fine we were
just having waffles and beans not exactly fine dining'.
Polly joked 'come in' Corey said 'Polly it's great to see
you' Dan said kissing her on the cheek.
'You too darling is this your fiancée?' 'yes this is Lizzie'.
'Polly great to meet you I'm such a big fan' 'you too'.
'Come in' Polly said taking their coats.

She loved playing hostess 'bucks fizz?' Polly offered 'yes please' 'coming up' Lizzie had frizzy dark brown hair. She wasn't the best looking but not the worst either she was a slim size eight with a strong Dublin accent.

'I didn't know you were coming round' Corey said 'we decided to see a film' Daniel said 'hey Dougie'.

'Have a good day out?' Daniel asked 'we went to the London Aquarium' 'sounds good'.

'So Polly have you just got back from New York?' 'yeah'.

'She's a bit jet lagged' Corey said in the hope they wouldn't stay long 'sorry' 'it's fine really' Polly said. Polly made tea as Corey forced a smile 'so you didn't see a film then?' Corey asked 'no we went shopping'.

'Looking for anything in particular?' Corey asked.

'An engagement ring Lizzie lost it down the drain'.

'That's such a shame' Polly said 'I know' Corey wondered if she'd secretly pawned it to get some money. She wouldn't put it past her 'anyway she's found one'.

'That's good' 'so do you have a job yet?' Corey asked Lizzie 'yes as a waitress at Pete's'.

'It's an upcoming new restaurant'. 'it'll help us save up for the wedding' Lizzie said.

'What about your record producing?' Lizzie asked Corey.

'I'm producing a girlband with Andy from the band'.

'Oh that's great so he does keyboards and programming and you do the vocals' 'no we both do the music'.

'I can use a mixing desk I've been doing it for four years'.

'Great' 'Corey's multi-talented she even let me produce a song on my album' Polly said.

'I said Quincy Jones doesn't have anything to worry about' Polly joked and so the evening went on.

With Lizzie asking questions with suitable put downs when they finally left Corey was happy.

Usually she loved hanging out with her brother but Lizzie made it hard 'she didn't seem too bad' Polly said.

Corey had an angry look on her face 'did you see the way she put me down' 'she was a bit off with you'.

'What does he see in her?' 'she's not the worst looking'.

'And what the f**k does she know about the music industry!' 'I wouldn't let her get to you'.

'Seriously of all the people my brother could choose to go out with!' 'maybe it won't last long' 'I hope not'.

'Hey I'm sure he'll see what she's like' 'I wouldn't bet on it of all the people he could get engaged to'.

'She looks like a tramp' 'maybe she is' they laughed.

'He's more than my brother he's my best friend' 'I know darling but it's his decision to be with her'.

Corey decided to try and forget Lizzie.

She loved the fact that Douglas was now on summer
holidays and they could enjoy hanging out together.
Corey knew she was more like his sister than his mum but
they had a good relationship.
Hopefully her brother would split up with Lizzie soon.
Stacey and Polly were attending a family meal up north.
They all went to Andy's place in Lytham St Anne's it was
nice all of them being together as a family.
Along with Wendy, Simon Polly's half-sister Emily and her
brother Christian as they sat round a big table.
'Potatoes?' Andy asked Stacey 'please' 'seeing anyone?'
he asked 'I want to be single focus on my career'.
'I want you to find someone nice to be with' 'so do I Andy
but I don't think there is anyone' 'don't say that'.
'You'll find someone nice what's that saying love will
come when you least expect it' 'I know you're right'.
'You won't be on your own you've got me' 'and Kim' Polly
said 'I know' 'I'm fine really this food is so good'.
'Almost as good as Veronica's' Veronica was Stacey's aunt
and Marcee's sister who she loved very much.
And reminded her of the cook Rusty Lee Stacey and Polly
helped themselves to as many potatoes as possible.
And stuffing 'you two have got big appetites' Andy said.
'That's rich coming from you' Stacey joked.

'Don't be cheeky!' Wendy served them ice-cream with chocolate sauce 'this is so nice' Polly said 'it's the best'. Stacey said afterwards everyone chatted in the living room 'did you like that?' Polly asked Christian.

'Oh lovely nice food' 'and I love ice-cream with chocolate sauce' 'snap' Polly said 'Stacey looked nice'.

Christian said 'yeah we both love our food'.

'I love a curvy girl' Stacey was angry Christian had just called her curvy did he think she was fat?.

Christian went into the dining room 'having a good time?' Polly asked Stacey 'fine' 'what's up darling?'.

'Your brother just called me fat!' 'no he didn't! 'he called me curvy it's the same thing' 'it's just a word'.

'He may as well have called me fat is that what everyone thinks of me Susie?' 'course not!'.

'I know I've put on weight' 'Stace I'm sure he didn't mean it alright!' 'I hate your brother!'.

'You don't even know him listen you've gone from a size ten to a twelve it's not a big deal' 'is everything ok?'.

Christian asked Stacey walked off angry 'what's up?'.

'Stacey took offence to being called curvy' 'I'm sorry it just came out I don't think Stacey's fat'.

'Don't worry about it she's slimmer than I am but in her mind she's fat she'll be fine'.

Christian followed Stacey to the kitchen to apologise.
'I didn't mean to call you curvy' 'I know I've put on
weight recently but there's no need to call me that!'.
'You don't even know me!' 'I'm sorry' 'it's only because
I'm 5'2 if I put weight on it shows up on me'.
'More than someone who's taller' Polly joined Stacey
outside 'you alright' 'I'm sorry alright'.
'I know I overreacted but that comment upset me'
'Christian's really nice once you get to know him trust me'
'if you say so' 'he's almost single'.
'I think he's having problems with his girlfriend he might
be interested' 'you are joking!' 'why not?'.
'I'd rather be single than date your brother' 'if you just
got to know him whether you like it or not he's family'.
'He's my half-brother' they went back inside a few days
later Stacey decided to go shopping in London
She wore a white T-shirt with a pink palm tree and blue
denim pedal pushers and silver Sketchers trainers.
Stacey had lots of them since she had previously been the
face of Sketchers.
She wore her dark brown hair naturally curly blue
eyeshadow, mascara and some foundation.
Even though she'd made the effort to look nice Stacey still
hoped she wouldn't be recognised by anyone.

*She looked in Jane Norman as she spied someone who
looked like Christian it couldn't be him could it?.*
'Stacey' 'Christian' 'how are you?' he asked 'good'.
*'I'm just shopping' 'anything in particular' 'just browsing
I'm sorry about the other day having a go at you'.*
'It's fine I'm sorry too and your not fat'.
*'That's not what the magazines say' 'I think the media
should be banned from printing that rubbish'.*
'How come your shopping in women's clothes shops?'.
*'It's my sister's birthday in a few weeks time' 'how old is
she?' 'fourteen I also have a brother who's fifteen'.*
*'What about you any brothers or sisters?' 'I have a
half-sister she's a year younger'.*
*'We met when I was fourteen when I met my mum' 'sounds
interesting' 'I thought my dad Paul was my uncle'.*
*'Then when I was twelve I found out he was my dad and
that Wendy wasn't my mum she was my aunt'.*
*'It's confusing I don't know why they did it I guess so
I wouldn't feel different as a child not having a mum'.*
*'Wendy thought she couldn't have anymore children so she
was my mum and I didn't know about Jonathan'.*
*'My cousin she gave him up for adoption as a baby cause
she was in a violent relationship'.*
'When we lived in Ireland they found each other'.

'I met Jon at school I knew him before we found out anyway... you don't wanna hear about me' 'I do'.
'Besides we're family my dad's married to your aunt'.
'I think we're cousins by marriage' Stace said 'would you like to have a drink with me?' 'Christian asked 'yes'.
'If you're not doing anything' 'no but I have to meet someone at 2pm' 'I know a pub not far away'.
Stacey went with Christian she was still angry at him calling her curvy.
But decided she could just about forgive him the pub was nice as they sat down at a table 'what would you like?'.
'A coke and some cheese and onion crisps I don't drink much' 'neither do I' Christian ordered half a pint of beer.
Stacey wished she'd worn something else even though it was a nice weather.
She looked like she was ready for a day at the beach.
'So you never drink?' Christian asked 'sometimes my limit's two glasses of champagne or wine'.
'After that I'm gone I get really tipsy quickly'.
'You're like me then I'm the same two glasses' 'I can't take much alcohol dad's the same' Stacey said.
'You look like your dad' she said 'yeah I'm sorry for what I said your not fat you've got a great figure'.
'Not at the moment I ate too much junk food lately'.

*'I'll be back soon' Stacey watched as Christian walked
over to a tall girl with straight light brown hair.*

*A Sloane type they chatted he then returned 'who was
that?' Stacey asked curiously 'my ex-girlfriend Laura'.*

*'Are you gonna get back with her?' 'I don't think so that
ship has sailed' 'how long did you go out together?'.*

*'A year' 'that's a long time' 'Stacey' she looked over it was
her sieter Kim 'how did you know I was here?' 'I didn't'.*

'I wanted a drink and I was thirsty it's really hot outside'.

*'I'll go order what about you?' 'I'm fine I've already had a
drink' 'who's this?' Kim asked 'Christian'.*

'Polly's half- brother' 'hi we'll chat in a minute' 'ok'.

*Kim ordered a drink she returned sitting down at their
table 'I'm Kim' 'Christian' he smiled 'so are you single?'.*

*'Yes' 'Kim!' 'no it's fine you don't mind me chatting you up
I quite fancy a blonde haired blue eyed boyfriend'.*

'Have you ever dated a black girl before?' 'no' 'Kim'.

*'Christian's ex-girlfriend is over there' 'oh sorry I didn't
mean anything' 'it's fine'.*

*Stacey looked over as his ex-girlfriend gave Kim a look
she looked at Christian she clearly fancied him.*

*Stacey watched as his ex-girlfriend came over to their
table 'Laura this is Stacey and Kim'.*

'I see you're dating black girls now'.

'I'm not dating anyone but they do say variety is the spice of life' he joked Laura gave them a look .

'Well nice to meet everyone I'm leaving now bye Christian' she left the pub 'I don't think she likes me'.

'Don't worry she can be like that frosty sometimes' Christian said 'did you want a drink? Kim asked.

'I'm fine' 'I think Kim has a crush on you' Stacey said.

'Maybe I do' Kim smiled they decided to go play a game of pool Stacey chatted to Kim.

'Maybe you're being a bit forward' 'you think so' 'yes'.

'Well if you like someone there's no point in waiting around you don't fancy him do you?' 'course not'.

'Well then I guess you're right I shouldn't be too forward' 'so tell me what you know about him?' 'not much'.

'Polly just getting to know him he's privately school educated he lives in a mansion'.

'He has a brother and sister who are fourteen and fifteen' 'how do you know all this stuff?' 'Polly told me'.

'Anyway I doubt he'd want to go out with a black girl from Hackney' 'Kim said sadly you never know'.

'Well tell him to add me on Facebook if he wants' 'ok'.

'Game of pool?' Kim asked 'yes' Stacey said as they set up the pool table as Christian chatted to a man at the bar.

'He's gorgeous' Kim said Stacey could see she was taken with Christian they played Stacey won the game of pool.

'Listen I have to go now I'm cooking a meal for someone so I have to get home' Christian said.

'Ok well I enjoyed having a drink with you' Stacey said.

'Me too it was good to see you nice to meet you Kim'.

'You too' they watched as Christian left Stacey wondered who he was cooking a meal for probably a girlfriend.

'What shall we do now?' Stacey wondered 'let's go back shopping for a bit' the girls left the pub.

Going back into the sunshine as they shopped Stacey wanted to lose weight before buying new clothes.

So she helped Kim try on things afterwards they went to a café where they ordered jacket potatoes with cheese.

Chocolate fudge cake 'this is so good' Kim said 'I know'.

'I need to go on a diet' 'says who?' 'me I've put on weight don't pretend you haven't noticed' 'course I have'.

'But come on a size twelve is a good size to be' 'I guess'.

'You asked me and I'm telling you the truth it suits you'.

'I don't know' 'you look great men like women with curves' 'well I'm single so it doesn't matter'.

'And I'm releasing a new album soon and I want to look good so I'm going on a diet'.

'I'm getting a personal trainer' 'if it's what you want'.

'In a few years from now when the group splits up I am gonna gain weight get really fat and I am gonna love it'.

Stacey laughed Kim was part of girlband Crème all the members were mixed race they'd been big in the U.S.

Kim often struggled to keep her weight down Stacey loved her and couldn't imagine life before meeting her.

As Stacey got up to leave happy 'let's go back to yours' Kim suggested they linked arms.

As they went home to Stacey's they'd had a good day out together when they got home they listened to music.

Stacey thought about Christian she felt guilty that she had been off with him when they had first met.

That evening after Kim had left Stacey tried on some of her clothes which no longer fit.

Just to make herself feel worse Stacey decided she was going to attempt to get back her size ten figure.

She decided to hire a personal trainer to help her isn't that what all celebrities did? she would look into it.

The next day her dad announced he was coming round to visit Stacey couldn't wait she always missed him.

When she was away he was visiting friends in Essex she was dressed casually wearing a white T-shirt.

And jogging trousers 'dad' 'hello darling' he hugged her Stacey loved him so much.

And was a real daddy's girl 'you look nice' he said.

'Really' 'yes darling only you could look pretty in jogging trousers' Stacey made her dad tea.

As they sat down on the sofa 'how's things?' her dad asked 'any dates on the horizon?' 'not at the moment'.

'I just want you to find a nice man to settle down with'.

'I know me too' 'Justin and James they were too old for you I heard you and Christian got acquainted yesterday'.

'I thought you hated him' 'I did we got talking I think he's ok now we both said sorry' 'that's good'.

'Because he's part of the family now' 'I know' 'you know if he weren't family he'd be perfect for you'.

'He's not my type besides his ex-girlfriend is still around Kim has a crush on him they met at the pub yesterday'.

'We were shopping together' 'does he like her?' 'I think she was too full on she might have put him off'.

'Besides she's in America a lot with the band' 'talking of America I'm glad your back in the UK'.

'So am I dad I'm recording my new album it's mostly pop some ballads you'll like it' 'I'm sure I will'.

'Dad what do you think of me hiring a personal trainer?'.

'What for?' 'to lose weight' 'can't you do that by yourself?' 'I could but I need someone to motivate me'.

'I haven't exercised in months not even dance classes'.

'I think you look ok' 'thanks but I can't wear any of my old clothes' 'then just buy some new ones' 'very funny'.

'But I want to look good for when my album comes out'.

'If it's what you want I understand well then you should hire someone if you think you'll get a quicker result'.

'Just make sure it's not too expensive' 'ok dad I'll make sure it's reasonable it's Wendy's birthday tonight'.

'Christian will be there and Polly you said you get on ok now' 'yes' 'we'll have a nice dinner'.

'You find something nice to wear and I'll pick you up at six thirty and we've booked a table at a restaurant'.

'At seven' 'I can't wait did Wendy like my present?'.

'She loved it' 'good' Stacey had given her a beautiful silver necklace and matching earrings.

You couldn't go wrong her dad soon left as she planned what to wear that evening something glitzy.

Glamorous she decided she'd leave it till later Stacey had a late lunch doing pizza and mini quiches with some coke.

Heaven she thought she knew she'd have to start her diet soon but right now it could wait.

Finally around 5.20pm Stacey began getting ready doing her make-up it didn't take long.

As she found an outfit to wear a black jacket a white top underneath and a too tight silver glittery skirt .

It was a twelve but was more like a ten rather than buy a new wardrobe she decided she would lose weight soon.

Stacey hoped to book her personal trainer in the next few days she finished off the look with black tights.

And silver strappy high heels and a silver necklace she knew she looked good.

She waited for her dad to pick her up 'Stacey you look gorgeous' 'thanks' she got into the car.

As they arrived at the restaurant 'Stace' Wendy hugged her 'you look nice' 'thanks so do you'.

Wendy was wearing a red dress her wavy red hair down.

She looked great for forty six Stacey spied Polly and Christian they both looked good.

Polly was wearing a black glittery dress her red curly hair tied back she looked gorgeous.

Christian was wearing a navy top black jeans and boots smart but casual he looked nice Stacey thought.

'Right drinks' Wendy said 'Stace' 'just a coke' 'you always have a coke be more adventurous' Polly said.

'Ok vodka and orange' 'I'll have one too' Polly said 'Christian' 'a lemonade' 'alright coming up'.

'You never drink' Polly said 'I do on special occasions'.

'Well this is a special occasion' 'you're right I'll have one later'.

They sat down at a table the restaurant was nice and relaxing with wooden tables and red carpets.

They sat down Stacey could feel how tight her skirt was she sat next to her dad Polly next to Christian.

Who thought how pretty Stacey looked wearing her black jacket low cut white top.

The drinks soon arrived on a tray as Stacey sipped her drink while looking at the menu.

'I think I'll have vegetable lasagne and chips' Polly said.

'Sounds good I'll have that too' Christian said Polly spied Justin Stacey's ex-boyfriend as she looked over.

'It's Justin' Polly said 'I know he's with a girl Susie come on let's just concentrate on our dinner'

Stacey secretly looked over he was with a latino looking girl tanned with black hair he caught her eye.

As he came over 'Stacey' 'Justin' 'hey baby I haven't seen you in a long time' 'I know' 'come over for a chat'.

'If it's ok' 'Wendy's celebrating her birthday' 'well happy birthday' 'thankyou'.

'I'm sorry if I'm interrupting anything' 'it's fine Stace go on you have a chat'.

'Besides dinner will be at least ten minutes' 'thanks Wendy back soon' Stacey went over to his table.

As he put his arm round her 'won't your girlfriend mind'.

'No because she's my cousin' 'really' 'yes my uncle married a woman from Cuba this is Makita this is Stacey'.

'My ex' 'hi' 'I like your music' 'thanks' 'I'm gonna go get a drink you want one Stacey' 'ok'.

'I'll have another vodka and orange' 'so what are you up to?' 'just recording songs for my new album'.

'What about you?' 'DJing partying when I get time Stacey you look nice I love the jacket very posh' 'thanks'.

'You look great are you single?' 'yes' 'Stacey will you go out with me?' 'I don't think so it didn't work out'.

'Nothing serious no strings attached just dating me and you that way no-one gets hurt no engagement ring'

'Just us having some fun I'll give you my new number'.

Stacey couldn't believe Justin wanted to go out with her she just wanted to be single for a while.

Makita returned with the drinks Stacey drank her vodka and orange quickly not wanting to be too long.

Getting back to Wendy's table 'I'll call you' 'I can't wait' Stacey returned to the others 'well what did he say?'.

'Polly asked 'we just chatted I had a drink' 'you're not getting back with him' 'no way'.

'I just want to be friends don't worry I don't intend to get heartbroken again' 'Fine as long as you don't'.

'I won't Susie ok I promise'.

Stacey had to wait longer than the others for her food but when it arrived it tasted delicious.

They had all had a nice family meal Christian went back to Polly's apartment Corey hadn't been able to go.

Because she felt ill 'how was it the dinner?' Corey asked. As she lay on the sofa 'the food was nice Stacey's saw Justin he asked her out she said no which I'm glad about'.

'His type their all the same she wants love Mr Right she said she wants what me and you have'.

'You know a special relationship'.

'I'm sure she'll meet someone soon' 'I know she will'.

One night stand

The next day Polly flew to New York she was happy to be there she'd brought her New York apartment not long ago.

And she loved it ever since she was a little girl Polly had always wanted to live in New York.

She was glad to be back in her apartment she employed a woman to come once every two weeks to clean.

Polly wanted to move there permanently rather than divide her time between there and London.

Instead of just having her New York apartment as a holiday home but she knew Corey wasn't keen.

Polly knew that Corey liked New York so maybe she would change her mind they'd decided to spend two weeks there.

Polly was promoting her new lingerie range while Douglas was back at school in Dublin.

Corey was looking forward to it she had forgotten how nice their apartment was as she admired the view.

She decided she was glad of a change of scenery for a while the next day they went shopping Corey loved it.

The shops were so good there and it was nice being with Polly often she would be doing TV apperances.

To promote her movie while she would be in London doing music now they were together and Corey loved it.

She thought the next time she could bring Douglas he'd like it there she thought.

As Corey looked around Macy's department store at the jewellery section she'd always loved jewellery.

And there was so much to look at she looked at a silver charmbraclet 'Corey' she heard a voice call.

She turned around 'Steve' 'how's my favourite Irish songbird?' 'I'm great' it was Steve.

He was an american actor they'd made two romantic comedy films together I Love New York & Paris.

They'd got on well become friends and kept in touch but hadn't seen each other for a while 'how are you?'.

Steve asked 'I'm good' 'it's great seeing you again'.

He kissed her on the cheek 'hello Polly' 'hi' 'so are you two busy?' he asked 'just shopping'.

'Would you like to have lunch somewhere?' Steve asked 'great idea' Polly agreed 'ok then'.

'Let me just buy this bracelet' Corey said 'let me' 'what'.

'I'm buying it' 'you can't do that!' 'I can' 'but it's expensive' 'so let me pay for it Corey'.

'Really you don't have to' 'I want to' 'ok thankyou'.

Corey reluctantly gave in Steve paid for the bracelet which of course looked gorgeous on her.

They had lunch at a nice café.

*'So how come you're in New York?' he asked 'Polly's
doing some press and promoting her lingerie range'.
'On the home shopping channel I thought I'd come for two
weeks' 'we're going to be apart for a while'.
'And I don't have any work commitments' 'it's really good
seeing you again Corey' 'you too how's your wife?'.
'Oh we've broken up' 'I'm sorry' 'it's ok we were having
problems' 'I'm sure you'll not be short of admirers'.
Polly joked 'I'm getting on now' 'I'm twenty seven now'
Corey said 'well try being almost forty' 'still young'.
'Where are you staying?' he asked 'Polly's got an
apartment in New York' 'feel free to come round anytime'.
Polly said 'thankyou that's very kind of you Polly'.
'Anytime' 'hey there's a party tonight eighties old skool
stuff you two fancy coming?' 'why not'.
'You're certainly making the most of being single'.
Polly said' 'yes I had a pretty bad time the last few months
so I'm trying to have fun' 'good for you'.
'so you'll come' 'course we will won't we Cor' 'yes'.
'Sounds great' so that evening they got ready to go out
Polly wore a blue sparkly dress and heels.
Corey wore trousers and a sparkly black top and silver
mini hoop earrings she looked great Polly thought.
They arrived for 8pm Steve was there with a friend.*

As they greeted the girls 'you two look gorgeous'.

Steve said 'thanks we like to make the effort' Polly said.

'You look sensational this is my friend Eddie this is Corey and Polly' 'Polly I'm such a big fan' 'thanks'.

'I love all your films' 'thanks' Polly said 'let's go party'

Steve said 'would you girls like a drink?' Eddie asked

'I'll just have a coke' Polly said 'are you sure?' 'I used to have a problem with drink' 'ok I understand' 'Corey'.

'A glass of white wine' 'coming up' 'nice club' Corey said 'oh it's great I've been coming here for years'.

'You look beautiful' Steve said to Corey 'thanks' she suspected Steve had a crush on her.

Despite the fact he knew she was a lesbian she didn't mind Steve was a good looking man for his age .

Corey sipped her white wine 'I'm so glad you're in New York' 'so am I' Corey smiled.

Polly was chatting to Eddie who was taken with her.

'Let's dance' Steve led Corey to the dancefloor as they danced together 'good dancer' Steve said 'thanks'.

'Your not bad yourself' 'no I'm terrible' 'there's far worse dancers trust me' they laughed.

Corey knew they had a great connection at the end of the night they went home she thought about Steve.

He seemed taken with her the next day she went shopping
Polly had a lie in as Corey wore a light blue strappy top.
And blue trousers and dark sunglasses as she looked
round some clothes shops she decided she liked New York.
As she came out of a shop clutching a shopping bag a
woman called after her 'hey' 'me' 'yes I saw you'.
'At that club last night I saw you dancing with my husband
coming on to him!' 'I was not!'.
'You must think I was born yesterday!' 'I'm married!'.
'Since when has that stopped anyone!' 'I'm married to a
woman I'm a lesbian ok!' 'whatever!'.
'Just stay away from my husband!' she walked away.
Giving Corey a look no wonder they were getting a
divorce she thought if that's what Steve had to put up with.
The woman obviously had issues as Corey returned home
Polly was eating toast in her fluffy pink dressing gown.
'Have a good time shopping?' 'great except Steve's wife
accused me of having an affair with him'.
'You are joking!' 'no she saw me last night at the club'.
'I tried to explain we were just dancing she went mad at
me' 'no wonder he's divorcing her he's nice Steve'.
Polly said 'yeah we get on well' 'maybe we can all go out
together' 'sounds good' Corey agreed.

A few days later Polly did a slot on the home shopping channel Steve rang a few days later.

He wanted to come round Polly was out visiting her friend Maggie who was from Liverpool.

Who'd moved to New York a few years ago they'd met on a boat trip there Corey didn't mind being left alone.

Besides she loved New York she heard the doorbell ring she went to answer it 'Steve' 'Corey you look great'.

'I'm wearing a T-shirt and jogging trousers'.

'You look gorgeous anyway' 'would you like some homemade cookies?' 'I'd love some' 'a drink?' 'sure'.

'Juice' 'yeah' Corey brought out a plate of cookies and some squash 'nice cookies' 'Polly loves to cook'.

'Tell her I love them' 'ok I will' 'did I tell you I love your Irish accent' you'll have to come visit me in Dublin'.

'I'd love to' 'I have a nice house I'll show you round'.

'I'd love that I came round because I wanted to apologise about my wife' 'oh it's fine really' 'no it's not'.

'You didn't deserve that it's our divorce she was just taking it out on you the fact that she shouted at you in the street'.

'She doesn't even know you' 'really it's fine' 'it's not fine you are the nicest person and she's a bitch'.

'You're calling your ex-wife a bitch' 'yes I am'.

'You're right she's a bitch'.

'How could you be married to her for so many years'.
They laughed 'maybe I just never met the right girl'.
'Do you have any children together?' 'two sons teenagers
we married in our mid-twenties we fell out of love'.
'Like many couples do when they've been too long
together' Steve smiled at her.
He was making it obvious he fancied her 'I'm sure you'll
meet someone else' 'I'm not getting any younger'.
'Age is just a number it's how you feel inside' 'that is so
true' 'I know' 'you are so beautiful' Corey smiled.
She didn't know what to say to him 'your not so bad
yourself' 'thanks'
Corey realised how much she enjoyed Steve's company.
'I've had a great time' he said 'me too' 'will I see you
soon?' 'how soon?' 'tomorrow' Corey said.
'Ok what time?' 'eleven' 'sounds good' Steve smiled.
'Can I kiss you goodbye?' 'course' he kissed her on the
cheek 'bye gorgeous' 'bye Steve' he was great company.
They got on well the age gap didn't matter the next
morning Steve arrived for 11am.
Corey was wearing jeans a white T-shirt and blue hoop
earrings she had an eye infection.
So couldn't wear her contacts she was wearing glasses.
'You look great' Steve said 'so do you' 'I like the glasses'.

'I have no choice my eyes are playing me up so no contacts this week' 'well you look nice' 'thanks'.

'Let's go would you mind if we went to an Art gallery?'. Steve asked 'course not it's a great idea I paint' 'really'.

'I'll have to see some of your paintings some time'.

'Well I don't get much of a chance these days with being a mother and acting and singing but I love Art'.

'Visiting the galleries and exhibitions' 'well you'll love this exhibition I've wanted to see it for weeks' Steve was right.

Corey did love the exhibition it was great after he took her to a restaurant which she loved.

He also took her out on a boat cruise to see the Statue Of Liberty it was great breathing in the fresh air. He had his hands round her waist as they sat together.

Corey had butterflies in her stomach she questioned why she was feeling like this she felt confused.

She decided it was ok to fancy men even if she was a lesbian maybe she was bi-curious.

When the cruise came to an end they walked alongside the river 'Corey can I give you a kiss?' 'what kind of kiss?'.

'On the cheek' 'ok' Steve kissed her on the cheek she loved it 'was that ok?' he asked 'it was great'.

'What shall we do now?' Corey asked 'I know an Irish bar if you want' 'great let's go' they soon arrived at O'Brien's.

'You'll love it here' Steve said 'it's popular with the Irish-Americans and the Irish what do you want?'.

'A pint of anything' 'ok I'll have one too' Corey took off her jacket 'let me take it for you' Steve took it.

Hanging it in the corner they were playing traditional Irish music it had a warm atmosphere Corey loved it.

Except for the Mousse head in the corner 'who's this?'.

The barman asked Steve 'this is Corey my friend who starred with me in I Love New York' 'great'.

'I loved that film you were great' 'thanks' 'so are you really Irish?' 'yes I'm from Dublin' 'I love the Irish'.

'That's why I work in an Irish bar what you having?'.

'A pint of your best stuff and one for Corey' 'coming right up' 'it's not bad here' 'I told you you'd love it here'.

The drinks arrived as Corey sipped her pint 'game of pool' she asked 'ok why not' they took their drinks over.

As Steve chatted to various people he introduced Corey everyone seemed so nice.

She decided she'd let Polly know about it later as she got up and danced Corey loved it.

It was just like being at home in Ireland a traditional Irish pub they left around 8pm.

Before going back to Steve's place which was a nice apartment 'it's great' 'I'm glad you like it'.

'Thanks for taking me out tonight you take me to the best places' 'well I want you to enjoy New York'.

'I'm having a great time' 'that's good because I like spending time with you we have a great time together'.

'I know you're a good friend' Corey said 'well I'll be going now' 'ok say hi to Polly for me' Steve kissed her. On the cheek 'night' she waved as she hailed a taxi home. Polly was in as she rang the bell 'Cor darling come in I've just put some pasta on where have you been?'.

'I had a day out with Steve' 'where did you go?' 'we went to an Art gallery then we had a boat cruise'.

'Then we went to an Irish bar it was great called O'Brien's' 'oh Maggie told me about it is it good?'.

'Oh it was great we had fun I'm sorry I was late home'.

'It's fine listen Cor I'm gonna be busy so it's probably time for you to go back home' 'oh right'.

'I know it's really hard for us to be apart I guess it's just my job I did take some time off'.

'I know it's ok really we'll be together again soon before you know it' they watched a DVD before going to sleep. Corey felt a bit sad that she would be going home the next day Polly woke early for her business meeting. As Corey lay in rising around 9.30am as she got dressed.

She decided to go and see Steve to explain that she was going back to the UK she knocked on the door.
As it opened 'Corey isn't it' it was his wife 'sorry have I come at a bad time?' 'yes actually' 'I'm sorry'.
Corey turned to leave 'so tell me are you having a relationship with my husband?' 'no I told you'.
'I'm a married woman' 'that doesn't stop anyone you could be bi-sexual'.
'I know a woman who left her partner for a man it happens' 'I love Polly she's my wife'.
'Why do I have to explain my relationship to you! I'm not having an affair with your husband'.
'Besides I thought you were getting a divorce I'm leaving ok I'm going back to the UK and you have issues!'.
'I do not!' 'you're just jealous of any woman who's friends with your husband'.
'So every girl Steve speaks to he's having an affair with!'.
'I didn't say that!' 'I'm going!' 'Corey!' Steve called.
'Don't leave Angela was going!' 'I just came to see you'.
'I'm so sorry about that come in how are you?'.
'I'm good I had a good time yesterday' 'me too' 'I came to tell you Polly's busy business meetings movie stuff'.
'So I'm gonna be going home back to the UK' 'I'll miss you' 'I've had a great time hanging out with you'.

'Me too' 'you'll have to come visit me' Corey said 'I'd love that' Steve smiled 'I've never been to Ireland before'.

'Well I'll show you round' 'that would be great she tried to change my mind about me getting a divorce'.

'I said no chance she's gone now' 'good' 'it's just the two of us' Corey knew what Steve was implying.

'Shall we go somewhere since it's my last day in New York' 'let's go see a movie' Steve suggested.

'Ok which one?' 'your choice' after dinner they went out to see a movie Corey loved it she went home afterwards.

They arranged to meet that evening so Steve could take her out to a restaurant Corey was looking forward to it.

So that evening she put on her make-up getting ready to go out with Steve Corey wore a navy jacket.

And mini skirt black tights and a gold heart pendent she looked good Steve knocked on the door she opened.

He was wearing a navy suit which looked good with his dark blonde hair he looked good she thought.

As he handed her some roses 'flowers for me' 'yeah'.

'I remembered you like roses' 'I love them thanks let me put them in a vase' Corey found one.

Putting them in water before they left For their evening out it didn't take long to get to the restaurant.

As they arrived Corey felt happy in Steve's company.

She ordered a pasta dish it tasted delicious as jazz music played in the background it set the scene.

A single red rose on the table it was the kind of restaurants she used to go out with Polly.

Before her career and children took over they chatted enjoying good food and wine Corey loved it.

She couldn't believe it when she saw Polly on the other side of the restaurant with Tom Hanks.

Hopefully she wouldn't be seen 'I've really enjoyed tonight' Steve said 'me too' 'desert' 'I don't know'.

Usually Corey would have said yes but she wanted to get out of the restaurant as quickly as possible.

Without being seen 'I've really enjoyed tonight' Steve said 'it's been great' 'please have desert' 'ok'.

Corey ordered a chocolate brownie with ice-cream usually she would have enjoyed it.

But ate it as quickly as she could 'shall I pay?' 'no it's my treat' Steve said 'enjoy that' 'yes thanks' Steve paid.

As they left now she could finally relax Corey knew she was playing a dangerous game.

Going out on dates with Steve when she was married but she'd never felt this way about any other man before.

It scared and excited her she kept telling herself she was gay and it was just an infatuation.

*That a trip to an Art Gallery and a boat cruise was
perfectly innocent that they were just good friends.
It was no good she knew she fancied Steve Corey felt
guilty she was married she loved Polly.
Why was she attracted to someone else there had always
been a spark between them they were friends.
Nothing more they'd shared a kiss now she felt confused.
Corey received a text on her phone it was Polly to say
she'd be back around 11.30pm.
She decided to invite Steve back they drank wine chatted
as she drank glass after glass of wine.
Corey couldn't remember how many glasses she'd had was
it four or five Steve made it obvious he fancied her.
This time she accepted her feelings as they kissed they
couldn't stop he took her upstairs as she took off her skirt.
He undid his jeans as he reached for a condom hastily
putting it on they had sex it was great Corey loved it.
It felt magical like an episode of Sex & The City a sense
of excitement running through her body.
Finally it was over she felt on a high after she changed
her clothes putting on a T-shirt and jogging bottoms.
'You are so gorgeous' 'so are you?' Corey couldn't believe
what she'd done had sex with a man.
Only the second time in her life the first as a teenager.*

Before she realised she was a lesbian 'listen Steve please don't tell anyone about this' 'course not' 'I'm married'.

'I enjoyed it but it should never have happened' 'I know'.

'I'm sorry it was my fault' Steve said 'don't be sorry it was great I've loved spending time with you really'

'I'm going home to London tomorrow' 'so soon'.

'I have to go home I have to get back to my daughter'.

'I understand' 'we'll keep in touch come see me ok'.

'It's a deal' at that moment Polly arrived home ' did you get my text?' Polly asked 'yes did you have a great time?'.

'Yeah I had dinner with Tom Hanks he's so nice can you believe it?' 'no it's great I was just saying goodbye'.

'To Steve since I'm flying home tomorrow' 'Steve hiya' 'hey Polly it's been great seeing you both' 'you too darling keep in touch' Polly said 'I'll be going now'.

'Night everyone' Steve kissed them both on the cheek.

'Bye Steve' 'bye Corey' he waved Corey knew she would miss him 'he's lovely' Polly said 'I know' they went to bed. The next morning Corey woke early as she said goodbye to Polly then went to visit Steve.

She wanted to say goodbye to him properly she knocked on the door 'hey gorgeous'.

'I thought you were flying home' 'I am I just wanted to say bye' 'it's been fun' Steve said 'well thanks'.

'For making me feel like Carrie Bradshaw from
Sex And The City' 'with pleasure can I give you a kiss?'.
'On the cheek' 'ok I'll be a gentlemen' Steve kissed her it
was innocent 'you're a good friend the sex was amazing'.
'I don't regret it but it shouldn't have happened'.
Corey said trying to make herself feel better 'can we still
be friends?' Steve asked 'course' Steve hugged Corey.
'I have to go' 'have a safe journey home call me when you
get back' 'I don't have your number'.
Steve handed her a piece of paper with his number on.
'You do now' 'I'm married' 'I know it's ok we'll forget
what happened' 'I love Polly'.
'What happened can never happen again' 'I understand'.
'I just want to be your friend' 'thanks Steve I wish I didn't
have to go but I do' 'I'll come visit you in London'.
'I'll look forward to it then' 'bye darling' Corey waved she
knew she'd done the right thing finished the affair.
Corey knew she could've stayed longer in New York but
what would have happened? more sex more dates.
She'd acted responsibly she loved Polly the last thing she
ever wanted to do was break her heart it was a mistake.
That anyone could make it would never happen again
Corey flew home she fantasied about the things she and
Steve could have done but she liked it that way

Sometimes the fantasy was better than the reality no-one got hurt that way you could switch off.

Whenever you liked as Corey arrived home in London she caught a taxi home as she unpacked took her make-up off Put on some more comfortable clothes as she listened to her answerphone messages she had one from Daniel.

He was having an engagement party he was marrying Lizzie she thought he had better taste in women.

He wanted her to come he thought they could get to know each other better she wanted to say no.

But he was her brother maybe she could bring a friend.

Then it wouldn't be so bad Stacey had decided to hire a personal trainer Louie who worked with other celebrities.

He was gay sweet camp as soon as Stacey met him she knew she really liked him he knew Polly.

Who he'd met recently and was a big fan of if anyone could motivate her to lose weight get her back into shape.

He could 'Stacey you have way too much fat in your diet'.

He said as she told him her diet she agreed he was putting her on a low fat diet.

Stacey was prepared to put a hundred per cent into her new regime Corey couldn't stand Louie.

She'd met him once which was enough he was someone who made Alan Carr and Louie Spence look butch.

He gave her a headache he was so over the top at least now Polly was in New York she wouldn't have to put up with him in the house and now she had to attend her brother's engagement party.

Love and hate

They were getting married on May 1st a Spring wedding.
Corey wished they weren't getting married she had no
interest in welcoming Lizzie to the family.
She decided to invite Stacey to Dublin with her Corey also
planned to see Carol.
The evening after they arrived it was the engagement
party she wore a dark blue dress silver earrings.
Corey knew she looked good Stacey wore a black jacket,
short skirt and heels she looked nice still it wouldn't be
hard to upstage Lizzie Corey thought.
Since she looked like a tramp the party was being held at
a five star hotel the girls were impressed it was nice.
Free food and drink as long as she stayed away from
Lizzie it should be ok Corey thought to herself.
They realised they'd arrived early the party didn't start till
7pm they decided to take a walk.
As they soon spied Carol with John her step-dad 'Corey
how are you?' John asked 'I'm good' Carol hugged her.
It felt nice after spending her whole life not getting on with
Marie you look great off to a party?' John asked.
'My brother's engagement party' 'when is he getting
married?' 'May 1st' 'that's a way off' 'I know'.

'She's doing some Art course and is re-doing her house so won't have time to have one apparently'.

'She's not my cup of tea' 'he must love her' Carol said 'what about you? off somewhere nice' Stacey asked.

'We're off for a romantic dinner celebrating our wedding anniversary eighteen years together' Carol said.

'That's great congratulations' 'thankyou' 'if you want to come along later you can' Corey said.

'We wouldn't want to gate crash your brother's engagement party' 'you wouldn't'.

'I'm sure he'd be fine with it you know the St James Hotel' 'yes' 'well it's on till eleven if you change your mind' 'ok'.

'We might come if not I'll call you ok' Carol said kissing her on the cheek.

Having Carol in her life made her feel better about things the problems with her parents 'I'll see you later'.

Carol waved they went back to the hotel they decided to order some drinks play a game of pool.

Wearing tight fitting clothes Corey hoped there wouldn't be any men ogling her 'Corey' she heard a voice call.

'Dan' 'you look great' 'thanks' 'nice dress I remember when you were seventeen you hated dresses'.

'Well it's a special occasion it's not very often I get to dress up' 'Stacey you look good you always look good'.

Stacey smiled Corey thought if only he'd gotten together with Stacey instead of Lizzie it was wishful thinking.

'Is Lizzie here?' 'course' 'I brought a present' 'great I'll go get her' 'great' the less time spent with her the better.

Lizzie arrived wearing a black dress and pearls her hair up she'd clearly made the effort 'you look great'.

'So do you Corey can't say I know about pool it's more of a man's game' 'lots of women play I got you a present'.

'Thanks' Corey handed her a jewellery box with a silver necklace 'nice'.

Corey had wanted to get her something terrible but she thought Daniel might realise how much she hated her.

'I'll put it with the other presents dinner will be ready soon' 'I'll see you soon'.

As she walked away Corey decided she really couldn't stand Lizzie surely Daniel could have picked better.

He was a good looking guy 'I don't like her' Stacey said.

'Join the club I'm only here for my brother and the food and drink' Corey couldn't wait for the night to be over.

They looked around the hotel was nice classy they decided to order a coke each at the bar.

Before the engagement dinner 'Corey' a voice called.

'Victoria what are you doing here?' 'me I was supposed to be meeting someone but I was stood up' she said sadly.

'A man?' 'no my real mother' 'you're back in contact?'.
Stacey asked 'yeah we've been e-mailing and chatting on
Facebook she said she's ill I don't know if it's true or not'.
'Maybe I'm not good enough' she said 'don't worry these
things happen' 'thanks I'll be ok maybe we'll re-arrange'.
'It was a big deal you know…' 'if she's stood you up
maybe she's not worth meeting' Stacey said.
Trying to make her feel better 'maybe you're right'.
'Listen we'll get you a drink' Stacey said 'thanks'.
'Something alcoholic to forget your troubles' 'yes please'.
'Vodka and gin' 'coming right up' 'what are you two here
for?' 'well we thought we'd spend the night together'.
'In a luxurious hotel seen as Polly's not here only joking!'
Stacey said 'you had me for a minute' 'no seriously'.
'Corey's brother's getting married and it's their
engagement party' 'that's great'.
'You always said how your brother was looking for love'
'well she's not that nice in fact she's a bitch'.
'But we kind of have to keep up pretences for the
occasion' Stacey said 'why don't you stay'.
 Corey suggested 'but I haven't been invited' 'Dan won't
mind' 'if you're sure' 'we're having dinner in a minute'.
'Have you eaten?' Stacey asked 'no I was supposed to
with my mother' 'then it's fate have dinner'.

'We can have a few drinks relax' 'thanks you're the best'.

'What are friends for' Stacey said 'I'll be back in a minute I have to make sure my mascara is ok' Victoria said.

As she went to the ladies 'I wonder what happened with her mum?' Stacey said.

'I remember once I was doing a gig with a band at this hotel I saw her crying it was her mam's wedding'.

'And her sister was really horrible jealous I think Victoria hadn't been invited' 'I always wondered why she left her'.

'Why they were estranged' Stacey said curious 'she left when she was a child to marry that other man'.

'Her step-dad I guess maybe they drifted apart' Corey wondered 'I know but I'm a mum now'.

'And I couldn't imagine leaving my daughter' Stacey said.

'I mean I understand people have joint custody but you know abandoning her and her dad as well'.

'I know my mum had alcohol issues but at least I got to know her as a teenager Victoria never had that'.

'And then her uncle abusing her' Stacey said sadly.

'I wish I'd known at school me and Polly then we could have helped her' 'Mrs Rayworth said that as well'.

'You saw Mrs Rayworth?' Stacey asked 'a few years ago'.

'When I left school when I was at Art College'.

'She was a great headmistress'.

'I know' 'better than Mrs McGowan she was vile'.

Stacey said 'a right bitch' 'hi I'm back' 'vodka and gin'.

'Thanks hopefully it'll make me feel better' 'I might need one later having to pretend to like Lizzie' Corey joked.

'What's she like?' 'not very nice' 'she's always making comments about Corey' Stacey informed Victoria.

'You'll see when you meet her later still hopefully the food will be nice' 'everyone dinner is served'.

'Everyone be seated champagne will also be served'.

The host said Stacey noticed a reserved sign on the seat next to he she put it in front of Victoria.

They looked at their menu's as they ordered their starters 'dough balls for us three' 'thanks' Victoria said to Stacey.

Main course was pasta in a creamy sauce as Corey looked around the table she spied an old friend Colin he smiled.

Maybe the evening wouldn't be so bad a waiter served wine as he poured a millimetre of wine into Stacey's glass.

'Where's the rest?' she asked 'maybe because it's exclusive their tight with portion sizes' Corey joked.

'So exclusive their serving child size portions' Stacey joked they laughed 'I know what you mean'.

Victoria agreed as she looked at her tiny piece of chocolate cake Lizzie gave them a look they looked away.

'Did you see that?' Corey said 'I know'.

'So we're not allowed to enjoy ourselves' Stacey said.

'What does he see in her?' 'I have no idea' Corey replied.

After dinner everyone chatted Lizzie approached them.

'Hi' 'hi Lizzie' Corey said smiling keeping up her act of pretending to like her 'Corey who's this then?' she said.

Looking at Victoria 'she's our cousin' 'oh ok I'm Lizzie'.

'Victoria' 'well I hope everyone's enjoying themselves'.

'Immensely the food was great' Stacey said 'I know'.

'I'm full up must go' 'you must be the only one the size of the portions' Stacey said 'what?'.

'I said you are the only one who could carry off such a great dress' 'thanks see you round people to see'.

'That was close' Victoria said 'I know and quick thinking saying Victoria's your cousin' Stacey said.

'I was worried I might get thrown out' 'no you're with us we wouldn't allow it besides she doesn't own the hotel'.

Corey said as Victoria relaxed a bit more the music started as they disco began Corey chatted to Colin.

'How are you?' he asked 'great you?' 'grand you look fantastic where's Douglas?' 'he was ill'.

'He couldn't make it' 'that's a shame' 'I know' as Corey looked over she couldn't believe it.

She saw Douglas was chatting to Lizzie and Daniel.

'I'll see you in a minute' Corey said walking over to them.

Lizzie seemed to be enjoying herself Corey thought.

'Corey you know when we get married I'll be like Douglas's aunty' 'I know' 'I guess it'll be good'.

'To get to know him since Dan has custody' Corey wanted to say that she also had joint custody.

But didn't want to start a row 'having a good time?'.

Lizzie asked Corey 'great nice hotel' 'just getting a drink back soon' 'great night isn't it'.

'Yes I thought Dougie was too ill to come' Corey said.

Angry at her brother 'he's better now he took some aspirin does the trick' 'does she know that we have joint custody'.

'Don't worry I've explained everything' 'great' 'I saw you talking with Colin' 'I haven't seen him in ages'.

'It was good to catch up' 'I'll see you later' Dan said.

'Oh does Dougie want a drink?' 'it's ok I've got him a coke' Lizzie said 'see you then'.

Corey went over to the bar to see Colin "I see Douglas over there' 'yeah Dan gave him an aspirin'.

'So he could come he's getting to know Lizzie' 'you sound like you don't like her' 'I don't like her'.

'I can't stand her either' Colin said smiling at least she wasn't the only one who didn't like Lizzie.

'Never mind if they do make it up the aisle it won't last more than three months' 'that's true'.

'Maybe a year if she's cunning enough what about you?'.
Corey asked 'just dating looking for the right girl imagine
if we'd stayed together and you hadn't become a lesbian'.
'I was thirteen we were and I didn't choose to become a
lesbian it's just something that's in me'.
'So does Douglas know about me?' 'no I want to tell him'.
'It's about timing I'm thinking maybe I should wait till he's
sixteen' 'I understand he's a lovely lad'.
'Does he ever ask about me?' 'sometimes I will tell him
when he's older I promise' 'so is Stacey single?' 'why?'.
'Do you fancy her?' 'she's gorgeous how can her ex cheat
on her' 'she left him because he cheated on her'.
'She's happy being single I think' Corey received a text
from Carol saying she couldn't make it.
But did they want to meet tomorrow she said yes.
'Who is it?' 'Carol my real mam I said she could come to
the party but she wants to see me tomorrow'.
'Do you mind if I go soon?' 'no message me on Facebook'
'will do' Colin hugged her she went to get Stacey.
'Mind if we go?' Corey asked 'no come on' they left Corey
was glad she felt uncomfortable the whole night.
The next day Daniel came to visit with Lizzie and Douglas
she couldn't even relax in her own home.
Without her being there she welcomed them.

A forced smile 'great party last night' Corey said.

'This is Megan and Timmy' Lizzie led in two young children that was all she needed other people's children. Who were uninvited Marie was also scared of other children she didn't know at the best of times.

'My sister's kids you don't mind' 'course not' Corey lied.

'Tea' 'yes please' Corey went to make the tea as Stacey sat next to her Corey was grateful for her company.

What would she do without her 'so tell me you're half Irish?' Lizzie asked Stacey 'yes my dad is his parents'.

'Great is it true your mixed you look white' Corey couldn't believe Lizzie so now she was interrogating Stacey.

'My mum's mixed race so technically I'm a quarter black' 'right ok so what about your daughter?'.

'Isn't her father black' 'he's black Italian' 'so I guess she'd be half black then French and Italian'.

'Mixed race kids come in all different shades not everyone looks like Mel B or Halle Berry'.

Stacey was offended at Lizzie's dissecting of her and her daughter's black heritage she didn't say anything.

But felt upset at what she'd said Corey returned with the tea 'so what you up to today?' Corey asked.

'We're going shopping' 'great' 'bridesmaids dresses then we're taking Douglas to a film after' 'sounds good'.

Corey felt angry she was his mother she had joint custody Lizzie was acting like she wasn't in the picture.

She didn't want to make a scene fall out with her brother because of her.

Stacey had decided she couldn't stand Lizzie 'I was just saying to Stacey about her being mixed'.

'Weird how genes work how come your skin's so pale?'.

'It's my Irish side my dad's a redhead with green eyes or he was till he lost his hair so's my aunt'.

'When I was younger had olive skin but then it got lighter' Stacey felt upset by Lizzie's questioning.

She'd only just gotten over dealing with the fact she looked different from her mum and sister.

Now she felt unconfident about herself Corey noticed how sad she looked she decided to change the subject.

'So tell us about the dress?' Corey asked 'it's red' 'really'.

'Yes it's the fashion now ever see Jodie Marsh takes it up the aisle' 'no I didn't'.

'Well the wedding's gonna be gothic in a medieval castle'.

'With candles it'll look great in May we might even get a may pole' Dan said.

Corey couldn't imagine her brother wanting a gothic wedding he was very much a traditionalist.

Lizzie definitely seemed to be in charge.

'The bridesmaids will be wearing red too' 'great'.

Corey didn't know how much longer she could pretend to like Lizzie she'd have to tell her brother how she felt.

The children were also behaving badly so much that Marie started crying upstairs she hated any kind of noise.

The little boy was the worst jumping on Corey's back.

Something she wasn't pleased about since as a teenager her dad had left her with marks on her back.

After belting her so hard something she wasn't about to tell Lizzie finally they left.

Corey didn't think she could take anymore of Lizzie's pretending to be nice to her act.

'I thought she'd never go' 'I know' Stacey agreed.

'I can't believe that bitch is marrying my brother'.

'I hate her so much and every time I see her I have to pretend to like her' Corey noticed Stacey looked upset.

'What's wrong?' 'I'm sorry I'll be ok' 'don't be is it what she said? she is such a bitch the things she was asking'.

'About you and your daughter' 'I always felt different from my family I know it shouldn't matter'.

'I only just started feeling ok about everything I have vertigo I never told anyone it's a skin condition'.

'People think I have naturally pale skin but I didn't when I was a kid I was tanned dark olive'.

'Then when I was eleven I got these patches so by the time I was thirteen I looked white' 'I'm sorry'.

'You never told me' 'I don't tell anyone I don't mind how I look like I'm not gonna go get a tan'.

'Just because of anyone but I was just starting to feel good about myself' 'and she made you feel bad about yourself?'.

'You don't have to explain please don't let that bitch feel bad about yourself she's not worth it'.

'You should be proud to be mixed-race' 'thanks I'll try not to let her bother me'.

'Listen she is never coming round my house again my brother does not want a gothic wedding'.

'He's a traditionalist did you see the way that boy jumped on me?' 'I know and she didn't tell him off'.

'Lizzie is a bitch and she doesn't care that Douglas is my son if they get married I'll never see him'.

'You've got custody' 'joint custody I only see him in the school holidays and soon I won't see him at all' 'you will'.

'She'll take him on days out' 'can't you say something'.

'Maybe not without falling out with my brother' 'if you told him what she's really like' 'he's in love with her'.

'Maybe he's marrying her because he doesn't want to be alone' 'maybe I doubt it my brother's really good looking'.

'He could have anyone he wants and he picks a tramp'.

'Like her I guess some men will date anyone I hope he's not marrying her cause she's pregnant' 'let's hope not'. Stacey replied 'shall we go see my mam?' Corey asked. It was now 4pm but Corey needed to get out of the house. As she arrived with Stacey she was happy meeting her mother was the best thing to happen to her.

Carol had a day off work 'how are you?' 'great' they were offered tea and biscuits 'is John at work?' 'yeah'.

'And the boys are at school it's a shame they'd love to see you' 'I know tell them I say hi they can come see me'.

'In London anytime' 'so how was the engagement party?' 'don't ask actually it was ok Colin was there my ex Dougie's father we chatted and we saw Victoria'.

'The food was ok it's her I can't stand Lizzie neither can Stacey I mean what is my brother thinking'.

'It's like I have to pretend to like her' 'that's not good'. 'Maybe you should tell him how you feel' Carol suggested. 'Then he might never speak to me again' 'he's your brother I'm sure he'd value your opinion'.

'Even if I said I hated Lizzie' 'you've got to be honest'. 'Maybe I could I wouldn't want to ruin our relationship'. 'You wouldn't maybe he'd appreciate you being so honest with him' 'he's my brother I want him to be happy'.

'But she's not right for him' 'are you gonna be a bridesmaid?' 'no way she hasn't asked me'.

'I don't even know her if she did I'd say no their having a gothic wedding red dresses' 'sounds cool'.

'Maybe it's not my brother's thing' 'I know him he wouldn't want that' 'don't worry it probably won't last'.

'Maybe a few months then you can say I told you so how are you Stacey?' 'I'm great' 'how's your little girl?'.

'She's at home I can't wait to see her' 'you know you can come to my house anytime you like'.

'I'm surrounded by men a lot of the time it's nice to have some female company' 'it's good to see you' Corey said 'you too' Corey wished she had met Carol sooner but now they were making up for lost time they chatted for a while.

When she left she decided to invite Carol to London soon.

That afternoon she went to see Douglas Lizzie wasn't there she decided she'd talk to Daniel.

Tell him what she really thought of her not yet though Corey said her goodbyes as she left for the UK with Stacey who was eager to start working out again.

With Louie she had been doing well on her new diet plan.

And she looked better he was great he kept her motivated at all times he was also being strict with her.

But Stacey knew it was for her own good.

Corey was writing songs with the band it took her mind off things her affair with Steve.

Now she was back in England it made her feel even more guilty Corey told herself that it had been a mistake.

It was wrong that Friday afternoon Corey decided to go see Stacey.

As she arrived she could see through the window that she was working out with Louie great Corey thought.

She almost decided to leave but changed her mind surely she could just about manage an hour.

With an annoying camp queen Corey knocked on the door Stacey went to open it 'come in I'm working out'.

'Bad time' 'no we'll be done in ten minutes we're just about to do some cooling down exercises'.

'Make a drink if you want' 'ok' Corey had some orange juice she watched them working out.

Stacey seemed in the zone while Louie looked full of energy Corey wondered how anyone could be that hyper.

Without taking drugs Stacey and Louie cooled down.

She wondered why Stacey didn't just go back to doing dance classes 'I'm finished'.

'I think I'll have some orange juice' 'hard workout'.

'It'll be worth it you'll see I'm just gonna go have a shower back soon'.

Now she was being left alone with Louie 'how was Ireland?' 'great apart from my brother's fiancé'
'Bitch is she?' 'something like that' 'I love Loose Women' he said happily Stacey soon returned.
'Did you enjoy your workout?' Louie asked 'yes it was great' Stacey said.
'Why don't you just do dance classes?' Corey asked.
'Because she's employed my services it's better this way quicker results' 'if you think so'.
'I always thought personal trainers were a waste of time'.
'I help people to lose weight how is it a waste of time'.
'Because people can motivate themselves to lose weight'.
'Are you telling me you've never put on weight' 'yes'.
'After I had Marie I motivated myself to lose weight to exercise personal trainers are a waste of money'.
'What about personal stylists when people can dress themselves' 'I was just giving my opinion!'.
'So you can give it but you can't take it' 'oh I can take it!'.
Corey said angry 'even off bitchy queens!' 'someone get her a feather boa!' Stacey was shocked.
At the frosty atmosphere between them she realised that Corey and Louie weren't going to be the best of friends. Corey scowled at him 'oh I don't have a stylist I dress myself for your information!' 'who dressed you today'.

'M & S' 'come on what do you take? to be that hyper all the time E's and amphetamines' 'how dare you!'.

'Some people are naturally high! how dare you accuse me of taking illegal substances!'.

'Just because you used to do drugs!' 'I don't do drugs!'.

'I haven't taken them for five years' 'well then don't accuse other people!' 'please don't row!' Stacey said.

'Have you always been this sarcastic?' 'oh always'.

Corey replied 'not always not at school' Stacey said.

'Really Stacey' 'yes' 'maybe I wasn't' 'so what were you like at school?' 'I was on all the sports teams'.

'Netball, hockey, rounders see I know my sport I was an average C student it was a private school'.

'Me and Stacey went to Angelsfields it's outside Dublin I started when I was eleven Polly and Stacey later'.

'They were almost thirteen my dad dealt in race horses some other dodgy stuff'.

Flashback

'That's how he paid for the fees' as Corey arrived home from school it was a beautiful Friday afternoon.

November and quite cold Corey was hiding a secret she was eight months pregnant.

She'd taken to putting her bag in front of her stomach.

When travelling in public transport she couldn't take any risks that she would be found out her dad would hate that.

He'd demanded she keep it a secret it was becoming harder Corey couldn't tell any of her friends.

In case they told someone she had to pretend she was ok.

Act as if everything was normal luckily she'd only just started showing no-one had suspected anything.

As she arrived home her dad appeared to be in a good mood 'dad' 'how's my little girl'.

'I miss you so much when your at school how's things?'.

'Great no-one's suspected anything' 'you haven't told anyone'.

'What your think I'm gonna tell the whole class?' 'good'.

'The sooner you have the baby get it adopted the better'.

Corey felt angry at her dad she knew she was too young to have a baby.

And she wouldn't want to raise any child around her
alcoholic father and uncontrollable temper.

But he was completely ignoring her feelings her sadness
the fact that she would have to part with her baby.

Almost as soon as it was born 'this is a problem for all of
us I don't want anyone knowing your pregnant!'.

'Well neither do I no-one knows!' 'good that's how it'll
stay understand! Corine I love'.

'You this is for the best for you and the baby' 'I know that'.

'It's just really hard pretending not to be pregnant'.

'Well do something to take your mind off things here's
some money go have a night out at a disco'.

'It's on me' 'thanks' 'no problem oh and I know you're a
lesbian' 'what?' 'I saw you kissing a girl in town'.

'When?' 'a few weeks ago' 'ok I like girls' 'I don't care
that you're a lesbian' 'you hate gays'.

'what two people do in the privacy of their own homes is
their business I don't care for gay men'.

'But I don't have a problem with lesbians' 'you don't have
to worry I'm not gonna bring anyone back with me'.

'You can but it's better I'm not here if you want your own
privacy' 'ok'.

She wasn't exactly going to bring anyone home the state
her father got himself into 'listen I'm off out'.

'For a few hours after tea I'll be back around eleven'.

'Off to the pub' Corey asked 'I have a date' 'who with?'.

'A woman she's gorgeous blonde tanned probably your type'.

'Now you're a lesbian you can appreciate the beauty of a woman so what type do you go for?'.

'I've only just realised I'm a lesbian I'm getting used to things when I find out I'll let you know'.

'As long as Dan's not gay' 'he's not trust me' 'good '.

'Then everything's grand' he kissed her on the cheek.

Even when he was being a bastard he could get her to forgive him a real charmer Corey listened to music.

Doing her homework before having an early night's sleep her dad came in around midnight singing.

Usually a good sign if he was smashing things up in the kitchen it was a bad sign.

And meant he was going to get violent Corey went back to sleep the next morning she woke at 10am.

Tired from her dad's singing 'you're showing now' 'I know don't worry when I go out I'll wear a black coat'.

'So no-one will know' 'you're going out?' 'yes I'm going to see my girlfriend and no I won't tell her' 'well have fun'.

'I'm going to the racecourse' 'enjoy yourself' after he left Corey looked around the kitchen was a mess.

Piles of dishes she was angry her father made the house a mess she was eight months pregnant.

And had terrible back pain she should have been resting not tiding up after her father she washed up.

Thinking about things at least once her baby was born he wouldn't be able to harm him.

Her dad had already hit her twice during her pregnancy.

Luckily she hadn't miscarried Corey got dressed and decided to go see her girlfriend it wasn't that serious.

They were only dating but she was happy to be out the closet that Monday Corey returned to school.

That morning she had stomach cramps she ignored by her second lesson they were worse she panicked.

Suddenly she realised she was going into labour.

'Miss I need to leave class' 'what's wrong Corey?'.

'I'm in pain I'm ill' 'ok you can leave' Corey grabbed her bag as she quickly rang a taxi grabbing her stomach.

She also rang her dad they arranged to meet at the hospital they put her in a wheelchair.

As she tried to breathe easily 'it'll be over before you know it' 'I hope so' 'it will'.

'And then everything can go back to normal' they got a bed for her as she lay there having contractions.

Trying to remain calm 'it'll be fine I know it hurts'.

'Dad listen please you don't have to stay it'll be ok I have the nurses with me' 'I'll stay'.

'But when it happens I'll sit outside' 'did you bring my overnight bag?' 'it's here' Corey lay there in pain.

Her brother eventually came at least Daniel was there her best friend 'does it hurt?' 'agony'.

'The sooner it's over the better' finally around 9pm her baby was born he looked small but gorgeous.

With fine red hair she'd fallen in love with him so had Daniel as they cooed over him.

'Don't get too attached we're only having him for a few weeks' her dad said.

Corey asked one of the nurses how to change a nappy.

They'd only have him a few weeks but she wanted to make sure he was looked after properly.

The next day they went home Corey began looking after him straight away.

Her father insisted she go back to school a few days longer people would suspect.

She acted as if everything was ok Corey adored her baby.

Occasionally her dad would shout that he'd had enough of the crying she was scared for her baby.

The sooner he was adopted the better her mother helped her find a family so he could be adopted.

Corey was sad he was going but she knew it was for the
best so he could have a better life someone else.
Somewhere safer three weeks later her mother said she'd
found a home for her baby Corey was pleased but sad.
She took the baby who she hadn't named to a couple in
their forties her mother said they were nice.
They couldn't have children at least Corey would be doing
something good for someone else.
'hello Corey' the woman said 'I haven't named him so you
can' 'thankyou' 'I know this must be hard for you'.
'It's ok I know he's gonna have a better life with you and
I know you can't have children' 'thankyou Corey'.
'My dad isn't good with babies he doesn't like them he has
a bad temper so I'm not sure our house is the best place'.
'To bring up a baby so this is for the best' 'we'll look after
him for you' 'thankyou oh he likes to be sung to'.
'To get him off to sleep' 'ok I'll do that well bye Corey'.
Corey looked back one more time knowing she'd never see
her baby again at least not until he was eighteen.
And decided to track her down she knew it was for the
best however upsetting it was for her 'I've got to go'.
'Why?' Stacey asked 'I just have to come round whenever
you like' 'Corey please don't go'.
'You've not been here long' 'I just have to'.

Stacey could see she was upset about something Corey
was shaken at her flashback as she returned home.
'Did I say something wrong?' Louie asked 'I don't know'.
'If I did tell her I'm sorry' 'I don't think it was you'.
Stacey said hoping Corey was ok as Corey saw her
answerphone go off she checked her messages.
She had one from Daniel saying he would be going with
Lizzie to Scotland with Douglas for a holiday.
Instead of bringing him to see her she was upset he only
had three days before he had to go back to school.
She was his mother now Lizzie was trying to take her role.
Corey left an angry message on Daniel's phone letting him
know how she felt about Lizzie and the situation.
Later that evening she heard a knock at the door it was
Daniel 'I didn't even know you were in England'.
'We need to talk' 'yes we do you never told me you had a
problem with Lizzie!' 'well I have now!' 'why?'.
'Where do I begin we have joint custody remember she's
trying to take over we have an arrangement'.
'We thought it would be nice for Douglas to go to
Scotland to explore new places'.
'And you're trying to make it difficult' 'how?' 'it's just a
two day trip' 'he only has a few days'.
'Before he goes back to school' 'so come home to Dublin'.

'Polly's away in America' 'most of my friends have normal jobs remember and you're loved up'.

'There's no need to be jealous!' 'why would I be jealous of her! she looks like a tramp'.

'Well I remember a few years ago you didn't dress so well as you do now' 'I don't like her ok'.

'Well I thought you did' 'I lied because she's your fiancée and you're in love with her and I want you to be happy'.

'Well why didn't you say so it makes sense now! what's up with you? imagine if Lizzie knew that you didn't like her'.

'If she'd heard that message on my phone then she'd know you hated her' 'I don't even know her'.

'Then how do you know you don't like her' 'I just do!'.

'She's not my type of person' 'she's good with Douglas'.

'Oh really! well I don't think Dougie is so keen on her'.

'They get on fine don't be like this' 'like what?' 'she's my fiancée and wants to take him places discover new places'.

'What's wrong with that?' 'she's trying to take him away from me!' 'no she's not!' 'yes she is Dan'.

'First mam and dad now Lizzie he's my son and you're trying to take him away from me' Corey cried.

She knew she was getting upset over nothing 'no-one's taking Douglas away from you what's wrong?'.

Daniel put his arms around her 'listen we won't go to Scotland if you don't want us to go'.

'We'll just bring him to you' 'no really it's ok you're right'.

'He should see different places it would do him good'.

'Are you sure?' 'yes' 'I don't want you being upset'.

'I won't be' 'but your upset now' 'I'm ok I'm not angry at Lizzie even though we don't get on I had a flashback'.

'To when mam took Douglas away I don't want it to happen again' 'it won't'.

'When we've finished our trip to Scotland we'll bring him here how's that?' 'thanks that'll be grand'.

Corey felt better her mind had been put at rest she still didn't like Lizzie and thought Dan could do better.

The next day Stacey came to visit Corey she was worried Louie had upset her Corey opened the door .

'It's freezing outside' Stacey said 'cup of tea?'.

'I'd love one I'm sorry about yesterday' Stacey said.

'It's fine really' 'I know Louie can be a bit full on but he's really sweet once you get to know him' 'it wasn't Louie'.

'Are you sure?' 'yes I had a flashback to when I had Douglas adopted or thought I did' 'I'm sorry'.

'It must have been hard for you' 'it's ok everything's good now' 'well you should have told me if you were upset'.

'I'm your best friend' Stacey gave Corey a hug.

'I know what would I do without you to talk to'.

'I can't believe how long we've known each other'.

Stacey said' 'I know since we were thirteen' 'do you think we've changed much?' Stacey said.

'I don't think you have maybe I have I loved those days'.

'Me too' 'I wish you'd told me what was going on with your dad' Stacey said.

'I didn't want anyone to know about my problems'.

'You should have told me' 'I know everything's ok now'.

'I miss those days too' Corey thought about Angelsfields. What a good school it had been how much she'd loved it. The friends she'd made it was a warm June evening Corey was getting ready to go to her waitressing job.

At O'Connor's a restaurant in Dublin a family run business now run by the owner and his brother.

It got her away from the house and her dad into the real world for three nights a week.

She did Fridays & Saturdays she earned the minimum wage as much as a sixteen year old could earn.

It helped to pay for her nights out Daniel also worked there.

At least they could bitch about how horrible the boss was together Corey did up the buttons on her white shirt. Before putting on a short black skirt and black tights.

And a pair of silver stud earrings she'd grown up as a tomboy.

Her waitressing job was the only chance she got to be girlie she applied some green eyeshadow.

And powder to her face Corey rarely wore make-up scared she wouldn't be able to apply it properly.

Polly knew all about make-up foundation, mascara fake eyelashes she was ready to go.

'Off out then' her dad asked 'yes' Corey said as Daniel joined her 'have fun' 'we will' Daniel said 'bye dad'.

'Bye Corey you look gorgeous in that outfit by the way'.

'Thanks dad' they left getting a ride with Colin Corey's ex-boyfriend to the restaurant they arrived for 6pm.

Ready for a busy night at the restaurant they checked in as they cleaned tables 'you look nice tonight' Colin said.

He'd recently started working there Corey knew he still fancied her they'd been an item for about eight months.

When she was twelve she had been thirteen when she'd had her baby he had a girlfriend.

But his crush on her was obvious he was always complimenting her he knew she was a lesbian.

But wouldn't leave it Corey didn't mind she liked him as a good friend 'you look gorgeous' 'you'll chase anyone'.

'In a skirt' 'that's not true' 'you've got a girlfriend'.

'I know I have' 'so what would she say if she knew you were flirting with other women' 'she wouldn't mind'.

'Yes she would and you know it listen thanks for the compliments but I'm not attracted to men in that way'.

'A waste if you ask me' 'I can't help it it's the way I am'.

'Well you know where I am if you change your mind'.

'I'm sure' 'ok well I tried my best' 'I like us being good friends if it's ok with you' 'it's a great idea'.

'Good I'd go crazy without you working here' 'Colin and you Corey' 'less chat more work' 'yes ok' Colin said.

As the boss left 'I'm only doing this till I leave school' Colin said 'if you don't get sacked before'.

'Better be careful what you say' Daniel said overhearing their conversation 'how about a kiss?' Colin asked.

'You've got a girlfriend just leave it!' 'you heard what my sister said' 'alright I was only playing with you'.

'Colin I'm a lesbian I've been out the closet for three years' 'alright' 'trust me if I was straight only you'.

'That's good to know so do you have a girlfriend?'.

'I'm always dating' Corey replied 'playing the field'.

'Maybe' 'slag' Daniel said joking 'just because you can't get a girlfriend' 'I can'.

'Actually I'm concentrating on my studies unlike some people I know' 'I am I want to get good grades'.

'So I can go to Art College' 'you'll get in' Daniel assured her 'I hope so' 'you will' Daniel spied a woman.

In her thirties with her partner 'table for two' 'yes Corey' 'Mrs Rayworth how are you?' 'I'm great'.

'I didn't know you worked here' 'oh for a while this is my brother Daniel' 'hello' 'come with me'.

'I'll show you to your table' Corey thought how good she looked for her age as Daniel went to get a drinks menu.

Corey waited for the next customers to arrive she didn't have to wait long she looked around.

Polly and Stacey had come with Polly's step-mum Wendy. And her dad Simon and Wendy's twin brothers Paul and Andy Corey was happy to see Polly.

She wished they could have stayed together she'd always dreamt of them having a lesbian wedding.

Now that she was with Andy there was no chance of that. Polly was clearly too into men Corey just hoped one day she'd find the girl of her dreams 'how are you?'.

'Great darling it's Jon's birthday' Polly replied.

'Happy birthday' 'thanks' Jon replied he was Polly's step-brother 'what would you like to drink?'.

'I'll have a coke' 'me too' Andy said 'I'll have a lemonade' Jon said 'ok coming up'.

Corey felt good she always did when Polly was around.

She still fancied her Corey looked over she was smiling at Andy it broke her heart.

To know that Polly didn't feel the same way about her anymore she knew she'd have to deal with it.

Polly thought how pretty Corey looked it was a shame it hadn't worked out between them

She was now in love with Andy 'I see Polly's here'.

Daniel said 'yeah it's Jon's birthday her step-brother their having a family meal' 'are you ok?' he asked 'I'm fine'.

'You have a sad look on your face' 'I was just thinking if only it had worked out between us' 'Polly likes men'.

'She's bi-sexual' 'maybe going with girls was just a phase' 'no Dan it wasn't like that' 'listen I love you'.

'You're my sister which is why you need to meet someone who's a hundred per cent gay'.

'Not someone who's bi-sexual or straight'.

'Polly's not straight' 'well almost I don't want you having your heart broken' 'I won't' 'you will'.

'Besides you said yourself she's leaving going back to England' 'I know your right'.

'Everything you've said is right' 'don't worry someone will come along when you least expect it' 'I know'.

'Here you go' Corey said as she brought the drinks on a tray 'thanks' Polly smiled Corey smiled back.

'You look nice tonight' Andy said 'tanks Mr O'Riley'.
'It's Andy' 'thanks' Corey couldn't hate Andy he was too
nice they ordered dinner she took their menus.
'If you need anything else call me' 'thankyou Corey'.
Andy said as she walked away Daniel gave her a look
'well did you chat to her?' 'not really she's busy'.
'It's a family meal' 'she's got a boyfriend?' 'yes I think it's
serious you're right I've got no chance' 'don't worry'.
'You'll meet someone soon' soon the orders were ready as
Corey took their plates over 'this looks nice' Andy said.
'I know thanks Cor' Polly said 'it's not me really'.
'It's compliments to the chef I'm just a waitress'.
'No darling you work hard' Polly said 'thanks listen I've
got other tables to serve I'll see you later' 'ok darling'.
Corey hated to be around her and Andy it upset her she
had never felt so jealous she thought she was over Polly.
But she knew she wasn't she still felt something for her she
wished she didn't that it was easier 'dad's here?'.
Daniel said 'what! why?' 'he's drunk at the bar' 'great!'.
'How can he just turn up here' 'I don't know you know
what he's like' Corey was angry.
How could her dad embarrass her at her workplace
'Corine' 'yes' 'get me a drink' 'you've had enough!'.

'No I haven't! get me one more speak to me with some respect! I'll get you one what your having?'.

'Nothing at work' 'come on now you need to loosen up' Corey went back to Polly's table to take orders for desserts 'hello I'm back' 'does that man come in here often?'.

Andy asked 'not very often' 'let me know if he gives you any trouble' 'I will do' 'Corey' she looked over.

As her dad was falling off the bar 'listen I'll be back'.

She walked over to him 'dad please! your making a scene!' 'oh really! I'll make an even bigger one'.

'If you don't give me a drink!' 'fine ok!' Corey had never been so angry as she asked the barman to order a pint.

Who just wanted him to be quiet the only time he was ever quiet was when he was drinking 'who's that man?'.

Polly asked 'my dad' 'really' 'yes he doesn't do this very often he was celebrating a friend's birthday' Corey lied.

What else could she say to them she wasn't about to admit her problems tell them her dad was an alcoholic.

Who hit her it would have to stay a secret 'listen I need to sort my dad out I'm glad you enjoyed your food'.

'Thanks Corey' Wendy said 'it's ok' Corey knew everything wasn't ok and never would be until she left home.

'Dad please go home do you want me to get sacked?'.

'I'm going ok' 'will you be ok to go home?' 'I'll take him'.

A man said 'great thanks' at least she wouldn't have to worry about her dad for the rest of the night.

'We're going now' Polly said as the others paid the bill.

'Thanks Cor for not saying anything about Andy' 'it's not really my business' 'I really appreciate it'.

'That's what friends are for' Polly had secretly started dating Andy who was their teacher.

And twenty two years older Corey knew Polly would be in trouble when her family found out 'well thanks darling'.

'Is your dad ok?' 'yeah someone's arranged for him to go home it's fine really I'll see you at school'.

'Alright bye darling' 'bye Corey' Wendy said as they left 'bye have a good night' Corey watched as Polly waved.

She realised how much she loved Polly she was unavailable but she would always be special to her.

And she would always love her somehow Corey knew she would have to find a way to deal with things.

Dan saw her watching Polly leave 'at least dad's gone home now' 'you enjoyed seeing Polly' 'yeah don't worry'.

'I'll find a way to move on' 'you'll find someone a nice girl to settle down with' 'I know'.

'I was just thinking back to those days tell Louie it wasn't his fault I got upset' 'I will are you missing Polly?'.

'Like crazy she's my other half I don't know what I'd do without her' 'she'll be back before you know it' 'I know'.

'You look really good' 'thanks I feel like I'm losing weight already' 'you look fine'.

'And if you feel you need to eat something do it you know those trainers can be too strict' 'it's for my own good'.

'Louie's great once you get to know him' 'I'm sure he is'.

'Trust me' Corey wasn't so sure there was definitely a personality clash maybe Louie was ok she thought.

But he did wind her up the kind of person who would give you a headache.

If you spent too much time in their company still she wouldn't say that in front of Stacey.

She was clearly taken with him three days later Daniel and Lizzie brought Douglas round to see her.

'Hello Dougie' he hugged her 'you ok?' 'yeah' 'he's grand' Lizzie said 'how was Scotland?' Corey asked.

'Good' Douglas said 'glad you enjoyed it' 'he did'.

'We had a great time' Lizzie said Corey felt as if she was trying to be his mother yet again .

'So how's the wedding plans going?' 'great May 1st it is we can't wait' 'I'm sure it'll be great' 'oh it will'.

'We've got the venues, invitations the dress it's gonna be great candles in the church really magical'.

'You'll love the venue' Daniel said 'I'm sure I will'.

'It's gonna be a good wedding we hope' 'yeah Dougie's gonna be a page boy'

Corey could tell from the look on his face he hated the idea 'great'.

She secretly hoped her brother would see sense and call off the wedding before they made it up the aisle.

Unfortunately it looked like they would be getting married as planned.

The wedding

'I was just wondering with the custody thing does the judge mind your part of a lesbian couple?' 'no'.

'Because I'm his mother it doesn't matter' 'but it's illegal in Ireland' 'I know'.

'I divide my time between Dublin and London so it's not an issue' 'but aren't you breaking the law?'.

'By being married to a woman I have joint custody for a reason it was the judges decision'.

'That me and Dan are the best people to look after Douglas how dare you! come here and criticise me'.

'You don't know me!' 'Corey!' 'no how dare she! you don't even have children you don't know the situation'.

'I do a good job looking after Douglas'.

'You think you can come in my house and judge me!'.

'I was only asking!' 'well I don't want to hear it! in fact why don't you just get out of my house!'

'Corey calm down!' 'no I won't calm down yes I'm a lesbian do you have a problem with it!'.

'I don't have a problem with it!' 'then shut the f**k up!'.

'Corey you apologise to Lizzie now!' 'no I won't!'.

'Yes you will!' Daniel said 'this is my house!' 'yeah well maybe you shouldn't be seeing Douglas!'.

'The state your in!' 'he's staying with me! we had an arrangement!' 'not when your like this!' Daniel said.

As Corey started to get angry 'come on we're going!'.

Daniel said to Lizzie as they left she was upset that she would use her sexuality against her.

As the door slammed shut she cried in her bedroom it seemed Lizzie and Dan were in control.

Telling her when she could see her own son Corey felt sad for the rest of the evening thinking about the row.

Later she heard a knock at the door 'Dan' 'I want a word with you!' 'she's not with you then!' 'Dougie's here'.

'But I'm only letting him in if you control your temper!'.

'Are you going to apologise to Lizzie?' 'why should I apologise to her! she had a go at me my sexuality!'.

'She didn't your overreacting!' 'I am not!' 'I think you are! she was just asking about our arrangement'.

Corey couldn't believe it Daniel really must have been in love with her to not be able to see what she was up to.

'You can tell her all the details you think it was ok for her to have a go at me your own sister for being gay'.

'She wasn't she was just asking!' 'she was not! I'm not apologising!' 'then your not coming to the wedding!'.

'Maybe I don't want to come!' 'I want you at my wedding your my sister you have to be'.

'Fine! tell her I'm sorry for using the f word I'm only apologising if she accepts what she did was wrong' 'ok'. 'I don't want any rows' 'neither do I Dougie I'm sorry about what happened your beds all made up' 'ok'. 'A drink?' 'yes please' 'ok coming up' 'I'll have one too'. Daniel said Corey was happy she'd made it up with her brother she still hated Lizzie.

She was annoyed she'd had to apologise to her when she had nothing to apologise for winding her up.

Over the court case the fact she was gay clearly she was a secret lesbian hater why couldn't her brother see that.

Still Corey decided it was better to apologise than to be at war with her brother she had Douglas for two days.

On the last day Lizzie came to pick him up she forced herself to say sorry

Secretly she couldn't stand to be anywhere near her that Saturday afternoon Stacey came to visit with Louie.

That was all she needed 'hi how are you?' Stacey asked .

'Fine come in cherryade?' Corey asked 'yes please both of us' she went to pour the drinks as Stacey joined her.

'Please don't row with Louie' 'I'll try not to' they sat down on the sofa as Corey brought them the cherryade.

'What happened with Lizzie?' Stacey asked 'don't ask'.

'It's that bad' 'I can't even see my own son'.

'Without asking permission she wound me up when she came round I don't even want to go to their wedding'.

'Dan made me apologise to Lizzie when she had a go at me about being a lesbian oh is it legal'.

'Your breaking the law to be married to another woman'.

'I swear she hates lesbians' 'bitch' Stacey said 'I know tell me about it I can't stand to be in the same room as her'.

'I suppose I have to go he is my brother after all we've always been close or we were before she came along'.

'Their so not right together he just can't see it'.

'Don't worry there's couples like that all the time everyone can see it except the couple in question' 'Louie's right'.

Stacey said 'trust me two years at the most' 'I bet they stay together just to prove everyone wrong'.

'It won't last though these things never do' Louie said.

'I hope it doesn't I give it a few months before they start having problems it'll be even worse if they have kids'.

'She's a bitch' Stacey said 'you should meet her'

'sounds like I don't want to' Louie said.

'Anyway I guess I'll have to get an outfit sorted'.

'I'll come with you' Stacey said 'thanks it's not for six weeks yet anyway what would I do without you'.

'Don't worry we'll get drunk together or try to'.

'Since I can't have more than two glasses of anything'.

'Where is the wedding?' Stacey asked 'a castle outside Dublin for the reception the wedding inside a church'.

'Maybe when they get to the speech I'll...you know'.

'Say something hen they say is there any reason why this person should not be married' 'you wouldn't'.

'I might I'll just have to deal with it the fact my brother's marrying Lizzie even though I hate her'.

'It's just really hard he's my best friend I don't want him having his heart broken' 'don't worry he'll see sense'.

Stacey assured Corey 'he knows everything about me'.

'There's nothing he doesn't know' 'everything?'

Stacey asked 'almost' 'don't worry about your brother'.

'I'm sure he'll see sense' 'I hope so' 'I'll be at the wedding we'll have fun' Stacey said.

Trying to make Corey feel better having Stacey there would make her feel better.

For the next few weeks Corey barely spoke to Daniel.

He said he wanted her at the wedding but wasn't acting like it she hated falling out with her brother.

It was all Lizzie's fault it had been fine until she came along ruined their relationship.

Corey decided she should plan a wedding outfit maybe something to upstage the bride.

She visited an exclusive boutique Stacey came with her.

Corey chose a berry coloured short dress satin as se=he
tried it on she realised it wouldn't do up .
She was usually a ten 'this dress isn't fitting me right'.
'I must have put on weight give me a twelve' she tried on a
bigger size it fit perfectly 'what do you think?'.
Corey asked 'it looks beautiful' the shop assistant said.
'Thanks I really like it' 'you look stunning' Stacey said.
'Really' 'definitely you should have been a model' 'thanks
Stace think it'll upstage the bride?' Corey joked.
'Definitely' Stacey thought how beautiful Corey looked in
the dress she chose some berry strappy sandals.
To go with the dress Stacey already had a green dress she
could wear that afternoon they watched DVD's together.
Ate Pringles she was enjoying some chill out time.
Corey still felt bad about the situation with her brother.
He was hardly talking to her at least she had Stacey and
bandmate Kitty to make her feel better.
She also had a new pastime eating and watching DVD's.
Occasionally venturing out to do the odd gig with the
band she didn't care she'd worked for years.
She deserved some chill out time Corey wondered why she
was craving more food than usual.
She decided it must be because she was a food addict
before she knew it Polly was returning home.

*From New York and Corey made sure she was waiting for
her it was now the end of April it was freezing cold.*

*As Corey wore a long black coat and hat Polly came
towards her looking gorgeous 'you look good' Corey said.
'Thanks I'm so glad to be back home' they went home as
Polly took off her coat she was so happy.*

*Polly was back home 'I've missed you much' 'you too'.
'I loved New York but I couldn't wait to get home how's
everyone?' 'great Stacey's lost loads of weight'.*

*'Working out with Louie' 'oh great I can't wait to see him
again how is he?' 'camp as ever' Corey said sarcastically.
'You seem a bit down' Polly noticed 'you would be if your
brother wasn't talking to you' 'the wedding'.*

*'Dan said he wants me to go so I am I've even brought a
dress just for the occasion'.*

*'He's changed ever since he took up with her' 'it's alright'.
'He knows what he's doing' 'and for the record because
I know for some reason you like her'.*

*'Me and Stacey can't stand her she's an evil bitch!'.
'I never said I liked her' 'you did and she's trying to stop
me seeing Dougie she tries to make arrangements'.*

*'For me not to see him when he hates her she hates
lesbians according to her we're not normal'.*

'I hate her so much' 'Cor listen I never said I liked her especially if she hates lesbians I'm sorry'.

'Why is she trying to change your arrangement with Dan?' 'why do you think'.

'So she can take him away from me' 'well he's stupid if he lets her' 'there's nothing I can do he's marrying her'.

'Don't worry I'll be there Stacey's coming too' 'and Victoria' 'it'll be ok it's just one day'.

'Then you don't have to see her again you said you've got a dress' Corey showed Polly the dress red satin.

As it took pride of place at the front of the wardrobe.

'Wow! it's gorgeous' 'I know' 'let's see it on' 'I don't know' 'why not go on' 'ok you can help me put it on' 'alright'.

Corey changed into the dress it wouldn't do up 'let me try again' Polly said she tried to zip it up 'it's no good'.

'It won't do up' 'don't worry ok' 'I've put on weight the last few weeks' 'I thought you did I didn't wanna say'.

'Too many Pringles' they laughed 'you look good'.

'Besides you can't have the figure you had when you were a teenager we're late twenties now' 'thanks'.

'What am I gonna do about the dress?' 'go back get a bigger size' 'what if they don't have one'.

'Course they will and don't worry they always cut things smaller in wedding shops' 'I know they do'.

'Thanks for making me feel better' 'you look great'.
'Tomorrow we'll go out get a bigger size give me a kiss'.
Polly asked as they kissed passionately the next day they
went back to the shop where Corey had brought the dress.
Luckily they had it in a size fourteen as she returned home
she tried it on Polly zipped her up it fit perfectly.
As Corey looked in the mirror she thought she looked
good 'stunning it's gorgeous' Polly said 'thanks'.
'You look beautiful' 'I love the dress' Corey was happy.
And Polly already had a crème suit and skirt she could
wear to the wedding Corey e-mailed her brother.
To find out who else was going apparently Carol hadn't
been given an invite she wasn't happy.
Daniel had always gotten on well with her even though
she was Corey's mum still it was his.
Or rather Lizzie's wedding he could invite who he wanted
the sooner it was over the better Corey thought.
Two weeks later it was the wedding May 1st in a church
just outside Dublin it wasn't a bad venue Corey thought.
She was dreading the wedding service the wedding took
place at 11am Polly, Corey & Stacey arrived together.
As they met Victoria outside the venue 'great church'.
She said 'shame about the weather' Polly said greeting her
'and the bride' Stacey said

'Never mind any excuse for a good wedding' Polly said.
Trying to lighten the mood Stacey was wearing a dark
green dress Victoria a berry coloured jacket and skirt.
'I feel like a wedding crasher' she joked 'well I bet half the
people who attend weddings only vaguely know the bride'.
'Or groom I reckon some are invited to make up the
numbers' 'I agree Susie' Stacey said.
'We'll have a good time nice meal at the reception and a
dance' Polly said 'everyone's going in' Corey said.
As they all took their seats inside the wedding hall she
spied Colin a few seats in front of them.
They said hello 'who's that?' Stacey asked 'Colin'.
'Dougie's father me and Dan are still good friends with
him' 'you look great' Colin said 'thanks so do you'.
As Corey looked around she couldn't believe it as she saw
her mother she was angry 'you are joking!' Polly said.
Looking around 'after all the things she said how could he
invite her!' 'I have no idea' Corey was beyond angry.
He'd even give evidence in court to say what a bad person
she was Corey suspected Lizzie had invited her.
Just to spite her or her mother had begged them to be
invited and had invited herself.
Either way she wasn't happy about it 'that bitch!'.
Polly said 'don't worry' 'stay calm' Stacey said.

Corey looked at the wedding programme the only thing she could do to take her mind off things 'Corey'.

'Uncle Tommy' 'how are you?' he asked 'I'm grand'.

'Your mam's over there' 'I know I just saw her I'm trying to avoid her if I can' 'I don't blame you'.

'Do you think Dan invited her' 'she probably invited herself knowing your mam'.

'After getting custody of Douglas how could he do that'.

'I don't know' 'don't worry I'll look out for you' 'thanks uncle Tommy' Corey felt better having family around. Even though Tommy wasn't her biological uncle she still thought of him as her uncle.

He'd paid for her to go to Art college finally it was time for Lizzie to make her arrival as she entered the church. Wearing her red dress her dark curly hair styled she would have looked pretty if she hadn't been such a bitch. Corey couldn't believe it when the music started Billy Idol White Wedding not exactly a romantic love song.

Behind her two young girls in crème dresses dropped red rose petals Lizzie gave Corey a look.

As she walked down the aisle 'did you see that?' 'I know' Stacey replied 'the sooner they get divorced the better'.

Corey whispered uncle Tommy smiled at her overhearing her comment 'the dress is nice though' Stacey said.

The service began 'we are gathered here today to witness the marriage
of Elizabeth Abigail O Hagen'.
'And Daniel Steven O'Hanlon Elizabeth do you take this man to be your lawful wedded husband?' 'yes I do'.
'And do you Daniel take Elizabeth to be your lawful wedded wife?' Corey hoped he'd say no.
'Yes' they were almost married now she thought 'if there is anyone present who objects to the marriage'.
'Of these persons here present let him speak now or forever hold his peace' Corey stood up Stacey smiled.
She had a feeling she was going to say something 'I do'.
'I object' 'Corine! sit down!' her mother said angry.
'You have something to say?' 'yes I do' 'bitch! ruining my wedding!' Lizzie looked angry.
All the more reason to say something 'let her say her piece' Daniel said looking at Corey.
'The reason I object is because your making a big mistake you could do so much better' 'it's my mistake to make'.
'Lizzie your not right for my brother I don't think you should get married' 'well we are so sit down and shut up!'.
'Before I have you thrown out! anything else!' 'no'.
'I've said my piece' Corey sat down Stacey was happy she'd told Lizzie how it was.

'Now you may exchange rings' Corey watched as they swapped rings 'now you may kiss the bride'.

Lizzie's side of the congregation cheered they were married now Corey knew her brother had made a mistake. He would regret she'd done all she could as Corey made her way out of the church first.

As she stood outside Lizzie's friends and family gave her dirty looks. 'you've got a feckin nerve!'.

'That's my daughter!' 'It's a free country' 'their married aren't they' 'Corine!' all she needed her mother.

'How could you ruin my son your own brother's wedding!'.

'The vicar said if anyone has any reason why these persons should not be married let him speak now'.

'Or forever hold his peace' 'alright I know it! I don't need a feckin sermon!' 'f**k off mam I've got nothing to say!'.

'I'll never forgive you for ruining their wedding!'.

'Well I'll never forgive you for ruining my life! you don't care who Dan's married to as long as he got married'.

'That's what you want the perfect life married two kids'.

'I have that but you don't see my marriage as real!'.

'This isn't about you!' 'great speech!' Daniel said approaching them 'your my sister'.

'Why couldn't you keep your mouth shut on our wedding day!' 'I was telling the truth' 'she's my wife!'.

'I hate her and she hates me!' 'your imagining everything how could you say those things at my wedding!'.

'She deliberately ruined our arrangements with Douglas' 'no she didn't!' 'yes she did!'.

'And you can tell her she's breaking the law!' 'how could you! how could you do that to me!'.

'I thought it might stop you marrying her!' 'well she's my wife and we're married whether you like it or not!'.

'And you! how could you invite mam!' 'she's my mother'.

'Even if she's not yours!' 'this is it! I am never speaking to you again!' 'and you invite her!' 'shut up mam!'.

'It's my wedding!' 'I'm your sister and I know you better than anyone else!' 'then you should be happy'.

'I've found someone to marry! you were always saying how I needed to settle down get married to someone'.

'Not her anyone but her!' 'your not to talk about Lizzie like that she's my wife your sister in-law now'.

'I'll be seeing you later' Marie said as she left.

'You invited mam after everything she said to me to Polly'.

'Everything she did!' 'she's our mother' 'that's it then me and you our relationship is over!' 'Corey'.

'Your no longer my brother! I no longer want anything to do with you!' 'don't be like that!'.

'You've made your choice disrespected me by inviting her to the wedding! and your a feckin idiot!'.

'Don't come to me in a few months when it's over!'.

'It won't be!' 'fine I'm going home!' 'please come to the reception we can sort this out' 'I'll see how I feel!'.

Corey left she went to her house to freshen up the reception had already started.

They chose to go later in the evening Daniel was upset his own sister and Polly who he'd always gotten on with.

As a friend they weren't at his reception it was too late. Now he'd invited his mother as he made speeches Daniel felt sad his sister his best friend wasn't there.

He hoped Corey was ok that she didn't mean what she'd said and that she'd forgive him for inviting their mother.

Later she returned with Stacey, Polly & Victoria there was no way she could've stayed.

With everyone giving her looks as they made their speeches Corey decided to keep a low profile.

'You've come back' Dan said spying her 'I can go if you want' 'no please I don't want you to go'.

'I'm not staying long oh I see mam's still here' 'listen'.

'No you listen! all the things she did saying to Polly it was her fault our daughter's autistic which isn't true'.

'And I can't believe you'd invite her after everything she's done!' 'I feel bad ok' 'you didn't have to invite her!'.

'Where's Douglas?' 'up there dancing' 'have some punch it might make you feel more relaxed' 'where's Lizzie?'.

'Around I'd stay out of her way' 'I'll try my best'.

'I'll see you later' Corey couldn't believe her mother coming towards her 'what are you doing here!'.

'Daniel invited me he's my brother' 'why didn't you stay at home you ruined the wedding!'.

'Now you've come here to ruin the reception!'.

'I didn't ruin the wedding! they got married I know how much you wanted to go to a proper wedding'.

'Since you didn't bother to come to mine! I know you don't class same sex weddings as real do you!' 'calm down!'.

'How can I stay calm with you around! you took my son away from me! lied to me about being my mam!'.

'Now you've taken Dan away from me!' 'you can't stand to see him happy with any girl I've got news for you'.

'You're no longer the special girl in his life anymore!'.

'You think I'm jealous!' 'you are and I know it!' 'you know nothing! you're a bitter nasty woman!'.

'You know one day you'll end up alone!'.

'I think it's the other way around! you love the fact that me and Daniel aren't speaking'.

'Just like you loved it when you stopped Dougie seeing me makes you feel powerful having control!'.

'Now Douglas knows what you're really like!' 'I'll get him back anyway! he's fourteen he's not a little kid anymore'.

'I have custody of him by law and if he says he doesn't want to live with you that's it' 'not in my book!'.

'You've only got joint custody there are things I could have said in court you know what I mean'.

'And when Daniel gets full custody you won't see him again! and what's gonna happen when he goes to school'.

'And they find out he's got two mams one of them is an ex-glamour model who used to get her chest out'.

'For a living!' 'the other has mental health issues!'.

Corey had never been so angry she grabbed her glass of wine tipping it over her mother 'you feckin bitch!'.

'And to think I was a mother to you for so many years!'.

'You never were! a mother to me you left me when I was seven years old you let my father beat me and Dan'.

'Don't tell me you didn't know he was a violent man you never cared about me!'.

'Because I wasn't your real daughter like Nicky! admit it you always loved Nicky more than me!'.

'You never wanted to be a real mother to me!'.

'Well I'm ashamed of what you've become!' 'what's that?'.

'Rich and successful!' 'no a bitch!' 'I'll never forgive you for this! ruining my son your brother's wedding'.

'You may think your high jinks are amusing no-one else does I'll never forgive you for this!'.

'Well I'll never forgive you for all the things you've done to me enjoy the reception!' Corey ran off.

As she went to the ladies toilets angry 'Corey' it was Stacey 'where have you been Polly's been looking for you'.

'I saw mam we had a fight' 'what happened?' 'she says she's gonna get Douglas back'.

'What if she tells the courts I've got mental problems and they give Dan full custody' 'they won't' 'they might'.

'You don't have mental problems' 'that's not what mam said' 'they wouldn't you've got joint custody'.

'She's just trying to play games get to you'

'I wish I'd never come to the wedding' 'Dan's your brother you've got every right to be here' 'you're right'.

'Please don't get upset you can't let her get to you'.

'I know I'll try not to' 'good I saw Colin he said he'd like to see you' 'where is he?'.

'The last time I saw him he was throwing shapes on the dancefloor' 'I'll go see him' 'see you in a minute'.

Stacey decided to wait for Corey outside 'Stacey' 'Dan'.
'Where's Corey?' 'around' 'tell me' 'she's upset your
mum's upset her she'll be ok' 'is she in there?' 'yes'.
'Corey' 'you shouldn't be in here it's the ladies toilets'.
'I came to see you are you ok?' 'I'll be fine I'm not staying
long' 'please stay as long as you like' 'I'm not welcome'.
'You are really' 'if I have to be in the same room as mam
or Lizzie' 'what happened with mam?'.
'I'm not talking about it' 'she told me you threw a glass of
wine over her' 'she deserved it' 'come on let's go dance'.
Corey went to the dancefloor with Daniel and Stacey
trying to have some fun. 'Cor there you are' Polly said.
'Let's dance' Corey forced a smile as she danced with
Polly she spied Lizzie as their eyes met.
Polly could feel the tension 'I'm only letting you stay
because of Dan! else I'd be asking you to leave'.
'Don't worry I'll be going soon' 'and I don't appreciate
being upstaged at my own wedding!'.
'What do you mean?' 'you know exactly what I mean!'.
'That speech the dress' 'what's wrong with my dress?'
Corey asked innocently 'you brought it just to upstage me'
'as if! I brought it cause I liked it' 'whatever!'
'Just make sure you're gone within the hour'.

*'Don't worry I will be' Corey was being kicked out of her
own brother's wedding could the evening get any worse.
She decided to head to the bar for another drink
'hello gorgeous' 'Colin' 'I heard about your row'.
'With your mam' 'she hated what I said about Lizzie'.
'I thought it was funny if you feel you had to say it' 'I did'.
'Maybe I shouldn't have' 'no if it's how you feel don't
worry they'll soon forget about it'.*

'Just between you and me I never liked your mam'.

*'Actually she's my ex-mother Carol's the only mother
I need who really cares about me'.*

'Do you know in America you can divorce your parents?'.

'Sounds like a good idea' 'are you ok?' 'I will be'.

*'I'm not staying long Lizzie told me if I'm not out of here
in an hour she'll kill me' 'I understand'.*

'If it's any consolation I can't stand her either'.

*'No-one can or uncle Tommy it wouldn't be so bad if she
wasn't trying to take my brother away from me'.*

'How can he like her let alone love her?' 'I have no idea'.

*'Don't worry he'll see sense you know it's one of those
relationships everyone around him can see it's wrong'.*

*'Except him' 'I know I can't stand her he invited mam can
you believe it? it was Lizzie's idea' 'I thought so'.*

'I don't wanna see my brother anymore' 'you don't mean that' 'I do he's my best friend but I can't see him anymore'.
'Without seeing her our relationship's over' 'I'll buy you another drink to make you feel better' 'thanks'.
Corey drowned her sorrows with another glass of champagne it made her feel better.
'You look gorgeous in that dress' 'thanks I see you were talking to Stacey earlier' 'yeah she's nice' 'I know'.
'Do you fancy her?' 'yeah shame she lives in London else I'd be making a pass for her' 'she's pretty' 'she's single'.
After a few glasses of wine Corey felt better she went back to the dancefloor with Colin she was having a good time.
She noticed Lizzie and her mum giving her dirty looks it was starting to annoy her she tried to ignore them.
'What the f**k are you looking at!' Corey said angry.
'Nothing why?' 'I'm trying to enjoy myself' 'well we don't want you here!' Lizzie's mum said.
'My brother he invited me' 'I never wanted you at our wedding especially not at our reception'.
'After what you said at my wedding!' 'I was just speaking the truth my brother can do so much better than you!'.
'Bitch! Corey look around no-one wants you here or your lesbian gang!' 'are you referring to Polly and Stacey?'.
'Who else would I be referring to!'.

Polly wanted to say something but decided to let Corey deal with Lizzie 'how dare you slag off my wife!'.

'I wasn't slagging Polly off' 'oh really! sounds like it to me!' 'you know you look like a tart in that dress!'.

'What's wrong with the dress?' 'well done Corey you showed me up! at my own wedding!' 'really'.

'And aren't lesbians supposed to dress like men you only brought that dress to show me up!' 'it's a dress!'.

'If I wanna wear a dress I will' 'why don't you get out!'.

'Make me!' 'no-one wants you here!' 'Corine!'.

'Mam stay out of this!'! 'maybe you should listen to your mam' 'maybe you should shut the f**k up!'.

'No-one ruins my wedding and gets away with it!'.

'Even your own parents don't want to know about you!'.

'Didn't your real mother give you up for adoption'.

Corey went for Lizzie as they started fighting 'you touch my daughter!' Corey had never been so angry.

'Your mother's right your are mental a psycho!'.

Corey hated her mother as much as Lizzie she wanted to smack her in the face.

Even though she wasn't a violent person 'you wouldn't want your kids being taken away now would you!'.

Daniel came over to see what the commotion was all about 'what's going on?'.

'This is all your fault!' Polly said shouting at Dan 'how?'
'take a guess! inviting your mum'.

'After all the things she's said' 'oh yes bring me into this!'.

'It's true she would put anyone in a mental clinic!'.

'Don't worry we're going! enjoy the rest of your reception!
hope you all enjoyed the scene!' Polly said.

As she gave Dan a look as they left Polly knew Corey was
upset and angry as she got home she cried.

Polly made her a cup of tea Corey felt like they were going
to push her over the edge 'it's what they want darling'.

'Polly's right they want you to be upset' Stacey said.

'I am upset ok!' 'don't worry you'll feel better in a few
days' Corey wanted to disappear the next day Carol rang.

Asking if she could see her she said she wasn't up to it.

Polly told her what had happened secretly Corey wanted
to see her mum but she didn't want to see her in a state.

Polly went out shopping as her mum came round anyway
Corey decided to tell her all about the wedding 'they
didn't want me there I shouldn't have gone'.

'Corey you're Daniel's sister you had every right to be at
the wedding'.

Corey & Louie

'They all hate me why did he have to marry her?'.
'Because he's a man and sometimes men will marry the first pretty girl they see'.
'Without thinking of the consequences' 'they were all laughing at me saying that I'm mental'.
'That I should be locked up' 'Corey your not mental you were probably drunk I hate to see you in a state'.
'I didn't want you to see me like this' 'I knew you were upset Polly told me but I wanted to see you anyway'.
'Try and make you feel better about things I love you and if I get hold of that girl Lizzie I will kill her myself'.
'Thanks I don't know what I'd do without you' 'me neither you know you should come round sometime'.
'See the boys' 'I will when I feel better I promise'.
Corey was glad her mum had come round meeting Carol had been the best thing that ever happened to her.
If only they had met sooner when she was a teenager all the things they could have talked about.
But it was better late than never a few days later she took her mother up on the offer of going round to see her.
And her step-brothers with Polly they had a nice time as they drank wine and talked watched telly.

Corey felt like part of a real family not one that was broken she felt sad at what had happened with Daniel. But she decided he had to be the one to make the first move screw her family she thought to herself.

She had Carol now and Polly Corey decided she didn't need anyone else she returned to London.

It had been an eventful few days now her head was clearer she decided to try and forget about Lizzie.

It was hard since she had to be in contact to speak to Douglas Stacey was continuing her workouts with Louie. She'd never felt better about herself and couldn't wait to come back with her new album.

He'd also become a good friend Polly adored him Corey however tried to avoid him she didn't get him.

Or the concept of camp although she realised she'd worn one or two dresses on stage that could be classed as camp The truth was she had little experience of hanging out with gay men Polly had her gay mafia which included George. And her uncle Sam Stacey filled Louie in on the wedding. Every little detail how Corey had stood up during the service asking her brother what he was doing with Lizzie. The rows with her brother and mum the big row with Lizzie and her mum how Lizzie had called her a tart. For wearing a sexy red dress and called her a psycho.

How she'd left in a state upset 'sounds like an episode of Eastenders' Louie said as they drank tea.

'I know I suppose these things happen at weddings don't they' 'not like that sounds bad glad their not my family'.

'They all hated her Lizzie was jealous Corey looked great in that dress Lizzie couldn't stand it' Stacey said.

'I suppose it's not a great idea to upstage the bride'.

'Can you blame her?' 'I suppose not she sounds like a bitch' 'she is Dan's so nice what was he thinking?'.

'You know men Stacey they think with their trousers'.

'Her mother or ex-mother she's vile she never cared about her she left her when she was seven'.

'Then only saw her in the holidays Carol's her mum now she's so nice' 'well at least now she has a mum'.

'They were so mean to her at the wedding Lizzie she's such a bitch they were calling her mental I was so angry'.

'Corey was in a state for days I know you don't get on but if you got to know her you'd like her'.

'She pretends to be tough doesn't let people in at first'.

'She never used to be like that at school I guess it's all the stuff she went through'.

'Anyway once she lets you in she's the sweetest kindest person and she has a really dry sense of humour'.

'I've noticed that' Louie said.

Sounding not convinced that they would get on he thought she was a tough cookie.

Stacey heard a knock at the door it was Corey 'hi'.

'Come in Louie's here' 'another workout' 'just chatting'.

'Lemonade?' Stacey offered 'yes please thanks' in the background Corey could see Louie dancing.

She still wasn't feeling that great after her fall out with Dan the last thing she needed was Louie.

A camp annoying aerobics instructor she sat on the sofa.

As Stacey made them tea 'I see ragdoll's here' 'who?'.

'Corey' 'why do you call her that?' 'because she's tall and slim and looks like one or she did'.

'Before she put on weight still we did recently have Easter' 'Louie! don't say that' Corey's been really stressed lately'.

'I know well my services are available if she wants to use me for a workout I'll give her a discount' 'Louie'.

'I'm not telling my best friend she needs to lose weight' 'why not?' 'because she'll never speak to me again'.

'I'm only offering my services' 'Corey's usually into keep fit' 'well she's clearly let things slip lately'.

'I put on a weight a few months ago' 'I know and look how I helped you' Stacey took in the lemonade 'Stacey' 'yes'.

'You can tell Louie I don't need his services to lose weight' 'I'm sorry you overheard us'.

'You know what Louie's like always trying to get business'
'I'm quite capable of losing weight myself! you can tell
Louie to take his business elsewhere!'.
'Why do you hang out with people like that!' 'he's my
friend he's nice once you get to know him'.
'Well he's not the kind of person I'd hang out with'.
'I'm sorry ok I'm sure he didn't mean what he said'.
'Course he did!' 'everything ok?' 'fine' Stacey lied.
Corey sipped her lemonade 'Louie' 'yes' 'for your
information I don't require your services to lose weight!'.
'Ok fine well I'm a qualified personal trainer'.
'How long for?' 'six years' 'so do you always go up to
people and tell them they need to lose weight!'.
'I'm sorry ok everyone puts on weight don't they?'.
Louie decided to change the subject 'how was the
wedding?' 'my brother's wedding'.
'Put it this way if someone had filmed it for a reality show
it would have made car crash TV'.
'Those things always happen at weddings especially the
Irish big drinkers and that' 'oh yes we love to start fights'.
'And get drunk' 'I didn't mean it like that' 'then what did
you mean!' 'listen I can see it's no good talking to you'.
'When your like this' 'like what? how do you expect me to
be when you bitch about me in the kitchen!'.

'You don't even know me! calling me fat do you know how it makes me feel! people like you annoy me'.

'Oh homosexual men!' 'no just you I'm going!'.

'Corey please don't go!' 'no Stace' 'please come back!'.

'Leave me alone!' Corey left slamming the door.

'I'm sorry' 'Louie! now look what happened!' 'I'll sort it' 'how she probably hates me too now' 'it'll be ok'.

'I promise I've got my car I'll go after her' 'I don't think that's a good idea Louie I think we should leave it'.

'Go round tomorrow' 'Polly will be mad at me' 'no Louie it'll be ok if you explain you're sorry'.

First Lizzie was being mean to her now Louie was calling her fat on top of that she wasn't speaking to her brother. Corey wondered could her life get any worse? a few days later she and Polly decided to go to Brighton.

For a few days anything to take her mind off things as soon as they returned home to London Corey felt better. The sea air had done her some good the next day Polly went for a meeting in London.

She was doing another lingerie range which she was excited about Corey tidied the house.

While playing with their daughter Marie she heard a knock at the door she looked out the window it was Louie.

All she needed to ruin her good mood Corey opened the
door 'I came round to apologise'.

'I'm sorry for what I said I didn't mean it' 'so you should
be! how dare you make comments about people's weight'.

'I'm sorry' 'what do you think would happen if I slagged
off every house guest I invited round'.

'I'd have no friends left!' 'I shouldn't have said what
I did' 'tropical juice?' Corey asked.

He was the last person she wanted to entertain but since
Louie was good friends with Stacey and Polly.

She had no choice but to try and be civil to him she didn't
want anymore rows.

'Darling I think we should try and get on with each other'.
'Since Polly's your wife and one of my best friends' 'ok'.

'I'm not that bad once you get to know me' 'how did you
meet Polly?' Corey asked 'at a charity do for something'.

'We were sat at the same table she was adorable the
sweetest person considering she's a big star'.

'I love that scouse accent at least you can understand her
I mean some of these wags' 'can you understand me?'.

'Perfectly I love the Irish see you've got me all wrong'
'I'm sure I have I always thought Polly's accent was
scouse mixed in with Lancashire she lived in Blackpool'.

'From the age of nine till she was eleven'.

'And then when she was with Andy' 'I love Blackpool if
I get married I'll have my stag do there'.
'It would be so much fun Polly said she'd show me some
of your wedding photos' 'I'll go get the albums'.
Corey couldn't believe how nosy he was being 'here we
are' 'great do you have any biscuits?'.
'There's cookies in the tin' 'great my favourites so Polly's
at a meeting?' 'yes her new lingerie range'.
'Listen I'm really sorry for what I said' 'it's ok'.
'Can we be friends?' 'ok why not' Louie looked through
photos of their wedding 'nice outfits' 'I know'.
'Five years we've been together' 'that's good' 'nowadays
so who asked who?' 'to get married' 'yes' 'I asked Polly'.
'We were in L.A' 'that's sweet so what did Polly's mum say
about it?' 'she was happy' 'what about your mum?'.
'She hated it not my real mam Carol Marie the person
I thought was my mam' 'why did she hate it?'.
'A long story' Corey got up collecting the empty glasses.
As she went to the kitchen the last thing she wanted to do
was talk about her mother or rather her ex-mother.
She returned again a glum look on her face 'listen thanks
for the lemonade I'd better go now busy day' Louie said.
'Glad you liked the lemonade and biscuits' 'bye' it was
awkward between them as Louie left.

Maybe they could be friends later that evening at 5pm
Polly returned home 'Cor guess who I met'.

'At the supermarket' 'Louie' 'Corey hello did I piss you off
earlier?' 'no' 'you don't have to lie you know'.

'I'm not lying' 'I can tell you are' 'you two please don't
row' 'I'm sorry darling' Louie said.

As Polly emptied her shopping bags on the table.

'I don't want to talk about my mam that's all' 'I really am
sorry I wasn't thinking I know she was a bitch to you'.

'Polly told me everything forgive me?' 'yes' 'really' 'good
darling I'll help prepare dinner' 'thanks'.

Polly said 'what is dinner?' Corey asked 'pasta in tomato
sauce and chocolate cake with crème'.

'I should be on a diet' Corey said 'f**k the diet it's gran's
chocolate cake recipe it's gonna taste lovely'.

Polly assured her 'I'm sure it will I can't wait' Corey said.

'Stacey's coming over at six with Andy' 'great'.

'And Marcee's coming as well and Christian it'll be good'
'I thought you hated Marcee' Corey said 'I did'.

'But she's Stacey's mum'.

'And she's better than your mum' 'well it'll be good all of us having dinner'.

Corey watched telly as Polly made dinner Louie sat on the sofa with Corey 'what's the deal with Stacey's mum?'.

'They don't get on' 'oh right' 'Polly's his ex-wife'.

'She was jealous but I think she knows now we've been together so long that's she's not a threat to her and Andy'.

'I suppose it must be awkward since Andy and Polly are such good friends' 'Andy invited Polly to the wedding'.

'She didn't go she didn't want a big row I think Andy really wanted her there'.

'Well it's good Polly is able to invite her round I've never met Christian Polly's brother' 'I don't know him that well'.

'He seems nice not sure if he gets on well with Stacey they had a row at a family dinner a few months back'.

'I think they made it up' 'I'll keep an eye out for that ooh tension happens in all families'.

They heard a knock at the door 'I'll get it' Louie said.

Getting up he opened the door as Stacey's mum came to the door with Andy 'hello' Marcee said 'hello I'm Louie'.

'I've heard so much about you from Stacey'.

'All good I hope' 'course she told me you were...' 'black'.

'Yes' 'pleased to meet you' Marcee said 'you too'.

Marcee smiled 'where's Stacey?' Louie asked.

'Oh she's coming with Wendy and Christian' 'I was gonna say their not an item are they?' Louie said.

'Stacey and Christian I doubt it she's not that keen on him after he called her curvy a while back at a family dinner' Andy said 'oh she told me about that' 'it was a pretty big row' Polly said joining them 'hello darling' Andy said.

'Hi' Polly said as Andy kissed her on the cheek she couldn't enjoy their friendly moment.

Worried Marcee wouldn't like it 'come in dinner's almost done I'm sorry it's nothing fancy'.

'Whatever it is I'm sure it'll be great' Andy said 'there's homemade chocolate for after' 'sounds great'.

They heard another knock at the door it was Wendy with Stacey and Christian 'hi' Wendy said.

As she hugged Polly 'come in' 'hi Susie' 'Stace you look good' Polly decided not to mention weight.

In case it reminded Stacey of her row with Christian.

'Hi' Christian said looking gorgeous as usual 'hi come in everyone dinner's ready'.

They made their way to the dining room Polly poured Bucks Fizz for everyone.

As she served pasta with tomato sauce she hoped Stacey and Christian wouldn't have another row.

She realised they were sat opposite each other.

At least they weren't sat next to each other Polly noticed
Stacey was quiet 'so does everyone like the pasta?'.
'Great darling' Andy said 'really nice Susie' 'thanks Stace'
'I always forget your name's Susan' Louie said 'it's fine'.
'Cor calls me Polly Rita calls me Sue in fact I have about
three different names' 'that's true' Corey said.
'I have to say this pasta is gorgeous and the sauce is
divine' Louie said 'I'm glad you like it'.
'So Christian how's the acting going?' Andy asked 'great'.
'I've got a part in a BBC drama King Arthur' 'so who are
you playing?' 'King Arthur' 'great'.
'Andy said you were studying stage management'.
Marcee said 'yeah at Uni when my friend said there was
an audition I should come along so I said ok'.
'That's great' Marcee said 'you don't know what
opportunities are just around the corner' 'I know'.
'I'm really enjoying it' 'that's good' 'you've got the right
look for those period dramas' Polly said 'thanks'.
'You've never done a period drama' 'I should I've got the
cleavage for it' Polly joked.
'I'd love to wear one of those old fashion dresses'.
'You'd be great' Stacey said 'I'll talk to my agent see what
I can do' Polly said she was happy.
Everyone seemed to be enjoying themselves.

After dinner they all watched telly Stacey helped Polly put away the dishes Marcee joined them 'how's things?'.

'Good' 'so no rows with Christian then' 'no' 'I think he seems really nice' 'he's lovely' Polly said.

'If I was twenty years younger' Marcee said 'you look twenty years younger anyway' Stacey said 'more like five'.

'You look good' 'he's single' Polly said 'I'm not interested he's not my type' Stacey said 'that's a shame'.

'Kim likes him' Stacey said 'really' 'we ran into him not long ago we had a drink at a pub she was all over him'.

'I don't think he was interested' 'don't worry you'll find someone nice soon' 'that's what everyone says'.

'You will' Marcee hugged Stacey she liked the fact that they were close.

The next day Polly arranged to go to the pub that afternoon with Stacey, Christian & Kim.

For some chill out time she was looking forward to it they went to her favourite London pub.

There was always a good atmosphere at least she got the chance to hang out with Kim who was excited.

At seeing Christian again she made it obvious she had a big crush on him Polly ordered them cokes.

Except Kim who had a vodka and lime 'he's so gorgeous' Kim said to Stacey 'I wish he was single' 'he might be'.

'Can you ask him out for me?' 'maybe' 'please Stace he's your family now since his dad married your aunt'.

'Ok I'll see what I can do' 'hello again' Christian said.

'Hi Christian' Kim said 'good to see you again congratulations on getting King Arthur' 'thanks'.

Kim was now looking adoringly into Christian's eyes. Stacey found it funny 'listen I'm just going to the ladies back soon' 'she likes you' Stacey said.

'I know she's sweet' 'not your type' 'no' 'because she's black' 'no I'm not racist in any way she's very pretty'.

'But just not my type' 'ok' Stacey knew that was his way of saying he wasn't into black girls.

'Did you like the meal?' Christian asked Stacey 'oh I like pasta I'm a vegetarian' 'I've been for a year'.

'Great do you know Wendy and Andy well?' Stacey asked.

'I've met Wendy a few times she's really nice' 'she's the best she's always been like a mum to me'.

'I'm glad you both liked my cooking' Polly joined them.

'Susie you're a great cook' 'I thought it was nice all of us being together as a family' 'really good' Stacey agreed.

'Back soon' Kim returned 'I need to talk to you' 'ok'.

Kim smiled 'I really like you' 'I like you too as a friend'.

'Don't take this the wrong way but you're not my type'.

'Because I'm black' 'course not you're gorgeous'.

'It's me not you' 'ok I understand' 'really you're not mad at me' 'no' 'cause I know you're Stacey's best friend'.
'Oh we're much more than that we're family' Polly re-joined them 'how's everyone?' 'good'.
'Does anyone fancy a game of pool?' Polly asked 'me'.
Kim said 'come on then I'll give you a game' Polly liked Kim she was always happy and smiling 'will she be ok?'.
Christian asked Stacey 'oh fine really she did recently break up with her boyfriend'.
'I think she just wants someone to replace him to help her get over him I told her she will' 'sorry to hear that'.
'It's fine someone's always breaking up with someone'.
'Can I ask you' 'I don't have much luck with men' 'maybe you haven't met the right person' 'probably'.
'Do you have a girlfriend?' 'Stacey asked.
'No I'm single too I'm too busy at the moment anyway with my acting career' Christian said,
Stacey knew she should have told Christian she was mixed race not white as most people assumed.
Explain everything about herself how she hadn't met her mum till she was fourteen.
Finding out her uncle was her dad when she was twelve and everything else how her mum was black.
And she looked white.

She didn't know Christian well enough to tell him.

'Can I get you another drink?' Christian offered 'ok coke'.

'I don't drink much' 'you said' Christian got the drinks
'you must think I'm really boring cause I don't drink'.

'Course not neither do I except on special occasions you
should see my mates at Uni their all getting drunk'.

'And I'm at the bar sipping orange juice' 'at least I'm not
the only one' 'listen I'm really sorry for what I said'.

'That time at that dinner' 'it's ok I had put on weight'.

'I still shouldn't have said it' 'I know I looked fat' 'you
weren't it's better to have curves than to be too thin'.

'Please forgive me' 'it's ok I've lost weight since'.

'Because of me?' 'no I wanted to Louie helped me I never
had a personal trainer before but he's so much fun'.

'He's gay camp he makes working out fun' Polly joined
them 'I saw you talking' 'I was just telling Christian'.

'About Louie he's nice quite full on though' Stacey said
'well sometimes' 'I think he's a bit full on for Corey'.

'I thought they made it up' Stacey said 'kind of'.

'It's a shame that my wife and one of my best friends don't
get on' 'maybe they'll make it up' 'I hope so'.

They soon left the pub Stacey realised when she got home
that she quite liked Christian possibly fancied him.

Not that she would tell anyone.

Stacey decided she'd forgiven him for what he'd said.

Polly was also pleased they'd been chatting.

She hoped Stacey and Christian might get together.

She decided to have a dinner party invite Stacey &
Christian, Louie, Kim and some other people.

It wouldd be fun Polly thought she enjoyed playing hostess
and arranged for some party food.

Crisps and pineapple and sausages on sticks cheese and
crackers the guests arrived for 6pm

Corey didn't feel so good she was upstairs in the bedroom
wishing she could be with the others.

But she didn't feel up to it 'darling loving the party food'.

Louie said as he kissed Polly on the cheek 'thanks'.

'I thought you'd like it since you're so obsessed with
healthy eating' Polly joked 'I am'.

'But it's nice to let yourself go now and again and I can't
resist a bit of sausage and pineapple' 'you're so naughty'.

'I know I am darling' 'that's why you love me where's
ragdoll?' 'who?' 'Corey her nickname' 'she's upstairs'.

'She's not feeling well she's in bed' 'well I'm sorry to hear
that' 'she might come down later if she's feeling better'.

'Well she's missing a nice evening' 'I know' 'I see your
brother's here he's gorgeous' 'Louie!' 'he is'.

'Well he likes women' 'a shame still nice to window shop'.

'He's only twenty' 'does he have a girlfriend?' 'he did'.
'He's single now I'm trying to set him up with Stacey'.
'Really I can see them together' 'I know she needs
someone nice' Louie agreed Christian's a nice lad'.
Polly said 'does he fancy her?' 'I'm not sure they were
chatting at the pub yesterday their both single'.
'They both love music they'd be perfect together'.
'Who would be?' Kim asked 'Stacey and Christian'.
Polly said 'I never thought about it now I know why he
wasn't interested in me I asked him out'.
'He said he just wanted to be friends' 'you think he likes
her?' Polly asked 'yeah'.
'Look at the way he's looking at her' 'I was saying to
Louie she needs someone nice' 'I agree'.
'I really want my sister to be with someone nice'.
'I miss having a sister' Louie said 'you used to' 'she died'.
'I'm sorry' 'one of those things' Louie said sadly.
'I'll be your sister if you like' Polly said 'ok darling'.
'I love having a sister Stacey's my best friend' Kim said.
'What about your dad? you said he remarried'.
'Do you have any other brothers or sisters?'.
Polly asked Kim 'a brother two sisters' 'do you see them?'
'no I don't see my dad' 'why not?' 'he doesn't love me'.

'He never phones me he only sends a card at Christmas'.
'I'm sorry' 'don't be Polly I'm used to it'.
'That's why I was so happy when I met Stacey someone
who's family who actually loves me and takes an interest'.
'And you've got your mum and Andy I can talk to him
about anything he's my step-dad now Andy's the best'.
'He's really good at listening to your problems' Polly felt
sorry for Kim.
She had no idea she had problems with her dad she liked
her a lot.
As Polly chatted to Louie Christian chatted to Stacey.
'Louie seems like fun' 'he is do you work out?'.
Stacey asked 'yeah I go to the gym' 'how often?'.
'Four times a week I put on weight really easily and
especially now I'm on telly I've got to make the effort'.
'You look fine to me' 'thanks by the way I really like your
music' 'really' 'yes my sister's a really big fan'.
'That's nice what music do you like?' Stacey asked.
'I like northern soul I like a lot of the stuff you like Wendy
told me you like Prince and Chaka Khan'
'Yeah music's my life' 'mine too' 'look at you two getting
cosy' Polly said 'we were just discussing music'.
Stacey said 'Louie you remember Christian'.
'Hello again' 'hi' 'you know you and Polly look alike'.

'Yeah we do' Polly said 'Louie's a personal trainer'.

'Yes darling so if you need anyone to help you work out'.

'Thanks for the offer but I've got my own personal gym'.

'That's good' 'Christian lives in a mansion' Polly said.

'That's interesting' 'my mum married my step-dad who's a lord' 'you are joking!' 'no' 'but their divorced'.

'She renounced her title so she could keep the house'.

'Sounds like a good deal to me' Louie said 'yeah it's a really nice house I should go soon though'.

'I'm almost twenty one' 'so in this mansion do you have a swimming pool?' 'Louie!' 'it's ok'.

'We do have a swimming pool and a Jacuzzi' 'sounds great' 'I'm sure you could come round' 'really?'.

Louie said looking interested 'yeah and Polly you haven't met my mum' 'no I haven't' Polly said 'well come round'.

'And the gardens are really nice in the summer it's a bit cold at the moment' 'well I'd love to and Louie will come'.

Louie seemed happy at the idea Corey had decided to make an appearance she still wasn't feeling herself.

'Cor you feeling better?' Polly asked 'a bit' 'maybe you've got a virus'

'everyone appears to be enjoying themselves'.

'Oh Louie likes my food' 'great party food' Louie said.

Corey forced a smile sitting on the sofa 'you look pale'.

'She'll be fine I'll get you a glass of clementine juice'.
'Any gossip?' Corey asked 'Polly's doing some
matchmaking' 'Christian and Stacey'.
'Don't you think they'd make a good couple?' 'yes'.
'I thought Stacey didn't like Christian' 'they've made it up
now' 'I hope she finds someone nice'.
They danced to music ate party food eventually it was time
to go around 11pm Christian wanted to see Stacey again.
He had a big crush on her he gave her his number.
'Call or text me' 'ok' Stacey was happy she really liked
him 'did he just give you his number?' 'yes' 'that's great'.
'You've got to tell me all the gossip' Polly said excited.
'I will' 'bye Kim' 'bye Polly I had a great time let's hang
out sometime' 'I'd love to'.
'You'll have to come round again' 'bye darling' Christian
said to Polly 'I'll arrange for you to come to the house'.
'Oh I can't wait and Louie' 'thanks Christian' Louie smiled
Polly was happy the evening had been a success.
'Everyone had a good time I'll tidy up' 'you don't have to'
Corey said 'I want to then in the morning I can relax'.
'Why did Louie call me ragdoll?' 'I don't know he says it's
his nickname for you' 'why?' 'maybe because you're tall'.
'Do I look like a doll?' 'not really' I don't look like a doll
you look more like one than I do' 'he said a ragdoll'.

'Oh tatty dolls no-one wants' 'Cor it's just a nickname'.
'Ask Louie next time he comes round' 'maybe I will'.
The next day Corey woke late after staying up to watch a
DVD by herself she felt alone.
She thought maybe she might call Stacey find out what
was going on with Christian.
Corey heard a knock at the door she answered it was
Louie 'Polly's not here she's in Liverpool visiting family'.
'I know that I thought you might want some company you
look tired' 'I went to bed too late last night'.
'I watched a film' 'which one?' 'Notting Hill' 'you like
Hugh Grant?' 'I like romantic films' 'me too'.
'See we could be great friends' Corey was too tired to
argue 'I thought we could work out together'.
'I am a personal trainer' 'oh now I know why you came
over' 'what do you mean?'.
'I know I've put on weight I don't need you to tell me'.
'I just came round to say hi we don't have to workout'.
'I don't mind aerobics but there's other sports' 'we can
play anything what about tennis?' Louie suggested.
'I don't mind it' 'badminton' 'I love badminton' 'fancy a
game?' 'why not' 'I'll drive us to the sports centre'.
Louie said 'ok give me five minutes to get ready' 'ok'.
'I'll wait here' Corey went to find a T-shirt and shorts.

She still wasn't convinced by Louie and didn't understand why he was so keen to be her friend.

As far as she was concerned they had nothing in common she grabbed a bottle of mineral water.

They were ready to go she got into the back of the car.

'Sit with me in the front' Corey sat next to Louie forcing a smile 'right let's go' five minutes later they arrived.

At the local sports centre Louie changed into a bright pink T-shirt 'nice T-shirt' Corey said 'I know darling'.

'Ready to play' 'yes I haven't done any exercise for a while' 'thought so' Louie said she felt angry.

As if at any moment she might hit him with her badminton racket Corey kept her composure 'you serve' 'ok darling'.

Louie served as they played Corey quickly got into it enjoying it 'you're good' 'thanks' she smiled.

'I did used to do a lot of exercise' 'what happened?'.

'I had my daughter and i've been busy with the band making films I lost my passion for it' 'that's a shame'.

'A bit of exercise never did anyone any harm' 'I know'.

'It's good for you' 'I bet you're missing Polly already'.

'Yes do you have a boyfriend?' 'no' 'I like being single' 'no-one likes being single' 'ok I hate it really'.

'I'm picky when it comes to boyfriends people tell me I'm hard work' 'that's not surprising'.

'I'm glad you think it's funny' Corey liked the fact she'd wound him up like he wound her up.

'I'm sure you could get someone' 'I always fall for straight men they tell me their gay then they leave me'.

'Tell me they were confused' 'maybe be more careful next time' 'I'll try' 'choose someone who's actually gay'.

'Well if they didn't lie to me I hate being lied to I want to be loved let's talk about something else' 'the weather'.

'Very funny' Louie was intrigued by Corey.

She was the only person he'd ever met who was almost as sarcastic as he was who could out wit him with words.

He was sure if he could break her down he could get to know the real her after an hour they stopped playing.

Corey felt tired better more alive 'enjoy it?' Louie asked.

'Yes I did I have a question why do you keep calling me ragdoll?' 'because you have the most gorgeous face'.

He said touching her cheek it still didn't answer her question Louie thought Corey was beautiful.

When she wasn't being so sarcastic she and Polly had to be two of the most beautiful lesbians Louie thought.

'I'm glad you enjoyed our game of badminton' Louie said.

'I did actually' 'good' they went to the cafe.

As Corey ordered a banana milkshake Louie a tea.

'Think how many calories are in that milkshake'.

'I'm really wanted a milkshake' 'I'm just saying'.

'You burned off all those calories and now you've put it back on' 'I don't care this milkshake is so good'.

'Well I'm glad you had a good time' 'I did' 'do it again?'.

Louie asked 'maybe why not' 'good darling I had a great time' Corey had actually enjoyed herself.

Louie wasn't so bad when he wasn't camping it up all the time he drove her home 'coming in for a bit?'.

'I would but I had a late night last night I need to get some rest' 'ok another time' 'course darling'.

'Great game of badminton' 'bye Louie' 'bye darling'.

Part of her found him annoying the other part thought he wasn't so bad he said he'd had a great time with her .

It was a nice thing to say Corey decided she would see him again maybe have another game of badminton.

It would be good fun as Louie drove away she decided to watch a DVD Four Weddings And A Funeral.

It was her favourite film she'd watched it so many times it was romantic and reminded her how lucky she was.

To have found the love of her life her gorgeous wife she was missing Polly already.

She hoped she was having a good time back in Liverpool.

After the film finished she had a cheese and tomato pizza and a coke heaven Corey knew Louie wouldn't approve .

Se didn't care he was Stacey's personal trainer not hers she was free to do what she wanted.

Later she had a bag of minstrels with a cup of tea Corey knew she should probably be on a diet.

But didn't have the willpower that evening Kitty phoned. It would be a few months until the band's new album came out she thought they should do a few gigs Corey agreed.

They would do two nights in London one in Manchester. Something for her to look forward to they quickly came up with their set list.

And planned to perform the songs in three weeks Corey decided to wear a nice black jacket and skirt .

Something slimming and glamorous the next day she decided to do some tiding up in the house.

In between practising her singing for the upcoming gigs as she dusted the living room.

Corey heard a knock at the door she looked out the window it was Louie 'hi' he said.

'I came round because I accidently left my car keys here yesterday' 'oh yeah I wondered who's keys they were'.

'Their mine' 'here you are' 'thanks I really need them'. 'Because I'm taking out a client' 'oh right' 'I say client'. 'More of a friend really we're gonna go to the sports centre playing a game of tennis'.

'She's been feeling really down lately maybe we'll go shopping later' 'sounds good' 'must be going bye'.

'Have fun' 'I will' Louie seemed distant with her different to the day before maybe he had things on his mind .

Or maybe he'd treated her like one of his clients she thought he'd been friendly genuine.

Now Corey wondered whether the game of badminton was part of a routine he did with everyone.

If she was right then she felt used by him Corey went out to do some shopping returning later.

As she watched This Morning as she read a celebrity magazine she didn't buy them very often anymore.

They'd not been nice to Polly in the past calling her fat.

Saying she needed to lose weight of course now she'd lost weight and had a successful film career.

They were begging her for an interview she only gave interviews for a select few Corey was the same.

As she read her magazine she came across an interview.

With Louie saying how he was a trainer to the stars.

Appearing on shows such a Lorraine and This Morning he name checked celebrities he'd worked with.

Several times of course Polly was mentioned.

'We hang out together all the time' surely he was exaggerating how was it possible.

When Polly was too busy making films for them to go clubbing together Corey wondered if she was being used. To add to his list of celebrity clients that evening Corey received a call from her old school friend Cassie.

To say she was on holiday in London with her mum and did they want to meet up.

She couldn't wait to see her again she wanted to look nice she wore a black coat with gold buttons.

And black trousers they'd arranged to have a day out. Shopping and some lunch at a café somewhere she thought she looked nice Cassie looked great.

As she greeted her she was wearing a pale blue jacket and skirt with matching heels 'you look great' Corey said.

'Me so do you' they hugged Corey was happy to see her as she lived in America she didn't get to see her very often.

They walked around town as they chatted 'so how long are you here for?' 'not long two days'.

'Then we're going to France and Italy' 'sounds great'.

'I hope you have a good time' 'oh I will' after shopping they had lunch at a café Corey took off her coat.

As she relaxed 'you look really pretty' Cassie said 'me'.

'You are joking! I've put on weight' 'so what if I was a lesbian I'd have a big crush on you' Corey laughed.

'Can I ask you a personal question?' Corey asked.

'You can ask me anything' 'have you had a boob job?'.

'Yes you noticed their bigger' 'yes since the last time we met I couldn't help noticing'.

'I always wanted to get them done I was too scared last year I was like I have to get them done so I did'.

'And I love them you don't think their too big do you?'.

'No they look great if something makes you happy you should do it' 'thanks I think so too' 'well it's true'.

Cassie couldn't help noticing Corey didn't seem herself 'how's Polly?' 'oh she's grand it's a shame you couldn't see her she's in Liverpool seeing family'.

'Maybe we could meet up in New York you said she has an apartment there' 'great idea you're welcome anytime'.

'I'll give you the address' 'oh thanks' 'I love what you're wearing' Corey said 'really thanks it's designer'.

'Mom works in a store they give her a discount I didn't realise it would be so cold'.

'I guess I'm so used to the good California weather'.

'It's been so cold it's almost March' 'oh our food's here'.

Cassie had ordered fish and chips 'oh very British'.

'I know and we had tea and scones in the hotel' 'it's here'.

Corey said admiring her big sandwich 'it looks great'.

She couldn't wait to tuck into her sandwich cheese, lettuce & tomato.

As she did it was heaven the nicest tasting bread ever.
It tasted amazing 'that must be pretty good' 'it's amazing'.
Corey said with a mouthful of bread she had missed
Cassie she was happy they were back hanging out
together 'shall we order a dessert?' Cassie suggested.
'I don't know' 'why not' 'I'm supposed to be on a diet'
'come on diets are boring you've got to have some fun'.
'I've spent the last ten years on a diet I hate it so much'.
'I'm doing two concerts with the band in less than three
weeks so I have to look good'.
'How am I gonna get in shape?' 'have you tried spanx?'.
'No' 'their great their like tights they go over your tummy
I swear you look a size smaller' 'I'll make sure I get some'.
'Seriously whatever you wear you'll look great'.
'Thanks we'll order a dessert how about we order a really
big expensive
ice-cream with all the toppings and share it'.
'Sounds like a great idea' Cassie agreed they ordered a
large ice-cream chocolate & mint sundae with sprinkles.
'Oh great!' Corey looked over it was Louie all she needed.
After having a nice day out with Cassie 'who is it?'.
'Stacey and Polly's personal trainer Louie he's so
annoying I thought he was ok'.
'He took me out for a game of badminton'.

'I thought he was being nice then I found out some things'.
'That he does it with everyone and he's been name dropping in celebrity magazines'.
'I don't want me and Polly being used in his career'.
'Oh I understand' Corey looked over as he headed towards their table.
With another very camp looking gay man 'Corey hey what are you doing here?' 'I'm with a friend this is Cassie'.
'Meet Louie' 'hello is that an American accent?' 'I'm from California' 'is this your new boyfriend?' Corey asked.
'This is Carl my ex we're still very good friends did you have anything nice to eat?' Corey knew he'd ask her that.
He was so predictable 'Cassie had fish and chips I had a cheese, tomato and lettuce sandwich'.
'And we shared a really big chocolate and mint ice-cream' 'they are nice here but so fattening'.
'I dread to think how many calories are in them'.
'Probably hundreds but Cassie's on holiday for a few days so I thought I'd treat her' 'sounds good'.
'Well we must be going now' 'oh did you have a good time with that client?' 'oh great time yes'.
'Nice meeting you Corey' Carl said 'bye girls' Louie said.
'He did seem a bit bitchy' Cassie said 'oh tell me about it'.
'I prefer to stay away from people like that'.

'Listen how about I go back to my hotel for a bit then we go out later tonight' Cassie suggested.

'Sounds like a great idea how about I pick you up at seven' 'ok then here's the name of the hotel'.

Cassie handed her a business card they said their goodbyes.

As Corey went home she decided she'd take Cassie out to a gay club make sure she had a good time.

She looked for something to wear she picked out a floaty black satin top and black trousers.

Corey was looking forward to it as arranged at 7pm she and Cassie went out to the clubs.

As she approached her usual club it wasn't open there was a sign outside 'closed for refurbishment you are joking!'.

'We can go somewhere else there's another gay club nearby Martins it's a bit seedy'.

'But the music's supposed to be good' the taxi dropped them off as they ventured inside.

It reminded them of the early eighties the music was good.

It was a mostly gay club for men usually anyone was welcome but clearly not there.

Corey decided they wouldn't stay too long she spotted Lucy a soft butch blonde haired lesbian.

From their usual club McCoy's 'hi Corey' 'hi Lucy'.

'Closed for refurbishment then' 'yeah that's why I thought I'd come here their not very friendly'.

'They gave me a dirty look when I came in I've never been to a gay male club before'.

'Well I've never come here either we won't be staying long this is Cassie my friend from America' 'hi'.

'I'll see you in a minute' Lucy said the music was good. They danced trying to have a good time 'Corey or is it Corine?' 'Louie hi' 'hello'.

'We seem to be bumping into each other a lot today anyone would think you're stalking me' 'McCoy's was shut'.

'So we thought we'd come here' 'you do know this is a gay club' 'I'm gay' 'I mean it's for gay men not lesbians'.

'Shouldn't everyone be allowed' 'I don't make the rules'.

'What happened to your boyfriend?' 'he's here he's an ex' 'I'm going to get a drink' 'word of advice don't stay long'.

'The owner hates dykes can't stand it' 'what is this some kind of exclusive club?' 'got it in one'.

Corey looked around there were some shady characters. Hardcore gay men not welcoming at all Corey wished she'd never brought Cassie 'listen Cas we'll get a drink'.

'And then we'll leave I hate this place' 'me too'.

Corey ordered the drinks as they chatted at the bar.

'This place is a joke McCoy's and Floats are much more welcoming' 'it's ok really' 'this place would be ok'.

'If it wasn't for the people in it good music lighting'.

The club was full of old skool neon signs they felt like they could have been in 1982.

Corey couldn't believe it as she looked around she spied Adrian 'Corey hello how's things?' 'fine' 'how's Polly?'.

'In Liverpool' 'really I thought she was supposed to be opening her new club' 'she is' 'it doesn't look like it to me'.

'I don't have to explain anything to you there's not one day that goes by when she's not on the phone to Sam'.

'Talking about music, lighting, layout I'm going stay away from Polly' 'with pleasure!' 'come on Cas'.

'Let's get out of here' they couldn't wait to leave 'bye Lucy' 'bye Corey see you in the club when it's been refurbished'.

'Me and Polly will come to the opening' 'bye darling'.

Corey called a taxi to take Cassie back to her hotel she said she'd meet her the next day.

Show her the attractions of London they'd have a better day tomorrow Corey felt tired as she took off her make-up.

Having a herbal tea before going to bed Louie seemed to come into her thoughts which annoyed her.

Corey felt he'd been bitchy to her at the club the next day she woke around 9am.

*She was looking forward to seeing Cassie again it would
be a better day.*

*Just as she was about to leave the house she heard a
knock at the door she looked out the window.*

*It was Louie what did he want? couldn't he leave her
alone she reluctantly opened the door 'Corey'.*

*'Forgotten your keys again' 'no I wanted to know why you
were so vile to me yesterday!' Louie said angry.*

*'Me! that's rich coming from you I could ask you the same
thing!' 'oh really since when was I vile to you!'.*

*'All the time oh how many calories are in that ice-cream
or do you know this club's for gay men!'.*

'They hate dykes here!' 'what was I supposed to say!'.

*'I was giving you some advice we don't go hanging round
lesbian bars!' 'McCoy's was shut!'.*

*'That's why we came there!' 'it wasn't that it was your
whole attitude!' 'my attitude how dare you!'.*

'You're pathetic you know that!' 'how am I pathetic?'.

*'Hanging out with celebs bragging to magazines about
your celebrity clients that you've worked with'.*

*'I don't go bragging about anything! they asked me who
I train' 'oh really!' 'yes I'm a qualified personal trainer!'.*

*'I train anyone famous or not famous! how dare you
accuse me of using my clients name to get famous!'.*

'And since when do you and Polly hang out all the time!'.
'Ask Polly we went clubbing in Brighton recently actually
I thought she would have told you since she's your wife'.
'Clearly not' 'me and Polly have a good relationship!'.
'You're single anyway what would you know!'.
'Listen darling I can get anyone! I have charm!'.
'Trust me you don't!' 'and you do!' 'I'm a nicer person
than you are!' 'oh really!'.
'Even your own brother doesn't want to know you!'.
'You know nothing about my brother!' 'I know enough!'.
'To know he didn't want you at his wedding because you
were jealous of his wife!' 'I wasn't jealous!'.
'I can't stand her! and I hate you!' 'I thought we were
friends!' Louie said.
'Since when did I ever say I wanted to be your friend'.
'If that's the way you feel!' 'it is!' 'what about the other
day when we had that game of badminton' 'you used me!'.
'And how did I use you! oh I know I was using you to get
famous that's right!'.
'How could I have even thought of hanging out with you!'.
'What's that supposed to mean!' 'you know you're the
nastiest piece of work I've ever come across!'.
'Oh me really you are joking!' 'you are such a bitch Corey
I'd like to know what Polly see's in you!'.

'She loves me!' 'I have no idea why you're a miserable fat Irish bitch!' 'I want nothing to do with you!' 'oh good'. 'That's fine by me!' Louie got into his car slamming the door as he drove off Corey began to cry.

How could he call her fat he knew she was sensitive about the fact she'd put on weight.

And using the word Irish wasn't that bordering on racism? she cried on the sofa for half an hour.

Vowing never to see Louie again she eventually got herself together so she could meet Cassie.

Outside Madame Tussauds she was with her mother .

'Hey Corey' 'hello' 'how are you?' 'I'm good'

Corey forced herself to say 'let's go in' they queued.

'I can't wait to see all the famous waxworks' Cassie said.

'Neither can I' 'you must come here a lot' Cassie said.

'No I'm busy working sometimes I come with Douglas'.

'I forgot you have a thirteen year old son' 'so do I sometimes' Corey reached for a tissue.

She was still upset over what Louie had said 'what's wrong? has someone upset you?' 'Louie'.

'You remember him from yesterday' 'the gay guy' 'yes'.

'What did he say to you?' 'don't worry forget it let's just try and have a really nice day together'.

'Ok I'm sorry I don't want to ruin your holiday'.

'You won't you make it better we get to hang out together'.
'Cassie's right she's always like I wonder what Corey's up
to' 'mom's right' 'well I'm happy you came to visit'.
'Next time stay longer' 'oh we will' 'I hope you enjoy
France and Italy' 'oh we'll post photos on Facebook'.
'I hope we can see each other soon' Corey said 'me too'.
'I'd like that' after seeing Madame Tussauds they went to
a café as they chatted 'I wish you could stay longer'.
'Next time I promise' 'good you know you can stay with me
and Polly' 'oh that's nice of you'.
'That's what friends are for' 'well you're the best friend
ever' Cassie said she got out her camera.
As she took a picture 'how's your brother?'.
'I wouldn't know we're not talking' 'why not?' 'it's a really
long story he married this girl Lizzie she's horrible'.
'She tried to come between us you know Daniel's my best
friend anyway she did'.
'I really didn't want him to marry her I even stood up at
the wedding her family were there'.
'I had a row with my mam my ex-mother as I like to call
her I just lost it at the wedding reception'.
'Her family called me a psycho' 'that's not very nice'.
'And she hated my dress because it was nice she said
I upstaged her' 'well I would have too'.

'Anyway it was awful and I haven't spoken to my brother since except about seeing Douglas'.

'I'm sure you'll speak to him again soon' 'I hope so'.

'You will he's probably just as upset as you are'.

'I'm glad you came to see me' Corey said 'me too I can't wait to see you again soon' 'me too'.

'And next time I'll take you on a proper night out'.

'Well I can't wait I guess I have to go now I'm so sad now' Cassie gave Corey a hug 'I'll miss you' 'until next time'.

Corey had enjoyed their short time together 'bye Corey'.

Cassie's mum said 'bye enjoy France and Italy' 'we will'.

'I'll put all the photos on Facebook' 'have a nice time'.

Corey said goodbye she'd enjoyed hanging out with Cassie even if it had only been for two days.

It had taken her mind off not speaking to Daniel and her row with Louie she returned home around 4pm.

Feeling a bit sad but happy to have seen Cassie and hoped to see her again soon she got herself a drink.

Of orange juice trying to relax she heard a knock at the door she didn't look out the window.

Corey hoped it wasn't Louie she opened the door 'Stace'.

'Corey' she felt relieved 'how are you?' she asked.

'I'm good Louie told me all about your row' 'oh great!'.

'He said you accused him of some things'.

'Of bragging about celebrity clients you've got it wrong Louie's not like that he's really good at what he does'.
'I never said he wasn't' 'he took you out for a game of badminton then he said you turned on him for no reason'
'I don't think so he used me' 'how?' 'he just did' 'explain' 'the next day he came round said he'd forgotten his keys'.
'So I gave them to him he was really off with me he said he was taking a client out for a game of badminton'.
'Then shopping see he does that with everyone' 'well he never took me out for a game of badminton'.
'I don't appreciate being used' 'how did he use you?'.
'I've told you' 'he was being friendly nice' 'Louie nice you are joking!' 'he's a good friend of mine' 'I know that'.
'I don't know how you can be friends with someone like that' 'why can't you get on?' 'because he hates me'.
'I can't stand him in fact I hate him!' 'hates a strong word' 'well I mean it!' 'you can't he wanted to be your friend'.
'I don't want to be his friend!' 'why not?' 'all he does is make comments about my weight'.
'I tried to go out to this club McCoy's was shut I saw him there he told me dykes weren't welcome'.
'He was trying to protect you because he knew what a dive that place was' 'I can protect myself'.
'He was looking out for you' 'I very much doubt it'.

'Why do you hate Louie so much?' 'where do I begin he talked about Lizzie he doesn't even know the situation'.

'I'm not jealous of her she ruined my relationship with my brother!' 'don't take it out on Louie' 'I'm not'.

'I'm just saying how it is do you know what he called me a fat Irish bitch!' 'he knows he went too far' 'too far!'.

'Listen he hates me cause I'm Irish' 'how can he I'm half Irish' 'he's always making jokes'.

'About how we drink too much I hardly drink!' 'why are you getting wound up?' 'because of him!'.

'It's probably my fault I wanted you to be friends and you don't get on I feel like it's my fault all these rows'.

'No it's not your fault ok it's just a personality clash that's all he's just not my type of person'.

'I'll tell him to stay out of your way are you still upset about Dan?' 'yes but I had a really nice day out'.

'With Cassie' 'how is she?' 'she's good she was only staying in London for two days then she's off to France'.

'And Italy' 'sounds good' 'she's gonna show us the photos' 'I love France and Italy so I can't wait to see them'.

'I'm sorry I had a go at you' Stacey said 'it's ok'.

'I wouldn't want us to fall out over Louie' 'we won't'.

'A drink?' 'yes please' 'I have J20' 'oh great I love J20'.

True love

'Coming right up' Corey returned with two glasses and the J20 'up to anything?' Corey asked 'just recording'.

'The album's nearly finished' 'that's great' 'thanks for the two songs you wrote for me' 'oh anytime'.

'So did you ring Christian?' 'not yet I will I just don't know what to say' 'invite him out on a date'.

'He gave you his number for a reason' 'I know you're right' 'I will call him'.

'He seems a lot nicer than most of your ex-boyfriends'.

'I know so you didn't like my ex-boyfriends?' 'not really'.

'Neither did Polly James was the best of a bad bunch'.

'He turned out to be the worst' 'it's true maybe I'll have better luck in the future' 'oh I know you will'.

'I would like to meet someone' the next day Stacey decided she should ring Christian.

She'd never had to ask anyone out on a date Justin she'd met in a nightclub.

And James she'd known through her record company.

Stacey didn't know what to say she felt like she didn't know Christian well enough she rang him around eleven.

As she waited for a reply 'hello' 'hi it's Stacey' 'I thought you'd forgotten about me or you weren't interested'.

'What made you think that?' 'it's been a few days since
I gave you my number I thought maybe I was too forward'.
'No I'm still interested' 'really' 'yes I'm not good on the
phone or even with texting'.
'I promise I haven't forgotten about you' Stacey assured
him 'I'm not very good on the phone either'.
'I thought you might be out filming' 'I have been but
I've finished now but I'm looking at other roles I can do'.
'I'm free if you want to go out somewhere together'.
'I'd really like that like a date' Stacey asked 'yes when are
you free?' 'anytime'.
'I've almost finished recording my album we're just
mixing it now' 'oh great how about today?' 'today'.
'If you're not doing anything' 'I'm not' 'I'm in the centre
of London I'm having a meeting with someone'.
'About an acting job then I can meet you' 'ok what time?'.
'Around two' 'how about I meet you outside the
Houses Of Parliament' Stacey suggested 'ok'.
'I'll be wearing a black coat' she said 'I'll see you then'.
'Ok bye' Stacey put down the phone she was happy.
After lunch she got ready applying some green eyeshadow
and black mascara she wanted to look nice.
She wore a stylish black velvet coat with silver buttons

*Stacey knew she looked good she left the house just after
1pm as she took a long walk along The Themes.*

*To pass the time she spied someone running as they came
closer she realised it was Louie with a client 'Louie'.*

*'Stacey' 'I don't know how you can work out when it's so
cold' 'oh darling it's fine once you get going'.*

'What are you doing here all alone?' 'I won't be alone'.

'Oh really tell me' 'I'm meeting Christian' 'like a date'.

*'Yes' 'that's great next time I see you I want all the gossip
I have to be going'.*

'If I stop for too long it ruins my flow' 'I understand'.

*'Bye darling I'll call you' Stacey looked on as Louie ran
she found a bench near the river she sat down.*

*As she watched families together she wished she had a
dad for her daughter.*

*But she knew she'd done the right thing by dumping James
once a cheat always a cheat.*

She was better off on her own 'Stacey' 'Steve' 'hello'.

*It was her manager Steve 'you look great' 'thanks how
come you're here?' Stacey asked 'I'm on a lunch break'.*

*'It's quarter to two' 'I know I'm so busy today' 'you work
too hard' 'what about you?' Steve asked.*

'I'm having a date' 'who?' 'Christian' 'who's Christian?'.

'Polly's half-brother' 'is he nice?' 'he's really nice'.

'Black' 'no white actually' 'interesting' 'I know
I've stopped going out with my usual type'.
'Variety is the spice of life' 'as long as you find a nice man
you're too nice to go out with anymore bastards'.
'I mean it you've been treated really badly in the past'.
'I never said anything but I'm saying it now' 'I agree'.
'I look back and I can't believe some of the people I went
out with' 'neither can I'.
'Justin we were better off as friends and the rest well
better best forgotten you know I think I'm older now'.
'And I know what I want from life I'd like to get married
one day like everyone else' 'take your time'.
'Next time find someone really nice who treats you like a
princess' 'I'll try to' 'so what does Christian do?'.
'He's an actor he recently left University he was studying
behind the scenes drama you know writing screenplays'.
'Directing and now he's doing acting' 'recently left
University how old is he?' 'twenty' 'oh toyboy then'.
'We're not going out yet it's just a date' 'that could lead to
something else' 'maybe it depends if he likes me'.
'Why wouldn't he your gorgeous and talented' 'thanks'.
'We didn't get on at first but now I like him' 'well that's
good then' 'I haven't been with anyone since James'.
'I feel it's time to start dating again'.

'We've talked once or twice Kim likes him' 'your sister'.
'Yes' 'how is she?' 'fine in America with the group I miss her she's my best friend in the world'.
'She asked Christian out he said no he was nice about it'.
'I don't think he's into black girls' 'does he know you're mixed race?' 'no it hasn't come up in conversation'.
'He just knows mum is married to Andy he's met her once at a family dinner he thinks she's a friend of the family .
'You are going to tell him' 'course I love my mum it's just how people always react when they find out about me'.
'It's started raining I knew it would' Stacey said 'how?'.
'I always watch the weather forecast' 'I wish I did it looks like it might get heavy'.
'I said I'd meet Christian by the Houses Of Parliament'.
'Let me see if he's there he's there' 'oh good' 'listen I have to go' 'don't worry call me tell me how it goes' 'bye'.
Stacey walked over as she stood opposite Christian it was now starting to rain heavily he was looking around.
He couldn't see her she crossed the road 'Christian'.
'Stacey there you are I was worried you might not come'.
'I was chatting to my manager I saw him over there by the river then I looked over and saw you' 'where is he now?'.
'He's over there he's gonna call me later I didn't want to be late for my date' 'this rain is heavy come on'.

'Let's find a café' Stacey was worried her make-up would start to run they found one nearby.

The one Polly always went to they found a table sitting down 'I should have checked the weather forecast'.

'I don't even have an umbrella' Stacey said 'I have one'.

'You're wearing a black coat too' Stacey said 'yeah you look nice' 'thanks even with the rain'.

'My hair it goes curly in the rain I have naturally curly hair I straighten it takes ages but it looks better on stage'.

'Shall we order?' Christian asked 'yes' they ordered hot chocolates 'so tell me what have you been up to?'.

'Not much I have a boring life' 'you're a pop star'.

'I'm just finishing off my new album in the recording studio and looking after my daughter' 'how old is she?'.

'Eight months' 'what's her name?' 'Tahilia I call her Tally' 'that's a nice name' 'thanks I think it suits her'.

'I can't stand these stupid celebrity names' Christian said.

'Me too some of them are awful' their hot chocolates arrived 'I have a photo I carry around'.

'If you're interested' 'oh yes' Stacey took out a photo from her purse 'she's cute' 'she's mixed race James my ex'.

'He's black Italian but he just looks full black I'm…Irish'.

'The name O'Riley it's Irish' 'I like your name' 'thanks'.

'My surnames Bell my step-dad's Scottish'.

'They've spilt up mum went back to her maiden name'.

'I kept his name I thought it sounded better for acting jobs'
Stacey decided she fancied Christian and liked him a lot.

'So how did your meeting go?' Stacey asked 'oh great'.

'I've got another acting role lined up' 'that's great'.

'I know I'm really enjoying it' 'I like acting too' 'my sister
she loved you in Imitation Of Life' 'you saw my film'.

'Yes my sister loved it so did I she was raving about it'.

'So I decided to see it I didn't think it would be as good as
the original I was wrong' 'you can't beat the original'.

'I always wondered if the girl in it was really mixed race'.

'The 1959 version' 'yes' 'she was Jewish-Mexican'.

'You've solved my mystery and your Irish'.

'I'm a few different things my great-grandparents on my
mother's side are Cuban and Italian'.

'I've never met them my great-grandfather's still alive'.

'He's like eighty five' 'is he latino looking?' 'I saw a photo
he has light coffee coloured skin'.

'My great-grandmother has dark curly hair and pale skin
like me are you gonna get into films?' 'you never know'.

'You should you would be good' 'thanks you haven't seen
my acting yet' 'I'm sure you're really good'.

'Stacey you're really pretty' 'even in the rain' 'even in the
rain' Christian said as they smiled at each other.

'I have something to tell you I've never been on a date before' Christian said 'neither have I' 'really?' 'yes'.

'Justin is a DJ at the club I go to James I knew through my record company so I've never been on a date either'.

'I was feeling really nervous about today now I don't feel so bad' 'me too are you single?' Stacey asked 'yes'.

'Kim wasn't your type' 'she's sweet but no' 'am I your type?' 'yes'.

'Sorry I couldn't have taken you out on an evening date'.

'I'm seeing friends tonight' 'I understand' 'would you like a boat cruise?' Christian asked 'down The Themes' 'yes'.

'I know it's cold but the sun's trying to come out' 'let's go'.

They left the café as they waited for a boat getting on with other tourists it was cold but Stacey enjoyed the fresh air.

As a strong breeze blew as the boat sailed down The Themes she was happy to be with Christian.

He was gorgeous he put his arm round her Stacey loved it feeling close to him she had a big crush on him.

And wanted him to be her boyfriend but she couldn't tell him he had to ask her out.

Stacey had lived in London most of her life but she had rarely had a chance to appreciate the landmarks.

Of London she'd had a good day out and was sad when the cruise came to an end 'I enjoyed that' Christian said.

*'Me too I loved it' 'we'll have to do it again sometime if
you want to' 'I'd love to' she looked at him.*

*She hoped he might kiss her 'listen Stacey I have to go
now' 'ok' she'd enjoyed spending time with Christian.*

*'I really want to see you again' 'me too I'll ring you and
that's a promise' he kissed her on the cheek.*

*'Have a good night' 'I will darling' Stacey watched him
walk away how she wished he'd kissed her on the lips.*

*Hopefully next time she would have to keep that fantasy to
herself for now that evening he texted her.*

*They arranged to meet up and go and see Corey and the
band in concert she told Polly all about their date.*

*And how they planned to meet again she was happy for
her Corey was busy preparing for some concerts.*

*With the rest of the band she had brought some spanx as
Cassie had suggested especially since some celebrity
magazines had picked up on the fact she'd put on weight.*

*She chose a black glittery jacket & skirt Corey looked
good she wished Polly could have been there.*

*Stacey & Christian came it was a good night they decided
to hang out at the bar after the show.*

Before going to see Corey and the band backstage.

*'It was a great show' 'thanks Stace' Kitty said 'I can't wait
for us to do a proper tour after the albums released'.*

'You'll come' 'I wouldn't miss it you're a great band'.
'You were great' Christian said 'thanks so are you going
out now?' Corey asked 'we went on a date' Stacey said.
Corey was curious to know about it but she could see they
were getting to know each other 'I love your jacket'.
Stacey said to Corey 'black makes me look slimmer'.
'You look fine to me' 'that's not what Louie thinks' 'I think
he went too far he didn't mean it you know what he's like'.
'He called me a fat Irish bitch!' 'I know it was a horrible
thing to say I'm sure he feels bad about it' 'I doubt it!'.
'Anyway it doesn't matter you're not a bitch' 'Stacey's
right you're a lovely person' Kitty said.
'Listen I've got to go now I'm tired but I'll call you'.
'Ok Stace' 'see you all soon I'll text you' Stacey said.
'And Christian it was nice meeting you' Kitty said 'bye
everyone' Christian called a taxi home for Stacey.
They promised to see each other again soon Corey and
Kitty tried to relax after their gig.
Kitty noticed Corey seemed distracted 'what's up?'.
'Nothing' 'tell me' 'really it's nothing' 'you're not still
upset over what Louie said' 'it's the way he said it' 'Cor'.
'He's just some nasty bitchy queen' 'I know' 'how dare he
say that about you!' 'maybe it's true' 'you are joking!'.

'And what right did he have to bring that bitch Lizzie and your brother into it I mean seriously he's not your friend'.
'He doesn't know you and he says that stuff' 'Kitty's right if you want me to deck him for you' Mike said.
'It's ok thanks for the offer' 'don't worry if I see him I'll say something'.
'And he doesn't want to mess with me when I'm angry'.
Kitty said Corey was grateful for Kitty's friendship she was more than just her bandmate.
They'd known each other since she was nineteen 'he said I was fat and it's probably true'.
'I mean I know I've put on weight' 'Cor so what! you're gorgeous whatever size you are'.
'Besides you've probably got PCOS I mean you don't eat much more than me why else would you put on weight'.
'Just like that' 'maybe you're right' 'Cor you know I'm right' 'Kitty's right there's lots of medical reasons why you might put on weight'.
'Maybe an underactive thyroid' 'thanks Mike' 'game of cards to cheer you up' 'ok why not' 'I'll deal' he said.
As he shuffled the cards Kitty went to the top of the tour bus as they continued playing 'you always beat me'.
Mike joked 'how is that possible to be beaten by a girl'.
'Maybe I'm not like other girls' 'you're right there'.

'Your special' 'me are you sure you're talking to the right person' 'course remember when we first met'.

'How could I forget you were sixteen you worked at that restaurant then later we met again'.

'In that bar you were singing with that awful band you had a voice a cross between Cathy Dennis and K.D Lang'.

'You still have a great voice' 'thanks' 'I remember you saw me play in that pub singing' 'you both great'.

'I mean it you've always been special to me' 'well we've known each other such a long time'.

'Well you've always been a good friend to me' 'more than a friend' Mike had a serious look on his face.

'What do you mean?' Corey asked 'I never told you this I always had a crush on you' 'you are joking'.

'No I mean it I'm telling you now' 'why didn't you ever say?' 'I was married to a woman you were a lesbian'.

'Are you upset with me?' 'no it's fine' 'don't worry I'm not gonna come on to you or anything'.

'I don't mind the fact you have a crush on me' 'well it was more than a crush I was always in love with you'.

'I feel bad I never read the signs' 'it's fine unrequited love have you ever had that feeling'.

'You know had a crush on someone that you wanted and couldn't have' 'yes Polly for years at school'.

'She liked men and women when she fell in love with Andy it broke my heart for years even though I loved Amy'.

'My ex fiancé but Polly it was always something else something really special' 'I know'.

'I always loved her so much' 'well you got the girl of your dreams in the end'.

'I'm really lucky to be with someone that I love so much'.

'I hope I get what you have' 'I'm sorry your marriage never worked out' 'it's ok really it wasn't meant to be'.

'I got my little girl out of it' 'you'll find someone'.

'I'm getting on thirty now' it's not that old' 'your right'.

'I'm not that old' 'you know I am' they laughed Mike kissed Corey on the cheek they looked at each other.

As she kissed him passionately he responded it felt nice.

'What was that?' he asked 'I'm married and I'm a lesbian but I wanted to make your dreams come true'.

'Well you did and I won't tell anyone' 'thanks'.

Corey felt tired as she went to bed she'd been feeling tired a lot lately and didn't know why.

A few days later after their short tour was over she woke in her own bed Corey thought about her kiss with Mike.

She didn't see the harm maybe it had been wrong but it was only innocent she had never had feelings for him.

As she had breakfast and some orange juice she felt more alive already she remembered Kitty was coming round.

She tidied up as the doorbell rang 'Cor how are you?'.

'Fine you look nice compared to me' 'it's called make-up'.

'You should have seen me this morning' 'I had a late night last night' 'you look tired Cor' 'I am'.

'It's like I have no energy' 'we can stay in if you like'.

'No I want us to go out it'll do me good the fresh air help me feel more alive' 'we'll go shopping' Kitty suggested

'I'm not sure I want to until I lose weight' 'you look fine'.

'You don't have to say that' 'it's true maybe you should take a leaf out of Polly's book' 'what do you mean?'.

'Well her wardrobe she's got her thin clothes her medium clothes and her fat clothes'.

'I did something bad the other day'. Corey confessed.

'Tell me' 'I kissed Mike' 'I know I saw you I thought you were joking around' 'we kind of were I'm still a lesbian'.

'He said he always had a crush on me we were chatting'.

'We'd had a few drinks he said he'd always fancied me'.

'That he'd always loved me I suppose I wanted to make his fantasy come true it was nice'.

'But I don't want Polly to find out I mean it meant nothing' 'I understand none of us will say a word'.

'What happens on the tour bus stays on the tour bus'.

'Thanks' 'everyone makes mistakes and you'd had a few drinks let's go shopping take your mind off things' 'ok' Corey was glad Kitty had come to see her she was also glad of the fresh air as they walked around town.

They went to Harrods where Corey chose a green satin dress for Kitty's birthday party.

As they looked around the clothes department Corey was sure she could hear a familiar voice 'oh fecking great!'.

'What's wrong?' 'it's Louie' 'where?' 'over there'.

Louie was with a female friend Corey was hoping he wouldn't see her 'Corey hello listen I'm really sorry'.

'About our row the other day' 'please leave me alone!'.

'I feel really bad' 'so you should how dare you speak to my friend like that! your scum what you said!' Kitty said.

'I know what I said was wrong' 'why don't you stay away from her and keep your vile comments to yourself'.

'She doesn't want anything to do with you!' 'can't she speak for herself now'.

Kitty watched as Corey collapsed on the floor 'Cor!'.

'Now look what you've done!' 'I haven't done anything!'.

'It's you! causing her stress' 'how I didn't know we were going to see each other' Corey sat up.

'Cor are you ok?' Kitty asked 'I'm fine I just feel really hot' 'come on let's get you outside'.

'Listen let me apologise' Louie said 'we're going!'.

Kitty said angry 'say anything about my friend again and
I won't be happy!' they walked out angry at Louie.

'Are you ok?' 'I'm fine now I'm outside in the fresh air'.

'Maybe you're ill maybe you should see a doctor' 'really
I'm fine it was too hot in there I needed to cool down'.

'As long as you feel ok' 'I feel fine' later when Corey got
back home she felt fine.

Clearly she'd just been having an off day she really
wished she didn't keep bumping into Louie.

They didn't get on and could never be friends the next
morning Stacey woke after a good night's sleep.

Thank god for nannies she thought she couldn't think of
anything worse than being woken at 6am.

The time when babies & young children tended to wake up
she loved being a mum.

But really wished James would take more of an interest in
his daughter which he never had.

She had her breakfast free range eggs with soldiers and
freshly squeezed orange juice she went upstairs.

About to start on her make-up the doorbell rang
'who is it?' 'Christian' her nanny Destiny called.

'Just a sec tell him I'll be down in a minute'.

'I'm going now I'll be back this afternoon' 'ok'.

Stacey hated the idea of Christian seeing her without her make-up 'Stacey do you mind me coming?'.

'Turning up like this' 'listen give me ten minutes I need to make myself look decent' 'you look fine to me'.

'I'll be back soon help yourself to a drink' 'thanks'.

Stacey found something suitable to wear applying some mascara and dark blue eyeshadow.

She looked much better she added a teddy bear gold pendent her hair was naturally curly.

She didn't have time to straighten it she wore it up in a ponytail Christian was waiting for her 'you look nice'.

'Thanks' 'and you looked fine before and you look just as pretty without make-up and I like your hair curly'.

'Thanks' 'nice necklace a present from anyone?' 'no'.

'Just myself since I've been single I buy presents for myself helps me feel better sad I know' 'it's not sad'.

'I'd do the same thing' Christian still wasn't sure if Stacey wanted to be his girlfriend.

When Kitty had asked she had just said they were on a date 'I'm glad you came over' Stacey said.

'Really you don't mind me just turning up' 'no it's fine' Stacey would rather he'd have called but any excuse to see him 'would you like to go out somewhere today?'.

'I'd love to but we have to take my daughter my nanny's out till late this afternoon'.

'I'd like to meet your daughter' 'come upstairs'.

Christian followed Stacey 'in here' 'she's gorgeous'.

'I know Destiny just changed her so she should be ok for a bit' 'how long are they in nappies for?'.

'Eighteen months apparently you can't train them till then but I wouldn't change her for the world'.

'I can't go out like I used to I have to remember to take stuff nappies, wipes, bottles' 'I understand'.

'Where shall we go?' Christian asked 'we could have a look at the London Aquarium' 'sounds like a good idea'.

'Douglas Corey's son likes to go there' 'Corey's son'.

'It's weird her having a fourteen year old son I mean she's only twenty eight' Stacey said

'I know I couldn't imagine it' they were soon ready to go. As Stacey called a taxi neither she or Christian could drive they soon arrived in town.

As they went into the London Aquarium they loved it watching the rays afterwards they went to a café To have lunch near the Themes 'looks nice here'.

Christian said they enjoyed the nice weather 'look the sun's out' Christian said 'it's still cold' 'hello' 'Steve'.

'Having a nice day?' 'yes' 'good you make a nice couple'.

'Christian this is Steve my manager' 'hello' 'I forgot how adorable your little girl is'.

'Steve was one of the first visitors after I gave birth'.

'I can't believe it's almost a year' Steve said.

'I guess at least one good thing came out of my relationship with James' 'I saw Adrian earlier'.

'With another man just between you and me he's been hovering around Polly's club a bit' 'why?'.

'He's pissed off she got the club he wanted to buy it'.

'I'm glad she has something he can't get he almost ruined her career' 'I know she's up in Liverpool'.

'So if you see her tell her I'm looking out for her' 'I will'.

'Adrian's just jealous because he knows he doesn't have a hold over her anymore' Stacey said 'who's Adrian?'.

Christian asked 'Polly's ex-manager he stole her credit card ripped her off took millions of her earnings'.

'It's like he's still obsessed with her' 'don't worry he'll get his comeuppance' 'thanks Steve you're the best'.

'Don't thank me darling I'll leave you two to enjoy the rest of your day' 'bye Steve' 'bye Stacey' 'he seems nice'.

'He is he's known me since I was eighteen he's like a dad or an uncle to me in a way'.

Later they went for a walk it was a nice day Christian had been desperate to buy Stacey some flowers.

But it hadn't been the right time attending a pop concert wasn't the right moment or that afternoon.

He wanted her to know how he felt they went home around 4pm 'I've had a really nice day' Christian said.

'Me too' 'we should do it again sometime'.

Stacey suggested 'I'd love to' Christian kissed her on the cheek again maybe he didn't want to be her boyfriend.

He hadn't kissed her properly yet she was confused.

But she'd had a nice day Stacey wondered if he minded the fact that she had a child after all he was only twenty.

Maybe he didn't want the responsibility he seemed ok about it maybe she was worrying about nothing.

That evening Stacey phoned Polly told her all the details of their day out she told her not to worry about anything.

That men were always sending out mixed signals and that she should be clear and tell him what she wanted.

The next day Stacey woke happy she'd had such a nice day with Christian and decided she liked him a lot.

'Delivery for you' Destiny said a smile on her face.

'Who from?' 'Royal Mail' it was a bouquet of red roses.

'Wow! for me' Stacey looked at the tag 'To Stacey love Christian P.S will you be my girlfriend?' 'that's so sweet'.

'I know he's so nice' Stacey finally had her answer as to whether Christian liked her as more than friends.

She was so happy that afternoon she phoned him thanking him for the flowers.

And saying that she did want to be his girlfriend Corey was excited at celebrating Kitty's twenty eighth birthday.

But she'd also not been feeling well somehow she managed to enjoy it.

She was happy Stacey and Christian were an item.

The day after Kitty's party Corey went for a drink at her local pub alone after being surrounded by people so much.

It was nice to be on her own she ordered a coke something non-alcoholic as Corey sat by herself.

As Tina Turner's Steamy Windows played on the jukebox 'what can I get you?' the barman asked 'an orange juice'.

Corey sipped her orange juice as she overheard a conversation 'don't you want one of our specials'.

'I can't afford it' Corey was sure she recognised the voice a mix of cockney and Welsh it was Romina.

She had been one of Polly's closest friends from school but had later tried to break up their marriage out of jealousy.

By claiming she had cheated with another girl Corey could never forgive her Romina turned around.

They looked at each other for a minute Romina was wearing a blue checked shirt and baggy trousers.

And blue trainers her dark blonde hair worn down,

A big surprise

Her hair down she decided not to approach Corey chances were she still hated her after what she'd done.

Instead Corey went to her she still looked pretty.

Romina thought but she'd put on weight and her hair was her natural chestnut brown colour.

Instead of dark red/brown as she often dyed it 'look I'm sorry for what I did trying to split you and Polly up'.

'What else can I say?' 'well I'm glad you're sorry for what you did you almost cost me my marriage' 'I'm sorry'.

'And Douglas the fact that I found out he's my son that's private family business' 'I did it for money'.

'Went to the papers with a good story we all need money'.

'Yeah it's ok for you and Stacey your famous and rich some of us have to live in the real world'.

'That's not my problem!' 'I'm just saying how it is I'm sorry I did it but I lost my job' 'why?' 'who needs a florist's anymore it's dying trade'.

'When you can just order flowers off the internet'.

'Some people might can't you get another assistant manager's job' 'I sent out my CV'.

'It still doesn't explain things why you tried to split me and Polly up' 'I was jealous ok I admit it'.

'Susie was my best friend the only person I ever had the only person who ever cared about me' 'you had friends'.
'At College' 'yeah some friends where are they now I make friends then they leave me'.
'Maybe if you tried being a nicer person' 'like your perfect' 'I never said I was still living in London?' 'yeah'.
'Where?' 'I'm homeless on the streets' 'really' 'yes' 'how long?' 'a while' 'why don't you go home?'.
'I fell out with mum' 'so you enjoy being homeless?' 'no'.
'Course I don't!' 'where do you live?' 'in a hostel nearby'.
'They give you tea that sort of thing' 'you look well' Romina said 'fat you mean you can say it' 'how come you've put on weight?' 'I don't know I like cake'.
Corey joked I think it might be PCOS my periods have been late' 'I heard about that'.
'I guess they even have medical names for when people are fat now' 'it's a medical condition' 'I know'.
'I don't sit around eating all day I do have a child to look after' 'I forgot your little girl how is she?' 'fine'.
Corey still hated Romina they had nothing in common and she hated her for what she'd done.
'I can't forgive what you did' 'I said I'm sorry' 'I know before you go I've got something for you' 'what?'.
Corey handed her a hundred pounds in cash.

'What's this?' 'for you it was for something else but you can have it' 'I don't want your money'.

'If someone offered me free money I'd take it' 'what for?'.
'To get yourself sorted take my advice and take the money use it to take the train home to Wales'.

'Buy some food and drink' 'I can make decisions for myself you know!' 'I know'.

'Besides maybe I don't want to go back to Wales'.

'Your family are there London is only good if you have money to do things'.

'There are lots of homeless people here because it's expensive to live here London's just a dream'.

'For many people I was lucky I made it as part of a succsessful band but many don't'.

'I'm giving you some good advice and if you want a job you'll stop smoking pot' 'how do you know I do?'.

'Your looking at someone who did it for years' 'thanks for the cash' 'anytime' Corey opened the door.

Romina left the pub as she watched her walk out the door.

'Oh Corey if you want my advice you'll stay off the pies'.

'I've never eaten pies in my life' 'not even a quiche thanks bye' Corey waved part of her felt guilty.

Maybe she could have put Romina up for a few nights but she knew she'd done the right thing.

Hopefully she would take her advice and go home to Wales Romina was now homeless.

Despite Polly paying for her to have a flat in Lytham St Anne's in Lancashire and then London Corey decided to go home to Dublin rather than staying alone in London she decided to take the ferry.

She could do with the sea air she couldn't believe how cold it was for March.

Corey drove to her house in Dublin it took a while she didn't mind once she arrived it was heaven it felt good.

To be home in Ireland she felt tired after a day's travelling Corey played with her daughter as she sat on a rug.

In the living room she watched telly before going to bed.

The next day she woke late having lunch before going to her local pub to relax she was glad to be inside.

From the cold outside it was gloomy day it looked as if it might rain at any moment 'Corey' 'uncle Tommy?'.

'What can I get you?' 'a vodka and tonic please'.

'Coming up you sit yourself down' Corey sat down at a nearby table as she looked around.

It was good to be back home 'you know the service here is second to none' Tommy joked she smiled.

'I saw your brother' 'when?' 'the other day things not going too well with his wife' 'Lizzie'.

'I never liked the look of her' 'she's not very nice'.

'Hopefully he'll find someone nice' Tommy said.

'If he see's sense she seems to have a hold over him'.

'Well you need to speak to him knock some sense into him'

'I'll try' 'how are you?' he asked 'I'm fine' 'seen Dougie lately?' 'no' 'I thought you had joint custody' 'it's Lizzie'.

'We don't get on so I'm just trying to avoid her if I can'.

'Well I don't like her he's better than that' Tommy said.

'Don't worry it won't last' 'I hope it doesn't he can do so much better' 'she has this hold over Dan'.

'I've noticed that between you and me I hope he see's sense and divorces the bitch'.

'What you said at the wedding was classic' 'maybe I shouldn't have said it' 'why not it was the truth'.

'And she tried to stop you seeing Dougie the courts gave you legal rights it's all there on paper'.

'Do you see your mam?' 'which one?' 'Carol yes not long ago she cheered me up after the wedding' 'that's good'.

'I saw her the other day I can see where you get your looks from you're a pretty girl' 'where was she?'.

'In town with her husband' 'John' 'they seem like a nice couple' 'oh their really in love it's nice'.

'She found happiness after all the things she went through she seems nice listen I've just seen an old friend of mine'.

'Don't mind if I leave you for a bit' 'no see you in a bit'.

Corey thought it was nice seeing uncle Tommy she'd not seen him for a while she sipped her pint 'Corine'.

Corey turned around it was Daniel they'd barely spoken since the row at the wedding 'I thought it was you'.

She said 'how have you been?' 'I've been ok' 'you look like you've put on weight but you still look good though'.

'For your information I've probably got PCOS if you know what that is' 'I've heard of it'.

'I should probably go to the doctor I've missed some periods' 'maybe you're pregnant' 'you're serious!'.

'I'm in a relationship with Polly don't you think I'd have to plan it first' 'you never know miracles happen'.

'Very funny' Corey smiled 'I like you like this' 'like what?' 'when your all sarcastic listen I'll be back in a minute'.

'You take your time' 'you can't have a woman drinking on her own in a pub' 'really I'm fine' Daniel disappeared.

As Corey sipped her pint secretly she was glad she'd seen her brother and that their reunion was so chilled out.

He returned 'where were you?' 'I was sorting something out finished your drink already another?'.

Corey was just about to say yes when she spied Lizzie they gave each other evil looks as their eyes met.

'I wondered when you'd turn up!' 'I live here!'.

'Why are you here? to wreck my marriage!' 'I'm pretty sure you're doing a good job of that by yourself!'.

'How dare you!' 'you don't like the truth!' 'the truth! you tried to ruin my marriage'.

'By what you said in the church!' 'you expect me to say nothing when my brother marries a tramp like you!'.

'You bitch! you ruined everything when you turned up at the reception! in that red dress trying to upstage me!'.

'And why would I want to do that?' 'because you like the attention!' 'that's rich coming from you!' Lizzie said.

'I think my brother deserves better than you!' Corey was getting angry 'don't you think you're going too far!' Daniel said trying to break up their row 'she's a feckin mental bitch! just like her mother!' 'what did you say?'.

Daniel said shocked at Lizzie's outburst 'you heard me!'.

'You dare say anything about Corey's mam!' Carol had spent time in a psychiatric unit.

After being abused at a mother and baby home in her late teens Daniel could see how upset Corey was.

'You're a sad dyke!' 'bitch!' Corey picked up a pint on the bar tipping it over Lizzie as she ran out the pub.

Angry and upset 'that was so feckin low!' Daniel said angry at Lizzie 'look what she just said to me!'.

'You deserved it!' 'how could you do that!' 'do what?'

'bring Corey's mother into it' 'your sister's a bitch!'.

'You're the bitch! how could I have ever married you what was I thinking!' 'Danny listen!'.

'Please don't call me that! in fact don't ever call me ever again! we're finished!' 'please don't leave me!'.

'We're over Lizzie finished my sister's my best friend what you said was low!' 'I hate your sister!' 'she hates you'.

'With good reason you're unbelievable! marrying you was one of the biggest mistakes of my life!'.

'You don't mean it!' 'I do good riddens to you!' 'Dan!'.

'F**k off get the message!' 'please listen!' 'I want you out of my life don't come near me again!' 'Dan!' 'get lost!'.

'Where are you going?' 'to find my sister!' 'that bitch!'.

'You're the bitch!' Daniel left the pub trying to find Corey. It had now began to rain heavily he walked down the road as fast as possible trying to find her 'Corey'.

'Where are you?' he finally saw her in the distance 'Corey!' she looked up 'leave me alone!' 'listen to me!'.

'There's nothing to listen to!' 'please what she said was low I told her that' 'did you hear what she said'.

'About my mam! all the things she went through in her life!' 'I'm sorry I had a go at her'.

'I don't know what you see in her you're better than that bitch trust me' 'I know ok'.

'So you've finally realised what she's like then' 'yes I know now marrying her was a big mistake'.

'I don't wanna have to see her everytime I want to have a conversation with my own brother it's me or her Dan'.

'You choose' 'I choose you everytime' 'you mean it' 'yes'.

'Your my sister and I love you' 'I love you too'.

He kissed her on the lips Corey was taken aback by his display of affection.

And the fact that he'd chosen her over Lizzie they spied a taxi as they both jumped in out of the rain.

Going back to Corey's house as they arrived they were soaking wet from the rain 'how are you?' he asked.

'I'm good' Daniel gave her a hug 'I'll make you a cup of tea' 'you always make a great cup of tea thanks'.

'How have you been?' he asked 'ok Polly's in Liverpool so I thought I'd come home for a bit I missed home'.

'Well I'm glad you did I've missed you I'm sorry about everything' 'it's ok' 'I should never have married Lizzie'.

'I realise that now I don't know what I was thinking I didn't know her well enough to marry her'.

'It's not just that it's the fact you invited mam to the wedding after all the horrible things she said about Polly'.

'She tried to stop me seeing Douglas my own son how could you do that to me?' 'it was Lizzie all of it was'.

'I didn't want to invite her to the wedding she insisted we even had a row' 'she was trying to get at me'.

'By inviting her' 'I know that now ok the whole wedding was taken out of my hands'.

'You think I wanted a gothic wedding red rose petals a rock song as I go up the aisle' 'rose petals sounds ok'.

'Not the rest of it' 'why didn't you call it off?' 'it was too late it was when you left before the speeches'.

'I looked over you weren't there Polly wasn't there everyone told me she was wrong for me I wouldn't listen'.

'Uncle Tommy' 'he was right' 'we were all right I expect mam will hate that you know her perfect son'.

'Getting a divorce' 'I suppose I felt it was time to settle down but I chose the wrong woman'.

'I won't make the same mistake again' 'you can be happy now find someone nice where's Dougie?' 'out'.

'At a friend's house staying the night' 'I'll see him tomorrow I've brought Marie with me'.

'How's my favourite niece?' 'she's good' 'think I'll have kids?' 'you'll make a great dad' 'I hope so'.

'I just have to pick the right woman why don't you come pick Dougie up from school tomorrow with me' 'ok'.

The next day Corey hung out with Daniel around 3pm she made her way to pick up Douglas from school.

As they waited for twenty minutes it was a nice sunny day he smiled as he saw her 'how are you?' 'good'.

They went home Corey went upstairs as she returned with a T-shirt and trousers 'it's from Polly'.

'The last time she was in America it's all designer stuff Dolce and Gabbana she wanted to buy it for you'.

'I told her not to spoil you but she insisted if you don't like it I'm sure we could change it' 'I like it'.

Douglas tried on the clothes 'it suits you' 'it's really nice'.

'I'll tell Polly you like it' 'where is she?' 'in Liverpool visiting family' 'do you miss her?' 'yes'.

'But she's coming back next week enjoying school?' 'not really' 'no-one likes school' Daniel said 'I did actually' Corey said 'you went to a private school' Daniel said.

'It was a really good school I can just imagine mam now Corine how do you think he paid for your education'.

'With all his dodgy dealings' 'what do you mean?'.

Douglas asked 'well your granddad was and is a criminal his money it usually went on drink and gambling'.

'He was a gangster' Daniel explained 'if he needs money he finds a way to get it he's a dangerous man'.

'He even killed a man' 'you're joking! he scares me' Douglas said 'he's a horrible man I'm ashamed to call him my father' 'me too' Corey said.

'So how's your Irish dancing coming along?' 'great'.

'I really like it I've only just started do you think it's ok for a man to dance?' 'of course'.

'Lots of men make a professional career out of being a dancer' Daniel said 'I really enjoy it'.

'It takes my mind off school' 'good keep at it' 'I missed you' Douglas said 'missed you too' Corey replied.

The next few days Corey had a great time with Daniel and Douglas she could have quite happily stayed in Ireland.

But knew she had to return to see Polly who was due to arrive back in London she made sure the house was tidy.

Marie had an obsession with Ker Plunk and building blocks anything colourful that made a noise.

Corey wore a black polo neck and some gold earrings some mascara she wanted to look nice.

For when Polly came home she was wearing a black coat and high heels she looked amazing Corey thought 'Cor'.

'Polly' they hugged 'I missed you' 'you too' Corey said as Polly smiled 'you look nice' Polly said 'me no'.

'You look amazing' 'thanks darling' Polly was glad to be back home 'I heard about your row with Louie'.

'He's just not my kind of person' 'it's a shame maybe if you just got to know him properly' 'I'm not interested'.

'I've seen enough of Louie to last me a lifetime'.

'Everywhere I go I seem to see him a café a nightclub and Harrods I can't stand him ok it's the way I feel'.

'I don't like him he called me a fat Irish bitch and you stay friends with people like that!' 'calm down!'.

'No I won't calm down you know I don't mind your uncle Sam he's very nice George is ok but Louie'.

'Is the most awful person I've ever met!' 'come on that's going too far!' 'no it's not'.

'If I have to spend another minute in the same room as him ever again!' 'I'm sorry you feel that way'.

'But he's my friend ok one of my closest friends' 'oh so you think it's ok what he said to me!' 'no I don't'.

'I'm really sorry he feels really bad he said to tried to apologise' 'I'm not interested' 'exactly give him a chance'.

'I just don't want to talk about him ok! I don't know him'.

'And I don't want to know him I'm still angry about what he said to me' 'I'm sure he didn't mean it'.

'Trust me he did' 'let's not row! we'll talk about something else' 'I'm sorry I got upset' 'it's alright'.

'How was Liverpool?' 'oh it's great I loved it being back home I went to the Theatre and The Wirral'.

'How's Daniel?' 'great we made it up he's split up with Lizzie' 'great she's such a bitch'.

'Dan was too good for her' 'that's exactly what I said'.

*'I'm so glad you made it up' 'so am I' 'and I'm glad to be
home' 'it's good to have you back' 'thanks darling'.
'How about we go shopping tomorrow to celebrate me
coming back home' 'sounds like a great idea'.
Corey agreed 'good darling' Polly said kissing her.
The next day Corey reluctantly agreed to go shopping with
Polly she'd begun to hate it due to her weight gain.
Still Polly had returned home and she would do anything
to make her happy so they set off before lunch.
Polly insisted on going to her favourite café near the
Houses Of Parliament 'I've missed my favourite café'.
'I'm having a cheese toastie what about you?' 'I'll have
the same and a tea and some coffee cake for after'.
'Me too' it soon arrived 'this is nice' Polly said Corey
realised how much she'd missed her.
After finishing their cheese toasties the tea and cake
arrived 'this is good' 'tell me about it' Corey agreed.
She thought it was the most gorgeous cake she'd ever
tasted with a lovely cup of tea she was in heaven.
It was so nice she could have ordered another one they
went shopping Corey helped Polly try on some clothes.
She began to feel hot as if she might pass out at any
moment 'there I've finished trying them on are you ok?'.
'Great' 'you look hot' 'I'm fine it's too hot for me in here'.*

'I won't be long I'll just pay for these' 'I'll be around' 'ok darling' Corey felt as if the room was spinning around. She felt ill not herself at all Polly paid for her items as she passed out on the carpet.

People went to see that she was ok Polly turned around wondering what was going on she realised it was Corey. Lying on the floor 'Cor! what's wrong?' she felt a pulse. She was conscious 'someone's called an ambulance'.

The security guard said 'thanks a lot' Polly was worried they soon arrived as they took Corey to hospital.

She wondered what was wrong they lay her down on a bed 'Cor wake up' she could hear Polly's voice 'Polly' 'Cor'. 'You're alright!' 'I'm ok I feel a bit out of it' 'it's ok you fainted your in hospital they'll find out what's wrong'.

A doctor was nearby 'she's woken up' 'Corey I'm doctor Jacob' 'what happened?' 'you passed out' 'why?'.

'Their not sure' Polly said 'can we ask a few questions?'. 'Yes' 'have you passed out any other time?' 'recently I was shopping with a friend in Harrods I passed out'.

'On the floor I thought it was nothing' 'have you suffered headaches or blurred vision?' 'no' 'stomach pains?' 'no'. 'I've just felt a bit ill lately that's all' 'right do you suffer with diabetes?' 'no' 'epilepsy' 'no' 'heart problems' 'no'.

'Have you lost or gained weight recently?' 'I've put on weight recently I don't know why I'm usually slimmer than this maybe there's a reason'.

'When did you last have a period?' 'two maybe three months ago' 'have you had an increased appetite?' 'yes'.

'You don't think your pregnant?' 'no I'm married to Polly I'm a lesbian' 'come on you are joking!' Polly said.

'We've been together over five years the only time she slept with a man was when she was thirteen'.

'Don't you think we'd have planned a baby' 'oh god!' Corey suddenly realised the time she'd slept with Steve in New York 'what?' Polly asked she just knew.

By the look on her face 'you are joking!' 'I'm sorry it was a one off' 'you slept with a man!' Polly was shocked.

'I'm sorry ok I was lonely!' 'Cor we're married since when have you fancied men!' 'I don't it was a one off'.

'I was really drunk I don't remember much of it' 'this is unbelievable!' 'I'm sorry' 'you're a lesbian'.

'You like women! think of how many women you slept with when you worked as an escort girl!' 'I know!'.

'So you're on the turn now!' 'no I love you!' 'yeah right!'.

'Maybe your bi-sexual!' 'I'm not!' 'you must be if you slept with a man!' 'it was a one off'.

'It'll never happen again but I need to find out if I'm pregnant' 'get on with it then!'.

Polly had never been so angry in her life Corey felt relieved.

If she did turn out to be pregnant it would explain a lot of things 'can I go home now?' she asked 'if you like'.

'But if you're not pregnant please see your GP' 'I will'.

'Thanks for everything' they left Polly was so angry she didn't say a word in the car as they went home.

She felt betrayed 'please don't be angry at me!'.

'Wouldn't you be! if it was the other way round and I'd slept with a man!' 'I know I'm sorry!' 'we're married'.

'Didn't our wedding mean anything to you!' 'of course it did I love you!' 'then why did you screw someone else!'.

'It won't ever happen again!' 'I bet you've been waiting for the perfect opportunity for me to do a film'.

'So you could go with someone else!' 'it's not true I'd never cheat on you' 'but you did and with another man!'.

'Should I get tested for an STI now?' 'no he's married or he was he's getting a divorce' 'this gets worse'.

'Does he have kids?' 'two sons' 'oh that's alright then!'.

'I thought I knew you I thought we told each other everything I feel like I don't know you anymore!'.

'You do I love you! your my wife!' Corey said upset.

'I thought you were putting on weight because you were eating too much now I know it's cause your pregnant'.

'You don't know I am!' 'we'll do the test I need to know so do you' 'ok I'll do it I'll find out if I'm pregnant'.

An hour later it came back positive Corey was hoping it wouldn't be but deep down she knew she was.

'What am I gonna tell everyone that my wife cheated on me!' 'I'm sorry' 'you should have thought of that'.

'Before you slept with someone else! you better make a doctor's appointment to find out how far gone you are'.

Corey reluctantly decided to make a doctor's appointment alone Polly was too angry to go with her the doctor.

Who confirmed that she was pregnant just over three months gone she arranged to have a scan.

Polly was still annoyed that Corey was pregnant and that they hadn't planned it together.

After Corey came home she didn't feel great she was angry at herself for sleeping with Steve.

'Well what did the doctor say?' Polly asked 'I am pregnant just over three months'.

'Don't expect me to be happy about it!' 'you think I wanted this to get pregnant!' 'I don't know!' 'well I didn't!'.

She hardly ever rowed with Polly she didn't want their to be an atmosphere 'Cor listen' Polly felt angry.

But she didn't want them to fall out over things they were married Corey was her wife .

She'd looked forward to returning home so they could spend some quality time together as a couple.

Only to find out Corey had slept with someone else a man she wouldn't tell her who it was.

She didn't actually care Polly felt like she wasn't good enough maybe it was her fault.

For going off to all her business meetings and acting jobs maybe she had neglected their marriage.

Even so what Corey had done was wrong she had been drunk if she had been sober it would have been different.

Or if it had been planned or if she'd had an affair maybe she could forgive her she didn't want them to split up.

Over a mistake Corey didn't sleep all night thinking about things as she ate breakfast the next morning.

'You hate me because I've ruined our marriage'

Corey said 'no I don't hate you' 'sounds like it to me'.

'I'm angry but I don't hate you I'm just pissed off why didn't you tell me you slept with someone else?'.

'Because I wish it never happened ok I just wanted to forget about it' 'you can't forget about it'.

'Not when your pregnant look if you said you were drunk then maybe we could move on pretend it never happened'.

'If I could take it back I would' 'who was it?' 'no-one'.

'Please tell me' 'it doesn't matter it was a mistake that should never have happened'.

'So you won't even tell me who the father is'.

'It's not that important' 'you're having a baby and who the father is isn't important' 'course it is who was it?'.

'Someone you know' 'maybe' 'one of the band Andy or Mike?' 'I wish their my bandmates' 'just tell me'.

'A friend' 'and he was married he was not now it meant nothing I was drunk it was a night that went too far'.

'I'm sorry I broke our marriage I do love you and I hate what I've done' 'I'm not happy about it '.

Since when have you been into men' 'I'm not ok it was a mistake I don't fancy men I like women'.

'Then why did you end up sleeping with a man?'.

'I don't know I was drunk it wasn't planned' 'the last thing I want is us splitting up over this' 'you hate me' 'no Cor'.

'Besides your pregnant' 'I'm fine' 'I don't care you should be looking after yourself I'll look after you'.

'No-one has to know do they' 'I never planned this to get pregnant again' 'I know'.

'We'll just have to find a way to deal with it' 'what do you mean?' 'you're having a baby' 'I could get rid of it'.

'I mean I don't want to but if it meant losing you'.

'I meant us having the baby course I don't want you to get rid of it we'll have the baby'.

'We were gonna have another baby at some point anyway'.

'Maybe it's fate you getting pregnant' 'you think' 'yes'.

'Your not leaving me' 'course not I love you' 'but your angry at me and with good reason'.

'I won't pretend I'm not but I love you Cor and what we have' 'I love you too I'm sorry I let you down'.

'I love you so much and I never meant to hurt you' 'Cor '.

'It's alright we can get over this me and you' Polly hugged her Corey felt better 'I'll make you a cup of tea' 'thanks'.

'I'm your wife I'm supposed to look after you'.

'What are we gonna tell people?' 'we don't have to tell them anything'.

'As far as their concerned we've been planning another baby no-one has to know anything or who the father is'.

'What if people ask?' 'just say it's a close friend'.

Corey felt better Polly had forgiven her she knew she didn't deserve to be forgiven she was just relieved. Everything was ok and was also glad she knew what was wrong with her Corey decided to e-mail Steve the news. She wondered how he'd take it what he'd think of her.

"Dear Steve I'm writing to you just because
I haven't seen you in ages also because I have
something to tell you there's no other way than to
just say it I'm pregnant'.
'And I haven't slept with anyone else since
I'm married so you're the father I don't expect
anything from you'.
'You don't have to worry about getting involved
Polly and me will look after the baby'.
'I have always thought of you as a good friend'.
'I know that me getting pregnant might ruin our
friendship I just wanted to say things as they are'.
'I would also appreciate it if you didn't say anything
about me being pregnant being a lesbian'.
'I don't want to have to explain to the media the
situation I'm just over three months gone'.
'So it's still early days I hope you have found happiness
after your ex-wife Corey xxx'.

Corey wondered what Steve would think once he received
her e-mail he'd probably be angry at her.
For bringing a child into the world he didn't want
Corey knew she'd done the right thing.
She'd said things as they were it was better than lying to
him finding out after the baby was born.

She was still getting used to the fact that she was pregnant again but decided to embrace the situation.

As best she could Stacey had been invited to Christian's house just outside London in the countryside.

She couldn't wait she'd be meeting his mum and brother and sister Stacey decided to invite Louie and Polly along. She decided it would be less nerve racking than meeting his family on her own they set off around 11am.

To be there for lunchtime it was a beautiful sunny day. Despite the chilly weather Louie drove them since none of the others could drive listening to Radio 2.

As they enjoyed the good weather as they arrived Stacey was slightly nervous meeting Christian's mum.

She was sure she'd be nice she was from Yorkshire people from up north were usually down to earth people.

They couldn't believe how big the house was like a National Trust property it reminded them of Angelsfields. Not quite as pretty but not far off they got out the car as they looked around 'the gardens are amazing!'.

Polly said 'look at this topiary love it!' Louie said.

'Come on let's go inside' they walked up the front steps as Christian opened to greet them 'hi' 'hello'.

'Your gardens are great' Louie said 'I know their really nice especially summertime come in'.

Falling to pieces

They made their way into the house 'it's nice' Stacey said.
'Oh I'm glad you like it come in' they followed him inside
They looked around paintings hung on the walls with tall
bookcases they heard someone come down the stairs.
'This is my mum' Christian said she was wearing a crème
suit her blonde hair up wearing a pearl necklace.
And high heeled court shoes she arrived at the bottom of
the staircase 'mum this is Polly' 'hiya' 'hello Polly'.
'I've heard so much about you you're Christian's
half-sister' 'oh I just think of her as my sister now'.
'Forget the half' 'yeah we've become close really good
friends' Polly said 'where's Corey?'.
'She wasn't feeling well she's pregnant'' 'really' 'yeah'.
'It's our second child together' 'you have a son' 'Luke'.
'And Marie she's five' 'how does that work? I mean who's
the father?' 'Andy my ex-husband' 'what about your son'.
'Oh he has a different father I got pregnant at thirteen'.
'I made a mistake but I wouldn't change anything' 'mum'.
'This is Stacey' 'hi' Stacey said smiling 'hello Stacey'.
'Hello I've heard a lot about you all good it's nice to meet
you I'll see you later' 'with that she was gone.
'She looks good your mum' Polly said 'oh yes'.

'She always likes to look presentable I'll show you round the house'.

Stacey had been nervous about meeting Christian's mum. She got less than a few seconds talking to her maybe she was busy they followed Christian 'I'll show you upstairs'.

'I'm so scared in case I break something' Louie said.

'It's such a gorgeous house' 'oh I love it here it's tempting to stay and not move out I should'.

'This is my brother's room he's fifteen' 'I remember you telling me you had a brother' Polly said.

'This is my sister's room Maria she's fourteen' 'is that a poster of me?' Polly asked curiously 'yeah'.

'She's your biggest fan she'll love the fact that you came round' 'wish I could have met her' 'hopefully soon'.

'When it's the school holidays here's a photo' 'oh she's really pretty her parents were Italian mum adopted her'.

'When she was three we're really close' 'that's nice I like your house' 'I'm glad you finally came round'.

'And got to meet mum the amount of times I've been to your house and you never came to mine'.

'Well I'm glad we got the chance to come round'

They looked upstairs Polly thought it reminded her of Victoria's house in Ireland she thought of her.

And decided she wanted to see her again soon.

It was soon time for lunch which was served in the dining room Stacey noticed suits of armour a red carpet.

The table was dark brown with plenty of seats she sat down next to Christian Polly and Louie sat opposite .

He was dressed surprisingly conservative in a black top and blue jeans Christian's mum joined them.

'Stacey I did you pasta since I know you and Christian are vegetarian' 'thanks' 'sounds nice' Polly said.

'Oh everything's freshly made here we have our own garden and chef before that we've got a starter'.

'Tomato and basil soup here it is' a waiter served the soup Stacey sipped it she thought it tasted nice.

'It's really good' she said 'I'm glad you like it' after the main course was served Stacey liked her pasta.

She noticed some roast potatoes she reached over 'oh that's for later I've got you some carrots' 'oh right'.

Stacey smiled secretly she was angry so she wasn't even allowed to help herself to potatoes.

It wasn't like they couldn't afford to buy more Polly was enjoying her soup Louie seemed a lot less lively.

They were all trying to impress scared of saying the wrong thing 'so how did you meet dad?' Polly asked.

'I was working a long time ago in a hair salon briefly in the centre of London I met your dad'.

'We had a relationship for a few months I got pregnant'.
'Then not long after I married Christian's step-dad we're divorced now' 'you were a hairdresser'.
'I used to work as a Saturday girl when I was a teenager'.
'I was gonna do an NVQ in hairdressing after I left school then I got into glamour modelling' Polly said.
'It was only briefly' 'right' 'I never liked hairdressing' Stacey noticed she seemed uncomfortable maybe because she wanted to project a lady of the manor impression.
She wondered if it was hairdressing she wasn't keen on or work in general.
Since she obviously lived off her rich husband she'd taken an instant dislike to her but she couldn't tell Christian.
'So Stacey you've got a daughter' 'yes Tahilia she's nine months' 'does she see her dad?'.
'If you don't mind me asking?' 'she sees him sometimes but she still lives with me' 'do you have a nanny?' 'yes'.
'Destiny we're good friends she's the best' 'I mean it must be hard work being a single mum' 'I'm used to it now'.
Polly could see Stacey felt uncomfortable and didn't want to get into a conversation talking about James.
And the fact he wasn't interested in his daughter she decided to try and change the subject.
'You've got a nice house' Polly said 'thankyou'.

'I'm glad you like it' 'it's a lovely house' Louie said 'so Louie what do you do?' 'I'm a personal trainer'.

'Sometimes I'm on Daybreak do you watch it?' 'no'.

'I'm afraid I don't BBC breakfast for me'.

'What about This Morning?' 'I can't say I've seen you on there' 'well I'm not on that often'.

'My day job is with celebrity clients' 'Louie works with me' Stacey said 'right great'.

Stacey wondered if she was being off with Louie because he was gay 'room for more' 'course mum' Christian said.

For dessert it was Stacey's favourite black forest gateaux with crème 'tuck in' 'it looks nice'.

Stacey decided however nice the food was she couldn't wait to leave she hadn't warmed to his mum at all.

Hopefully they wouldn't have to stay much longer she sipped her tea as she finished her cake 'so Stacey'.

'Enjoy that?' she let out a burp 'sorry' Polly and Louie tried not to laugh Stacey felt bad.

She'd tried to make a good impression 'so are your brother and sister at school?' Louie asked.

Trying to change the subject 'yeah they are my sister's fourteen and my brother's fifteen' Christian said.

As his mum gave them dirty looks 'where else would they be?' she said abruptly.

Louie decided he really hated Christian's mum and thought she was rude.

After lunch they wanted to leave instead Christian took them on a tour of the gardens it wasn't so bad.

Since the weather was nice 'showing them round the gardens' Louie turned around 'the bitch is back'.

He muttered under his breath 'yeah and it's such a nice day' 'oh yes isn't it' Louie said 'I'll leave you to it'.

She wondered off to their relief it would have been a nice day but Christian's mum had put them in a bad mood.

'So fancy a go in the Jacuzzi?' Christian asked 'I didn't bring my costume' 'never mind you can come back again'.

'Yeah' Stacey said forcing a smile 'I hope you had a nice lunch' 'the food was good' Stacey said 'it's great'.

After a stroll round the gardens they found an excuse to leave Louie saying he had a client to train.

'Well I hope you had a great time' Christian said 'we did' Stacey lied 'I'll see you soon' he said.

Kissing her on the cheek 'I'll miss you' she said 'I'll miss you too' 'nice seeing you again Louie' 'you too darling'.

'It's great Stacey's found herself a nice man'

'bye everyone' 'we had a nice day' 'I'll see you soon' Christian said hugging Polly as they got into Louie's car.

They were secretly happy to be leaving Christian waved.

As they set off home Louie didn't look himself Polly
noticed unusual for him since he was usually so happy.
'Have a good time?' Polly asked 'I didn't like his mum'.
Louie said 'sorry Stace I know he's your boyfriend'.
'It's ok I didn't like her either I hated her please don't tell
Christian' 'it's ok darling my lips are sealed'.
'I thought she'd be nice I was really looking forward to
today' Stacey said 'darling don't worry'.
'It's one of those things she was vile did you see the look
she gave me?' Louie said 'I noticed I just didn't like her'.
'I know you really like him but whatever you do please
don't marry him imagine having her as a mother in law'.
'No-one's as bad as Marie' 'I agree Susie I guess I won't
be coming here again' 'don't worry darling'.
'He can just go round to yours' once they arrived back in
London they were relieved.
Stacey decided she'd try not to go back to his house it was
a shame especially since her family were welcoming.
The next day Louie came over to see Stacey she was
looking forward to it after the day before.
They could watch This Morning listen to music after lunch
bitch about what an awful time they'd had at Christian's.
Stacey loved Louie he'd become one of her closest friends
as he arrived at eleven she was happy to see him.

He seemed a lot cheerier than the day before 'Louie'.

'Stace you know I had this nightmare I was back at his house then I realised it was just a dream'.

'Louie that's not very nice!' 'I'm sorry Stace she was vile'.

'A horrible woman and he's so sweet as well' 'well I won't be going back to his house again' 'what if he asks'.

'I'll say I'm busy recording' 'good excuse' 'anyway he can come to mine he's an actor he'll be working'.

'In London' 'he's really nice Stace you picked well this time' 'I know I'm so happy I really like him a lot'.

'Even know his mother's vile' 'as long as I never have to see her again I'm fine'.

'So what do you think of Corey getting pregnant?'.

'I had no idea I thought she'd just put on weight' Stacey said 'Polly didn't tell you' 'no' 'I thought you were close'.

'We are usually' 'then why didn't she say anything'.

'She must have had her reasons maybe they were waiting till she was three months gone till she had the scan'.

'Maybe surely she should have told you your family cousin's step-sisters' 'I know it's weird'.

'We tell each other everything why wouldn't she tell me?'.

'I know they wanted another baby but it's strange all of a sudden Polly just announces she's pregnant'.

'At Christians mum's house without telling me'.

'And Corey never said anything she's my best friend'.

'All the times I called her fat I feel like a bitch why didn't Polly tell me'.

'More to the point if Corey knew she was why didn't she say anything?' 'maybe she didn't know' 'Stacey'.

'Two girls together it's not like a straight couple planning a baby they have to go to a clinic or at least organise it'.

'Arrange who the father is or whatever it has to be planned weeks or months in advance'.

'The fact Polly hasn't said anything seems odd to me and you're telling me Corey didn't know she's pregnant'.

'When she's the one carrying the baby' 'what are you getting at?' 'the whole thing is odd'.

'That they wouldn't tell anyone after they'd conceived'.

'Corey's three months gone' 'exactly once you get to three months no reason not to tell everyone'.

'Maybe they were being careful' 'or maybe Corey had a secret affair maybe she slept with a man'.

'Louie don't be ridiculous! Corey's gay she's never been with a man she even worked as a lesbian escort'.

'Stace look at that MP who left his wife for that lesbian or there was this gay guy I read in a magazine'.

'He'd been gay all his life he went with a woman now their planning a family sexuality is fluid' 'maybe'.

'Would you ever go out with a woman?' 'I doubt it but you can never say never to anything I love being gay though'.

Stacey smiled Louie made her laugh 'listen bet I'm right'.

'I doubt it I bet your not' 'we'll ask Polly then' Louie said.

'She didn't exactly seem happy about it' Louie said 'no she wasn't' 'I'll find out the truth'.

Stacey couldn't help thinking that maybe he was right.

That afternoon Polly came round 'Susie' 'Stace Louie'.

'Sarling come in we're just watching Loose Women their discussing bi-sexuality' Louie said 'oh right'.

'I'm a lesbian despite what people think' 'well I'm gay'.

'But I find it interesting' Polly definitely didn't look happy.

Stacey thought not herself 'listen I think we need a little chat' Louie said 'what about?'.

'I know you're not yourself' 'how?' 'I can tell and I think I know why I've suspected something'.

'Tell me if I'm wrong did Corey sleep with a man?'.

'How do you know?' 'I just guessed the fact I insulted Corey twice about her weight and she never said'.

'That she was pregnant the fact that you announced it at Christian's house without telling us'.

'You didn't seem happy about it and there was no mention of a trip to the clinic'.

'I know if you'd have planned this you'd be shouting it from the rooftops you don't look happy' 'it's true'.

'She slept with a man' 'wow! who?' 'I don't know I haven't really asked I don't want to know'.

'I can't believe she did it' 'neither can I darling' 'it's Cor'.

'She's been with loads of women in the past before she married me since when has she been bi-sexual'.

'She says it's a one off that she was drunk' 'it probably meant nothing' Louie said trying to make Polly feel better.

'I had a right go at her I was mad we talked I wanted us to have another baby maybe it was meant to happen'.

'Don't worry about it everything will be ok' Stacey assured her 'thanks what if people find out?'.

'They won't I won't say anything Stacey won't so no-one has to know anything do they' 'that's what I thought'.

Stacey agreed 'as far as they know you've planned a baby together' 'thanks darling give me a hug' Louie said.

Polly felt better talking to Louie she felt better about things 'Susie it'll be ok you'll have the baby'.

'And everything will go back to normal I mean if it was a one off and she was drunk it's not like a proper affair'.

'I mean I know it was still wrong' 'you're right Stace'.

'Everything will be ok' 'I'll get you a drink' 'thanks Stace' 'are you excited about the baby?' Louie asked 'yeah'.

*'We are' 'what sex is it?' 'we don't know yet and she's
having the scan in a few days want to be godmother?'.
'I'd love to' 'can I be godmother too?' Louie asked.
'Course you won't tell anyone about you know what'.
'Oh course not Susie not a word' Stacey assured Polly.
'Secret's safe with us' 'thanks what would I do without you
two in my life'.
'You won't say anything about the fact I hate Christian's
mum' Stacey said 'no darling she wasn't very nice'.
'Understatement of the year' 'it's just between us you make
a really good couple' 'it's all because of you'.
'Setting us up' 'I didn't do anything it was all you you look
great together' 'thanks I'm really happy' 'I'm happy too'.
The following evening Stacey had a date with Christian
she was happy she really liked him.
Later that afternoon Destiny went out she looked after
Tahilia after lunch Stacey watched telly.
She felt more relaxed she heard a knock at the door as she
looked out the window it was Kim.
She was happy to see her 'Kim' 'Stace' 'come in I'll get
you a drink' 'I'm not staying!' Kim looked angry at her.
'What's wrong?' 'how could you!' 'how could I what?'.
'You know what not tell Christian about mum'.*

'What do you mean?' 'Polly told me how you hadn't told him about mum so you're ashamed of her now!'.

'It's not like that!' 'then how is it!' 'this has nothing to do with race!' 'then what is it?'.

'I didn't know Christian well enough to tell him about things my family' 'we are your family me and mum'.

'So we're not good enough now!' 'it's complicated I didn't meet mum till I was fourteen'.

'And then when I found out when I was twelve my uncle was my dad' 'what's that got to do with it!'.

'You met his mum why can't you just admit you're ashamed of who you are!'.

'I've never been ashamed of who I am!' 'you're a liar Stacey!' 'no I'm not!' 'you are!'.

'You know I didn't care that you had pale skin that you look white you were still my sister'.

'I still thought of you as mixed you sing and dance like a black girl you love soul music'.

'Then now it's like your someone else! with your white boyfriend visiting him in his mansion'.

'Next you'll be horse riding and playing polo why don't you just admit it your ashamed of me and mum'.

'And you want to be white a real life Imitation Of Life story!'.

'You didn't see how his mum was when we met her' 'what's that got to do with anything!' 'some people aren't like us'. 'They can't see beyond race' 'us you're not black anymore!' 'I've never hidden my mixed heritage'. 'From anyone' 'whatever! enjoy your new rich lifestyle!'. 'Wouldn't want the black side of your family to bring you down!' Kim left slamming the door.

Stacey was shocked at her outburst how could Kim accuse her of denying her black side.

Maybe she should have told Christian but she found it hard always having to explain who she was.

Being judged for looking white the looks of surprise the talking behind her back she began to cry.

As Destiny comforted her she could see she was upset first her boyfriend's mum hated her now her sister hated her.

Could her life get any worse? Stacey felt so sad she spent the rest of the day feeling down her sister hated her.

Her mum would probably hate her too the next day she still felt bad about what Kim had said.

At 11am Stacey heard a knock at the door 'hello darling'. It was Louie smiling as usual 'thought you'd like to go shopping with me and Polly' 'I don't feel up to it'.

'It's ok' Stacey had texted Louie telling him what happened 'it'll take your mind off things' 'come on Stace'.

'Me and Louie will cheer you up' 'ok Susie' she reluctantly changed her mind applying some make-up.

A lilac pastel eyeshadow & berry coloured lipstick 'you look great' 'thanks Louie' they headed into town.

'I can't believe what Kim said she's a bitch! how could she say those things' 'Louie's right you know' Polly agreed.

'I feel like it's my fault' 'it's not your fault Stace you've never lied about who you are'.

'You even starred in a remake of Imitation Of Life'.

'It's hard having to explain to people about things'.

'Polly's right darling you don't have to explain to us'.

'I mean clearly Kim's got a complex that quip about horseriding and polo' 'I don't mix in those circles'.

'Darling why would you want to' 'well some people do'.

'Social climbers' 'like Christian's mother then' Louie said.

'When we were at his house I felt so uncomfortable' Stacey said 'we all did' Polly said.

'You're better off without Kim you don't need her you've got us I know she's your sister but let her sulk'.

'If she wants to' Louie said 'let's hit the shops' Polly said.

'Me and Louie are gonna help you forget your troubles'.

'Thanks are you gonna get some stuff for the baby?'.

'I want to Corey's worried about not being far enough gone she's never had a miscarriage'.

'But she won't let me buy anything for at least a month'.
'Let me know when you can I want to buy something for the baby' 'ok Stace'.
'I hope one day I have what you have with Corey'.
'You will darling very soon trust me' Polly assured her.
They hit the shops trying on clothes having fun Stacey couldn't believe it when they bumped into her mum.
Outside Dolce & Gabbana 'mum' 'Stace Kim told me about your row' 'listen mum let me explain'.
'I swear I'm not ashamed of who I am' 'I know darling'.
'It's nothing to do with race I just don't feel I know Christian well enough to explain everything'.
'About how I found out my uncle was my dad how I'm this mixed race girl who looks white'.
'Then his mum was horrible not nice at all' 'your gorgeous just as you are everyone looks different'.
'Christian seems really nice' Marcee said 'you know that time I met him at the family meal' 'he's lovely'.
'You call me ok anytime tell me all the gossip even if it's in the middle of the night' 'thanks mum'.
'So you're not angry at me?' 'no your my daughter I love you' 'love you too have a good day' 'you too Stace'.
'I'll see you soon' they hugged 'bye darling' 'bye mum'.
'Your mum always looks amazing' Louie said.

'Yeah she does' Stacey agreed with Louie 'see your mum's cool forget about what Kim said' Polly said.

'It's like she doesn't understand when I introduce people to my mum they look at me strangely'.

'Like they think she's not my real mum it's really hard'.

'I know it's hard for Kim too like I don't know what it's like to walk into a room and have people look at you'.

'Because of the colour of your skin but she could be more understanding she had a go at me'.

'For having a white boyfriend now who's being racist'.

'She's just jealous' Polly said 'because she probably still fancies Christian' 'we were so close Susie'.

'Now she'll never speak to me again' 'that's her problem'.

'Not yours you know me and Louie are here for you'.

Stacey had loved hanging out with Polly and Louie she still felt upset about her row with Kim.

Corey woke tired around 10am Polly was seeing a friend in London Daniel would be coming to visit.

He was in London making a career as a successful songwriter.

Louie was making his way over to see Polly he parked nearby as he arrived he saw a dark haired young man.

He was sure he recognised him 'hello your not by any chance related to Corey?' 'how did you know?'.

'I guessed by the Irish accent you do look alike I'm Louie'
'Daniel Corey's brother'.

'Polly told me she had a brother' 'are you the fitness instructor?' 'yes that's me nice meeting you'.

'I came round to see Polly' 'oh she's visiting a friend'.

'Corey said I think she'll be back later' 'maybe I'll come back another day' 'no come in'.

'I'm not sure that's such a good idea me and your sister don't really get on' 'how come?' 'personality clash'.

'Maybe you can make it up cup of tea?' 'why not?' 'hello' Daniel said as Corey answered 'how are you?'.

He hugged her 'I'm grand it's good to see you good to see you too so why didn't you tell me you were pregnant?'.

'We wanted to wait till I got past three months' 'you still could have told me I'm your brother'.

'We've always been close all of a sudden you can't even tell me that your having a baby' 'I'm sorry ok'.

'I know I should have told you' 'you must be excited'.

'Yeah' 'so I'm gonna be an uncle again?' 'yes looks like it' 'I bet your buying baby clothes already' 'no not yet'.

'Why not?' 'what if something happens I'm waiting a month'.

'Last time you were pregnant you couldn't wait to buy things for the baby' 'you know I want to be careful'.

'I just don't want to jinx anything' 'ok I understand
I'm really happy for you'.
'And I thought you were getting fat from too many pints of
Guinness' Corey laughed 'anyway it's just a quick visit'.
'Louie's here to see Polly' 'hi' 'I said I'd make him a cup
of tea' Daniel kissed her on the cheek.
She was happy to see him 'make yourselves at home'.
'I'll make the tea' Louie sat on the sofa 'oh he seems really
nice Louie' 'he's ok not my type of person' 'he seems ok'.
Daniel made the tea as they sat down 'back soon call of
nature' he said 'your brother seems very nice'.
'You came to see Polly' 'yes and you she said when she's
away she wanted someone to see that your ok' 'I am'.
'As you can see I don't need anyone' 'is this what you
always do? push people away' 'you called me names'.
'I'm sorry you didn't say you were pregnant you kept it a
secret from everyone' 'I didn't know I was'.
'And since I'm pregnant I can choose who I want to tell'.
'I know your secret' 'what secret?' 'that you slept with a
man' 'you can't tell anyone' 'I won't tell a soul'.
'I suppose you'll use that against me say how I don't
deserve Polly how I'm a bad person' 'no I won't'.
'It's your marriage Polly loves you' 'yes she does and
I love her too whatever you think of me' 'fine ok'.

'Why do you hate me so much because I'm a gay man'.
'I don't hate you what about you! that time in the
nightclub when you told me dykes weren't welcome'.
'It was a gay nightclub for men only what you said to me
was worse! in fact some of it was homophobic'.
'What about you! you used me!' Corey said 'what do you
mean?' 'that time you took me to play badminton'.
'When I had a milkshake we hung out together then I find
out you do that with everyone' 'I don't understand'.
'When you came to collect the keys the next day you said
you were off to play badminton have a drink'.
'With that girl exactly what you did with me' 'oh so you
think that's some spiel I do with everyone' 'yes'.
'Well it's not I only do that with people I like trust me
there's plenty of clients I'd rather not hang with'.
'After our session' I guess I misunderstood' 'I'm having a
bad week I apologise for being bitchy'.
'I had to go to a memorial service for my sister she you
know...ten years ago' 'I'm sorry' 'she was my best friend'.
'Me and Dan are like that best friends I don't know what
I'd do without him' 'I'd better be off' Louie said 'client'.
'No I need to go home' she noticed he looked sad 'bye'.
Corey wondered if it was something she'd said he was
obviously upset talking about his sister.

She thought about Louie and their conversation later that
evening Corey recieved a phone call it was Louie
'I'm sorry for asking about your sister's memorial service'
'it's fine really you were only making conversation'.
'It's fine I would rather grieve for her in my own way
instead of being forced to attend a memorial service'.
'With my mum and older sister I should have said no their
such hypocrites she never even got on with mum'.
'Or my sister they make out they were close to her but
I was the one she was close to we were best friends'.
'Next time I'll go by myself to her gravestone you should
have seen all the rubbish they've put there trinkets'.
'And things she would've hated it I took some of it off said
it was thieves who'd stolen it'.
'She would've just wanted a nice bouquet of flowers and
one wind chime I'm sorry I'm talking too much' 'it's ok'.
'You look really good for being pregnant' 'me are you
serious' 'you look great' 'you said I was fat'.
'I didn't know you were pregnant I'm sorry' 'apology
accepted' Corey smiled 'good I'll leave you now'.
'If it's ok' 'Dan's here he'll look after me' 'that's good'.
'I'll see you round' 'bye Louie' Corey couldn't believe
they'd managed to have a conversation without rowing.
Although they weren't quite friends yet.

They'd managed to be civil to each other Corey still felt guilty about being off with Louie.

But she was sure he'd forgiven her things would be ok now Stacey had decided to go clubbing.

To the same club she'd been going to since she was seventeen it played old school hip hop r & b.

It was a ragga night Stacey was still upset over not speaking to Kim.

Music was the only thing that took her mind off things she wore a black dress her hair up naturally curly.

Lots of mascara she entered the club as she found Justin DJing he saw her smiling she ordered a drink 'hey'.

'Justin' 'I'm glad you came' 'I really needed a night out'.

'Wanna dance?' he asked 'yes' as Stacey danced with Justin she loved it as they danced .

To Dawn Penn's No, No, No she knew Justin fancied her. But she wasn't interested in being anything more than friends Stacey felt good.

As Justin played some old school classics as their dancing got raunchier she was having fun.

'That's some good dancing' it was Sherri Kim's friend.

'Stacey how are you?' 'good' she was worried Sherri would think she was racist after Kim's accusations.

'How's Kim?' Stacey asked 'not too bad we had a row'.

'Why?' 'I don't know she's not been herself she's been pissed off about something I think it's her dad'.

'She keeps saying how she wants to meet him
I told her I didn't think it was a good idea'.

'We had a row too we're not speaking' 'I know she told me' 'I'm not a racist'.

'She didn't give me a chance to explain I love mum I'm not ashamed of who I am' 'I know that'.

'You wouldn't be in a hip hop club with black people if you were don't worry about Kim she'll sort herself out'.

'What about Justin? what was that dancing?' 'just dancing ragga music makes you move in a certain way'.

'So you're not back on then?' 'no I like just being friends'.

'Still with Christian?' 'yes we're together' they danced to the music she loved it forgetting her troubles.

Sherri danced close to her she was obviously getting into the music 'hey what do you say we hang out properly'.

'I'd love to come round my house anytime' 'thanks'.

Stacey was glad Sherri liked her and didn't think she was a racist despite what Kim thought she was happy.

She'd made a new friend Stacey focused on promoting her album in Europe it took her mind off things.

But she felt lonely and realised how much she missed Christian.

That afternoon Corey decided reluctantly to visit her father in prison.

He'd apparently been diagnosed with cancer and it didn't look good Corey wasn't even sure she believed him.

But she wanted to see for herself she couldn't believe she was going to visit him.

She didn't even want to be in the same room as him the abuse she'd had over the years.

As Corey drove to the prison she was searched they were gentle with her taking into account her condition.

As she entered the visiting room their eyes met he smiled.

She didn't trust him he'd let her down so many times and she remembered he was a violent man.

A dangerous criminal 'Corine you're pregnant' 'yes'.

'Was it planned?' 'we were planning another baby'.

'Still with that tart?' 'if you're referring to Polly she's not a tart she's my wife' 'she used to take her top off'.

'For lad's mags I'm sure there's a few floating around in here' 'she's a Hollywood actress BAFTA's Golden Globes'.

'Quite impressive' 'what have you ever achieved?' 'alright point taken you know being pregnant suits you'.

'Thanks so you've got cancer?' 'yes testicular cancer'.

'They've found a lump it's only early stage but my lawyer thinks if I play on it i'll get an early release I'll survive'.

'Don't worry I'll pray for you' 'your a good Catholic girl Corine I'm very proud of you'.

'Their transferring me in a few weeks I'll be going home to Ireland can't wait home sweet home' 'that'll be good'.

'Still organising crime from behind bars' 'I might be you know me your not so innocent yourself'.

'Why did you ask me here?' 'so I could see you' 'has Daniel come to see you?' 'no he won't see me'.

'I don't know why I knew you'd come and see me my little girl so do you see him much?' 'yes'.

'We've always been close' 'I know how close you are'.

'What's that supposed to mean?' 'you know Dan he's always fancied you' 'he's my brother' 'when has that ever stopped anyone' 'your sick you know that!'.

'It's the truth! I've seen the way he is with you I know his secret fantasy'.

'How dare you say I want to sleep with my brother!'.

'You don't always have to have sex with someone to have a relationship with them' 'I hate you!' 'Corey listen'.

'I'm pleased to see you I've missed you I love you so much you were always my little girl I adored you'.

'From the moment you were born I treated you like a princess' 'let me refresh your memory'

Reunited

'You hit me and Dan' 'just the odd smack what was the problem anyway it's all in the past no-one's perfect'.

'I always loved both of you darling' 'you beat me and Dan from the time we were kids'.

'You whipped me so hard with your belt I still have the scars I had to have a nose job at seventeen'.

'Because you tried to beat me once remember that!'.

'I was drunk ok I never meant it I love you so much'.

'I didn't want anyone else to have you' 'I'm your daughter I thought you loved me!' 'I do' 'you love me so much'.

'You beat your own children almost killed Douglas by kicking me in the stomach while I was pregnant'.

'I never knew what love was until I met Polly' 'I never mean to hurt you!' 'you're a feckin liar!'.

'A murderer, burglar & terrorist think I didn't know about that man you helped to kill' 'keep your voice down!'.

'Why did you invite me here?' 'I need some money' 'no!'.

'Corine!' 'no your not getting any from me! you'll be in prison for a long time! which is where you belong!'.

'You bitch! I want some money I'll pay you back!'.

'I need some money some compensation for all those years of abuse! I had to put up with I hate you!'.

'And I feel sorry for all those victims of your crimes' 'your not so innocent a former escort girl and drug addict!'.

'I haven't done drugs for years' Corey got up to leave.

'Where are you going?' 'home' 'you're not going yet!'.

He grabbed hold of her arm 'yes I am leave me and Polly alone!' 'you run back to your posh house'.

'Your perfect life that tart paid for with her glamour modelling taking her top off for men!'.

By this time everyone was listening to their conversation.

'Are you ok?' an officer came over 'I'll be fine I'm going'.

'Your not my father anymore! you'll be all alone just your fellow criminals for company!'.

'And you'll have no-one but yourself to blame!' 'Corine'.

'Don't go!' 'I'm going leave me alone! you need some money work for it go rob a bank'.

'If that's the way you feel!' 'I do!' 'please your my daughter and Dan your my only family my kids'.

He was playing mind games with her nice one minute nasty the next.

'I'll never forget what you did to me! the times you hit me!' 'I'm a bad man Corey' she looked at him.

His face expressionless like he didn't care 'I'm going'.

He rubbed his hands for money Corey took out her purse.

Taking out a pound coin 'do the lottery!'.

'If you want some money but don't come asking me for anymore money!' 'you bitch!'.

As she walked away he was angry she knew the kind of person he was an evil cruel money grabbing liar.

Corey knew she'd done the right thing in having nothing to do with him she walked out.

Wishing she'd never gone to visit him how could she have believed his lies that he was dying of cancer.

He was a con artist he'd say anything to get what he wanted as she reached the entrance of the prison.

She heard a voice call 'Corey' 'Louie what are you doing here?' 'I was visiting my brother'.

'You have a brother in prison' 'yes shall we got get a drink somewhere?' he asked 'ok'

As she sat in the back of the car she wished she'd never gone to visit her dad.

'Was that your dad you were rowing with?' 'yes'.

'I heard some of your conversation the end part anyway'.

'I recognised your Irish accent' 'what's your brother in for?' 'burglary he's a nice person?'.

'He hung around with the wrong people he got three years he's got six months to go what about your dad?'.

'He helped kill a man gangster terrorist he's burgled houses' 'I wish I never asked I thought I had problems'.

'You don't have anything to do with him' 'not for a long time me or Daniel' 'Polly told me everything'.

'And about your mum' 'then you know what she's like'.

'You never saw much of her growing up' 'no just in the holidays Nicky my step-sister she was the favourite'.

'I never knew why until I found out she wasn't my real mam' 'it must have been a shock'.

'It turned out for the best I get on well with my real mother Carol' 'that's good I'm sorry about your family'.

'It's ok I have Daniel my brother we're really close'.

'He seems really nice' 'you'd like him if you got to know him' Louie felt sorry for Corey.

A mother who never cared about her who tried to hide the fact she brought up her son as her own a father in prison.

At least she had her real mother and brother Louie had hated Corey at first.

Now he found himself wanting to be her friend 'I'm sorry'.

'About everything when we first met I didn't know you very well' 'it's ok I guess I'm sorry too' Corey said,

'I've never been around gay men camp you know not like Polly she has lots of gay male friends' 'we're alright'.

'Once you get to know us' Louie joked 'just a bunch of harmless queens I'm sorry what happened'.

'At the gay club let's go eat something'.

They found a nice cafe nearby as they found a table Corey
ordered a vegetarian sausage & potatoes Louie the same.
The food arrived 'looks nice' Louie said 'I am trying to eat
healthily I had some Pringles last night' Corey confessed.
'Oh love Pringles' 'you're a fitness instructor' 'I know but
sometimes it's nice to be naughty'.
'A bit of what you fancy does you good' 'I can't imagine
you ever eating unhealthy'.
'I do I have my naughty moments can I ask does the father
know about the baby?' 'yes he does'.
'What did he say about it?' I'm still waiting for a reply not
a good sign' 'you told him' 'I e-mailed him'.
'Who is he? if I'm allowed to ask' 'an actor' 'famous'.
'He's successful in Hollywood' 'american' 'you're not
gonna give up are you' 'you don't have to tell me'.
'I'm just curious' 'even Polly doesn't know I'd rather not
say he's a friend' 'ok then' 'he lives in America'.
'So it's not like I'm gonna be able to see him much'.
'You know you're not the first gay person to have a
straight fling' 'it was a one night stand no romance'.
'No affair I love Polly I made a mistake I was drunk'.
'I understand you know you're not the first person it's
happened to' 'I like women I know my own sexuality'.
'I only ever had one boyfriend when I was thirteen'.

'Really tell me' 'we had sex I was too young Colin we're still good friends that's how I got pregnant with Douglas'. 'A year later I came out as a lesbian I've been happy ever since did you ever have a girlfriend before you know...'.

'Before I came out' 'yes when I was a teenager I dated both men and women'.

'Did you have any sexual relationships?' 'once or twice'. 'It wasn't for me it never felt right when I was eighteen I knew I was gay that I liked men'.

'I had a relationship with a woman I was at College it didn't last long but it was special in a way'.

'Her name was Billie she was a great person we're still friends I've liked men since I was a teenager'.

'But I really liked her if you've got feelings for someone that's it' 'how long were you together?' 'four months'.

'What happened?' 'we drifted apart she ended up marrying a man she invited me to the wedding'.

'Besides it could never have worked out between us it would have only been so long before I saw a cute guy'.

'I just really liked her I was there in the moment young and in love with a girl there's my confession'.

'Even a queen like me can fancy a pretty girl it was a one off thing I'm gay and proud' 'let's have a toast'.

Louie suggested 'ok then' 'to being gay and proud'.

They raised their glasses of coke 'dessert' Louie asked.

'Of course' Corey replied 'I fancy some ice cream how about we order a knickerbocker glory between us'.

Louie suggested 'ok then' it soon arrived as they tucked in Corey was having a great time.

She'd almost forgotten her row with her dad she hoped she never had to visit a prison again 'I'm sorry we fell out'.

'And what I said about you being fat' 'you didn't know I was having a baby neither did I' 'I know but I shouldn't have said it and you look great' 'well thanks'.

Corey was surprised at how well they were getting on she decided Louie was a nice person after all.

'I'll drive you home' 'thanks I had a nice time' 'you had a bad day and I wanted to take your mind off things'.

They soon arrived home as Corey got out he parked her car in the drive 'bye' Corey said as she waved.

She couldn't believe she'd had dinner with Louie.

Stacey woke the next day to a rainy day in London she gave Tally breakfast before watching Daybreak.

Then she got dressed applying some make-up her hair straightened wearing heart shaped earrings.

Which she'd received as a gift from Justin when they were going out together.

It was strange to be wearing a gift from your ex-boyfriend
they looked nice she thought around 2pm Louie arrived.
As they went into town together Corey decided she needed
to get some maternity wear.
She thought she could window shop for things for the baby
she was actually enjoying her time off.
And was learning a script for her next film role and
couldn't wait for the band to release their next album.
Things were looking good after going round the
High Street shops they headed to Harrods.
Corey remembered how she'd fainted the last time now at
least she knew why.
She looked around the gift department her mum Carol was
coming to visit and Corey wanted to buy her something.
She found a Swarovski crystal dolphin figure her mum
loved them she hoped she'd like it 'it's really nice'.
Stacey said 'I know think she'll like it?' 'she'll love it'.
'Corey' 'Lucy' it was Corey's lesbian friend the last time
they'd met had been the night at the gay club.
With Cassie 'how are you?' 'fine you?' 'great' 'I can't
believe your pregnant again why didn't you say?'.
'Oh I didn't want to jinx anything' 'I understand the three
month thing' 'yes' 'well congratulations' 'thanks'.

'I think this will be my last one' 'well I can't wait to have a family soon when I meet the right girl'.

'You and Polly make such a nice couple' 'thanks she's the love of my life' 'your so lucky married with kids'.

'The last time we saw each other was in that gay club'.

'Oh yeah what a bad night that was' Lucy said 'tell me about it when's your club opening?' Corey asked.

'In a few weeks you'll come' 'I'd love to and Stacey'.

'That guy was vile wasn't he talk about bitchy queens'.

'I remember you saying how you'd rather top yourself than spend another moment in a room with him'

'Someone as vile and camp' Louie looked over at Corey. She hadn't realised he was there 'anyway we'll talk on Facebook come along to the opening we'll have fun'.

'Bye' Corey said as Lucy left the store Louie looked at her.

'Louie listen I'm sorry' 'like f**k you are! vile and camp am I you're a f***g two faced bitch!' 'Louie don't!'.

'Stacey shut up I don't give a f**k!' 'I don't care if you're pregnant! and I want nothing to do with you!'.

'I only took you out to lunch cause Polly told me to look out for you while she was away!'.

'I thought you liked me!' 'I never liked you I hate you!'.

'Louie you can't speak to a pregnant woman like that!' Stacey said angry 'I don't care I'm going!'.

Louie left Corey felt bad not that bad after all he'd
slagged her off called her a fat bitch 'I didn't mean it'.
'It was before we were friends I thought we were'.
'Now he's saying he only took me out to dinner because
Polly told him to!' 'I'm sure he didn't mean it'.
'He's just saying it because he's pissed off I thought it was
out of order your pregnant' 'so he doesn't care does he!'.
'I thought I could be friends with him I thought we'd made
it up' Stacey felt bad she was angry at Louie.
For what he'd said she knew Corey hadn't meant to say
what she did to swear at a pregnant woman was wrong.
They went home Corey was upset however hard she tried
she couldn't get his words out of her mind.
Later that evening after Stacey had gone home Corey
decided to go visit Louie as she rang the doorbell.
She got no answer knocking on the door 'I can see you
from the window what do you want?'.
'I thought we could talk' 'you thought wrong do me a
favour and f**k off!' Louie slammed the door.
Corey was still angry at what he'd said 'why did you call
me camp? I thought we were friends!' 'oh friends really!'.
'I called you those things before we were friends I never
meant them' 'I thought we were friends'.

'Then you tell me you only took me out for lunch because Polly asked you to look out for me I don't need your pity'.

'I didn't mean to call you vile and camp I didn't know you then but you just called me a fat bitch'.

'I thought you were being nice to me' 'I was and I do want to be your friend' Louie said.

'I think there's been a misunderstanding between us'.

'You can say that again!'.

'Come in' Corey sat down on the sofa 'I shouldn't have shouted at you I'm a terrible person'.

'I shouldn't have called you names your pregnant the way I spoke to you it was unforgivable I had a bad week'.

'I shouldn't have taken it out on you' 'I said things too'.

'I'm not good at talking things through my dad was violent as a child' Louie confessed 'my dad was violent too'.

'Polly told me' 'I try to block it out things that happened' Corey said 'me too' 'sometimes I get angry about things'.

'It's a throwback to my childhood' Louie said 'I know how you feel I get angry too' 'I had counselling'.

'Only a few sessions it felt strange talking to someone I don't know I'm usually such a calm person normally'.

Louie said 'my dad was always angry at me everything I did was wrong' Corey admitted.

'He always came back drunk from the pub I always knew when he was in a bad mood I'd get scared'.

'He'd get me into a corner hit me you know' 'how often?'.

'It would depend sometimes once a week sometimes he wouldn't do it for a few weeks'.

'Dan was the only person who knew how I felt did your dad punch you?' 'sometimes he gave me a black eye'.

'A few times he used to belt me when he was really angry'.

'He told me to lie down he took out his belt '.

'Left me with scars' 'I'm sorry I know how you feel darling it happened to me what about your mum?'.

'She left when I was seven I hardly saw her except for the holidays it wasn't a surprise when I found out'.

'She wasn't my real mam she said she didn't know he was hitting us he hit her that's why they split up'.

'We were never close dad could be ok sometimes we'd go out places with him he always had a wad of cash'.

'From his dodgy business deals we asked him where it came from we knew he didn't work not a nine to five job'.

'He said I was his princess he could be a charmer nice one minute mean the next'.

'You never knew what mood he would be in' 'sounds like a bastard' 'I had to clean the house we were kids'.

'We sometimes went out to dinner if relatives visited or we lived off ready meals I got sick of it so I learned to cook'.

'Mam taught me and my Aunt I brought him Guinness he was happy when he had a beer if not there was trouble'.

'You kept house for him' 'hovered dusted' 'that's awful'.

'You should have told him to do it himself' 'I can't my dad's a gypsy it's our culture the men go out to work'.

'The women keep house' 'but you said he doesn't work'.

'Well he commits crimes to get money' 'so your like Cinderella did you tell anyone what he was doing?' 'no'.

'There was no point besides I was scared if I told someone then I'd never see Dan again they'd split us up'.

'I hated my life so much I wanted to be like the other girls' 'straight you mean?' 'no other things' 'tell me'.

'You know when I told him I was gay he didn't care as long as Dan wasn't he even gave me money'.

'To go to gay clubs' 'one thing I suppose you said you wanted to be like other girls'.

'Everyone's got something they don't like about themselves I wanted a normal family I suppose'.

'A mam and dad who loved me he never even let me have dolls I loved dolls so much I grew up as a tomboy'.

'I always wanted a Tiny Tears or one of those dolls with a porcelain face dressed in Victorian clothes'.

'I played with them at school' 'you are serious you're telling me he wouldn't let you play with dolls'.

'Sometimes he was just being cruel what about your dad?' 'same story alcoholic violent he hit my mum'.

'He used to break my toy cars my Action Man he left when I was fourteen best thing that could have happened'.

'You should have told me about your dad' 'he died the drink killed him so I'm free of him now' 'that's good then'.

'Corey let's start again ok forget the rows' 'I'd like that too' Corey agreed 'can I be your friend?'.

'I'd love you to be my friend Louie' 'good darling'.
Louie hugged Corey she realised she liked Louie he
wound her up but he had a good heart.
They'd had a similar childhood the same experiences
'Louie thanks ok for being my counsellor' 'I never thought
of myself like that take my advice don't visit your dad'.
'You don't need him you've got plenty of friends who love
you' 'I know thanks Carol's coming to visit me next week'.
'My real mother' 'is she nice?' 'she's great you'd really
like her you know'.
'Is that an invite to come round your house?' 'yes' 'thanks
I'd love to come round meet your mother' 'great'.
'I have to go now see my little girl' 'I forgot you're a mum'
'I don't like to leave her for too long' 'it's ok'.
Corey made her way to the front door Louie opened the
door playing the gentlemen he kissed her on the cheek.
'Bye' 'bye Corey do you want a lift home?' 'I'm ok you
don't live too far away from me I drove here'.
'Well take care bye darling' Louie said blowing air kisses.
Corey was happy they'd finally made it up she'd been
wrong about Louie she'd gotten to like him.
Now maybe they could be friends Stacey was busy
promoting her new album she loved performing live.
That afternoon she came back from an interview.

On This Morning to find the biggest bunch of red roses
they were from Christian.
She still couldn't stop thinking about him 'their gorgeous!'
Destiny said 'I know I love red roses'.
'I wonder if he knows their my favourite' 'maybe'.
'Polly probably told him Stacey he likes you he wouldn't
be sending flowers for the second time in a few days'.
'If he didn't really like you he seems really nice forget
about what happened with his mum if you can avoid her'.
'It'll be fine you deserve to be happy after
Justin and James' 'thanks for being there for me'.
'I hate to see you unhappy' 'you're more than my nanny'.
'You're a friend to me' 'well your one of my favourite
employers' Stacey liked having Destiny around.
She was more than her nanny she was a good friend.
That evening Stacey prepared for a gig she was excited
about touring her mum usually did backing vocals.
Along with two of her singers but she was ill and couldn't
make it she hit the stage at 7.30pm.
Where she sang her heart out for an hour and a half till
9pm Stacey drank mineral water refreshing herself.
As she touched up her make-up before meeting some fans
backstage she looked over she saw a familiar face.
It was Christian 'hi' Stacey said pleased to see him.

'Hi I saw your concert you were good' 'thanks I'm glad you enjoyed it' 'this is Maria my sister'.

'She's your biggest fan' 'hi pleased to meet you'.

Stacey said as a girl with dark shoulder length curly hair and olive skin smiled 'pleased to meet you too'.

'I liked your show' 'thanks' 'you're really pretty' she said as Stacey smiled 'I wish I had straight hair like yours'.

'I don't actually my hair's naturally curly like yours'.

'My parents were Italian I'm adopted that's why I look different to Christian'.

'Didn't you say your great grandmother was Italian?'.

Christian asked Stacey 'yes but I never met her she died did you pay to come to the concert?' 'yes'.

'Well next time I'll get you a VIP pass then you can get in for free' 'thanks you didn't mind us coming?'.

Christian said 'course not' 'I'm sorry about everything my mum the house' 'it's ok thanks for the flowers'.

'Did Polly tell you I liked roses?' 'yes' 'I thought so Stacey I really like you will you be my girlfriend?' 'yes' 'really'.

'Yes I like you too' they kissed Stacey knew she could trust Christian he wasn't like Justin or James.

He seemed interested in her he was kind and caring she was in love with him.

And knew they could have a relationship.

'I'll text you' he kissed her on the cheek 'bye'.

Maria waved 'bye' Stacey said feeling happy.

It was a Friday Corey's favourite day of the week she woke around 9am she liked having the bed to herself.

She chose a black T-shirt black elasticated trousers there was nothing in the house to eat.

Corey knew she would have to go shopping her nanny had broken her leg and couldn't walk far

As she walked into her local supermarket she decided she looked reasonably presentable.

As she selected milk, bread, juice and whatever else she fancied she was trying to eat healthily.

Eating lettuce and carrots but couldn't resist a few treats.

Her favourite foods pizza, ice cream, crisps and anything else that took her fancy.

She wondered through the aisles she heard someone calling her name 'Corey' it was Stacey 'hi how are you?'.

Stacey asked 'I'm fine my back's killing me I'll be fine'.

'How come you're shopping on your own?' 'someone's got to do it the nanny's got a broken leg'.

'You should have asked someone I mean in your condition' 'it's fine' 'what would Polly say about it'.

'She probably wouldn't like it I needed some fresh air to get out the house' 'and you shouldn't shop by yourself'.

'Carrying all that shopping' 'I'm fine' 'let me help you shop' 'I couldn't ask you to do that for me' 'why not?'.

'Corey how are you?' Christian asked 'I'm fine are you together?' 'yes' Stacey said smiling 'that's great'.

'Corey's doing her shopping by herself and I said she should have some help with her shopping'.

'Really I'm fine' 'Stacey's right in your condition let us help you' 'ok but I'm not finished shopping'.

'Neither are we' Stacey said 'ok thanks if you don't mind hanging out with a pregnant woman' 'course not'.

'Remember when I was pregnant and I'd split up with James and you looked after me' 'I always hated James'.

'And Polly' 'I know that now I wish you said a year of my life wasted on someone I didn't even like let alone love'.

'At least he gave you your daughter' 'I know I guess everything happens for a reason' 'definitely'.

Corey agreed when she got to the till she was tired from all the walking around.

Stacey and Christian helped her with the shopping as they cancelled the taxi that had brought them there.

And went home with Corey 'thanks' she said as they arrived home the nanny was playing with Marie.

Who was at home for the holidays she could enjoy lies ins and some extra help Corey made some tea.

As she chatted to Stacey in the kitchen 'Christian sent me more red roses' 'that's really nice of him'.

'And he came to see my concert last night backstage with his sister Maria she's fourteen she was really nice'.

'I was still upset about what happened with his mum at the house he said sorry and he said he really liked me'.

'He wants me to be his girlfriend' 'that's great' 'I know'.

'What did you say?' 'that I liked him too' 'let me know when there's a wedding invitation'.

'Oh I think that's a while away I want to get to know him'.

'I think he's the one' 'I really hope he is' Corey said happy for Stacey she deserved to find someone nice.

'Have you thought about names for the baby?' 'a few we're still looking I'll let you know when we decide'.

'Are you gonna have a baby shower?' 'I don't know'.

'Please say yes' 'maybe I had one last time I was pregnant' 'so you can have another one'.

'Do something different this time' 'maybe' 'that's a yes'.

Corey smiled she liked the fact that Stacey was around to talk to as a friend.

She was also happy Stacey had finally found someone nice to be with 'I thought we could go bowling tonight'.

'The three of us' Christian suggested 'I'd love to but I can't in my condition I don't think it's a good idea'.

'Lifting heavy objects' 'ok I understand Stacey'.

'Usually I'd say yes I'm not up to it' 'what's wrong?'.

'I fell out with my sister I found out something she said about me on Twitter' 'what did she say about you?'.

'That I don't deserve my success as a singer' 'how can she say that?' 'I don't understand she's a good singer'.

'Pretty in a successful group' 'she must be jealous of you'.

Christian suggested 'she's never been jealous our relationship's not like that she had a miscarriage'.

'So that's no reason to slag off your own sister she was only six weeks gone' 'there's no excuse for what she said' Corey said 'I don't know why she said it we used to get on so well she's my best friend now we aren't speaking'.

'She must have issues that have nothing to do with you'.

Christian said 'maybe I know she's been really upset lately about her dad I don't think she ever saw much of him'.

'She was talking trying to get in contact with him' 'it's not your problem' Corey said 'I know but she's still my sister'.

'Was she acting like your sister when she slagged you off' Corey said 'no I always wanted a sister and now I feel like that's it ever since I knew I had a sister'.

'Since the first time we met we clicked' 'don't worry ok'.

'I'm sure she'll realise what she said was wrong and apologise' 'I doubt it I'll be ok'.

'Do you and your sister look alike? Christian asked.

'It's Kim we're half-sisters same mum different dad's'.

'That explains why you look different I thought she was your best friend' 'she is she was'.

'Don't worry you'll make it up' 'I hope so' Stacey knew Christian was right she missed Kim.

Even though she was upset at what she'd said Stacey decided it was best just to leave Kim alone for a while.

Let her sort out whatever issues she was dealing with the next morning Stacey went to town.

As they went to a nice pub where they could get to know each other and chill out she was happy.

To have found Christian they enjoyed each other's company he treated her well.

Unlike her previous boyfriends who were only interested in sex 'so what are you drinking?' Christian asked.

'A coke' 'ok then I'll have the same' Stacey found a table.

'I like this pub' Stacey said it was the same one the first time he'd invited her to have a drink with him.

Christian sat down with her 'I wouldn't worry about your sister' 'it's ok she's my best friend'.

'I can talk to her about anything or I used to' 'you said your sister's in a group' 'their big in the states'.

'Their called Crème all the members are mixed-race'.

'Her dad's black and Egyptian I don't really know what her dad looks like he lives in America'.

'What about you is it just your brother and Maria?'.

'Yes and Polly' 'you know a lot about me now I'm a Libra and obsessed with Prince and James Brown' Stacey said.

'I remember your obsession with Prince' 'good'.

'Well I'm a Cancer and I love most music except heavy metal' 'me too'.

'I couldn't be with someone who doesn't like music'.

Stacey said 'and me you'll have to come round my house again I have a really good sound system'.

Stacey couldn't think of anything worse having to see his mother again 'I have a big record collection too'

'We'll have a music night' Christian suggested.

'Sounds great' 'back soon' he said Stacey went to the toilet as she returned she spied Christian chatting to a girl.

Suddenly she realised it was his ex she drank her coke she was angry what was she doing there? 'Christian' 'Stacey'.

'Laura was just going' 'says who?' 'just go away we're finished' 'you know you've done me a favour'.

'At least now I have a real man' 'really good it was over between us for a long time'.

'Then why did you get back with me?' Laura asked.

'I made a mistake I'm with Stacey I love her'.

'So Stacey you want a real man you won't find it not with Christian' 'what do you mean?' 'you like sex'.

'You were engaged' 'are you saying I'm easy I've slept with five men that's it' 'you have a kid' 'yes'.

'Put it this way you won't be getting any sex from Christian'.

'Why don't you leave us alone! I am so done with you Christian and that bitch!' 'there's only one bitch here!'. Stacey said as Laura left people stared at them.

'I'm sorry' Christian said to the barman 'it's ok we'll sort it out' 'Stacey I'm sorry she just showed up'.

'What were you thinking going out with her' 'I don't know I'm sorry she had a go at you she was angry at me'.

'And she took it out on you' 'she's not over you'.

'She better be because there's no way I will go anywhere near her again' 'good I love you' 'I love you too'.

'What did she mean no sex?' 'nothing' 'listen I don't care if there's some medical reason why you can't have sex'.

'Everything's ok Laura was just being bitchy comparing me to her other man he's Mr muscle owns a gym'.

'Oh I don't go for big muscles just normal sized men'.

'Good let's go back to yours' 'ok then' Stacey's anger at Laura faded away she loved Christian.

He was such a calm person he helped put her at ease .

They got back to her house as they went upstairs they
kissed on the bed 'I've got some condoms I mean...'.
'It's up to you' Stacey said 'I thought we could take it slow
get to know each other first' 'of course'.
'My last relationship didn't go very well except I got Tally
out of it at least'.
Stacey liked the fact Christian wanted to take things slow
that he didn't want to use her for sex like some men.
That evening Louie invited them out clubbing with him
Corey was also coming along Stacey was looking forward
to it her first proper night out with Christian.
Louie took them to a gay club as they entered the club
it was a good friendly vibe as Stacey looked up.
She saw a silver spinning glitter ball 'I've never been here
before' 'I know darling you'll love it' Louie said happy.
Stacey sensed he would be on the pull that night
'this is Donnie and Julian my gay friends' he said.
As two camp queens stood beside him 'hi' Stacey said.
'Oh hello darling you're even prettier in real life'
Donnie said 'thanks' 'see you later' they said walking off
'Your such a scene queen' Stacey joked 'I know and you're
a fag hag' 'not as bad as Polly' 'true'.
'Listen I'll get the drinks the usual?' 'yes thanks'.
'Back soon' 'are you ok?' she asked Corey 'I'm grand'.

'Do you think they mind having pregnant lesbians here?'.
'I'm sure they won't it seems friendly like a good club'.
They headed over to the bar to join Louie 'hi Christian'.
A man said in a northern accent 'hi' 'how are you?'.
'I'm good this is Stacey' 'you're together?' 'yes' 'Stacey
I'm such a big fan I think you're a great singer' 'thanks'.
'This is Ricky' 'hi pleased to meet you I'm an old friend'.
'Of Christian's' 'oh right' 'haven't seen you for a while'.
'Looking good as always I'll see you round' Ricky said he
walked off they all chatted as they had drinks.
Before hitting the dancefloor Louie returned with Donnie
and Julian Stacey danced with Christian.
As Lady Ga Ga's Just Dance came on they were all loving
it Corey felt had she not been five months pregnant.
She could have danced with the rest of them she spied a
familiar face 'Corey' 'Violet' 'how are you doing?'.
'I'm fine' 'expecting another baby? you are a busy girl'.
'How's your daughter?' 'she's good she's five now'.
'And she's gorgeous just like her mum' 'thanks'
'I've followed you in the press'.
'Your relationship with Polly' 'really' 'I used to buy OK
every week she's a gorgeous girl and so are you' 'thanks'.
'You're even prettier than I remember' Violet said 'your
not so bad yourself' 'me darling' 'I'm forty seven'.

'Well you look ten years younger' 'who's this?'
Louie asked 'this is Violet' 'I was Corey's sugar mummy'.
'When she was an escort girl' 'oh really I forgot about
that' 'Corey was a naughty girl so was I'.
'And she was very good at her job' 'oh really' 'this is
Louie' 'pleased to make your acquaintance'.
'Pleasures all mine Corey give me a hug it's been such a
long time' Violet gave her a hug.
Violet had been like a mum to her helping her to learn
French telling her where to shop.
Which restaurants to go to she'd missed her
'keep in touch let me give you my new mobile number'.
Corey keyed it into her purse 'text me darling' 'I will'.
As Violet left Corey decided she would definitely keep in
touch she ordered a glass of coke she enjoyed herself.
As she returned to the dancefloor as some drag queens
took centre stage.
Doing the moves to Beyoncé's Single Ladies as everyone
watched cheering Corey was glad she'd come out.
She was sure her baby wouldn't mind listening to some
good music she'd had a great time.
The next day she felt good Corey still had Beyoncé stuck
in her head as she put on 'Crazy In Love'.

Stacey was happy being with Christian she liked being part of a couple.

She was chilling out with Christian when she heard a knock at the door as she opened it was Kim.

What was she going to say? Stacey was still angry about what she'd said she wanted to tell her to go away.

But Stacey knew it would solve nothing she missed Kim.

Maybe she could forgive her sister 'Stacey' 'listen I'm sorry about everything' Kim asaid 'the things you said'.

'You said I didn't deserve my success as a singer it upset me you know' 'I know I was jealous of you' 'why'.

'You're in a successful girl band your really pretty and talented' 'so are you'.

'You said I was successful because I look white do you know how hurtful that is!'.

'You accuse me of being a racist your just as bad I don't care that you look black how can you say that about me!'.

'I was angry not at you ok at my dad I didn't mean it'.

'I never wanted us to fall out' 'yes you did mean it Kim!'.

'No I didn't I'm so sorry if I could take it all back I would please forgive me Stacey I can't stop thinking about you'.

'And what I said mum had a go at me' 'what's wrong?' Christian asked 'nothing' Stacey lied 'please Stacey!'.

'You're my best friend I had a miscarriage'.

'It screwed me up I know it's no excuse for what I said'.
'I'll let you sort it out I'll just be in the kitchen' 'is he your boyfriend yet?' Kim asked 'yes we're together properly'.
'He asked me to be his girlfriend the other night'.
'He's really nice' Stacey was slightly annoyed her sister was pretending as if nothing had happened between them.
'Kim I'm really upset about what you said' 'I'm sorry too I love you so much your my sister' she hugged Stacey.
'I love you too' 'really you forgive me?' 'yes course'.
'I'm sorry you had a miscarriage and about your dad'.
'Thanks' 'you don't need him ok you've got me and mum'.
'Thanks you're the best sister in the world what would I do without you Stacey'.
'I told Christian that we're half-sisters he thought we were best friends I mean we are but anyway...'
'I'm glad your with Christian' 'so am I' 'you make a really good couple Stacey your my sister and I love you'.
'Christian' 'you two made it up' 'yes' 'Stacey told you we're sisters'.
'If you ever get married I'll be your sister in-law' 'tea'.
Christian asked 'yes' 'biscuits' 'yes but I have to limit myself I'm on a diet' 'why?' Stacey asked Kim.
'My manager told me to lose weight' 'you look fine to me'.
'I put on weight when we were in America'.

'You know how it is' 'you look fine to me' 'thanks Christian' 'well I'm glad my manager's not like that'.

Stacey said 'you're so lucky my manager thinks he can control us' 'you should tell him where to go'.

'I wish besides I like being in the group too much I do what I have to do so have I missed any gossip?'.

'Corey's five months pregnant' 'I know' 'I'll change the subject' 'it's fine it just wasn't my time it's ok really'.

'You'll have a baby I know it' 'thanks I'm only twenty seven I've still got time' 'exactly and it's such hard work'.

'I can imagine Tally's so well behaved' 'I know I'm lucky and she seems to like Christian' 'that's good then'.

'Hey let's go to Ragga night at the club together'.

Kim suggested 'when?' 'two weeks time' 'ok then'.

Stacey agreed 'Christian you coming?' Kim asked

'I'd love to' 'good we'll all have fun together' Kim said.

Stacey was happy she'd made it up with Kim and couldn't wait for their night out together.

The next day Corey woke she was happy and excited her mum Carol was coming to visit along with John.

And their sons Douglas was with them they were on their summer holiday she couldn't wait to see them.

Corey did her make-up wanting to look presentable deciding what to wear she decided to wear black.

Anything to make her look slimmer she wore a gold necklace with a four leaf clover.

She received a phone call from Louie he was doing a workout with a client and did they want to meet.

After lunch on the river bank she said ok her mum wasn't due to come till about 2pm Corey called a taxi.

To take her there it was a nice sunny day she felt tired.

Louie came over full of energy as usual 'darling why are you wearing black?' 'because I'm pregnant'.

'So you should be showing it off instead of covering up'.

'I'm seeing my mam' 'really' 'yes so I don't want to look too big' 'well I think it's pretty obvious you're pregnant'.

'And more than halfway along' 'their my family my mam her husband and my two half-brothers and Douglas'.

'Ok point taken but you should still wear some more colours summer's nearly here'.

'I am trying to be more colourful' 'good darling because you're so pretty how old are your brothers?'.

'Fifteen and sixteen Graham and Connor my mam's called Carol my middle name will you stay and meet her?'

'Course darling I'd love to' they sat down 'I've got something for you' Louie pulled out a bag.

Revealing some baby clothes 'Louie listen you shouldn't have' 'I wanted to' 'thanks their really nice'.

'Polly will love them thanks Louie' 'anytime would you like a cushion?' 'I'd love one thanks my backs killing me'. 'I thought so I have one I've been using for sit-ups'. Louie gave her a cushion she instantly felt better 'thanks' 'well I have to look after you since Polly's away'.

Corey realised how much she missed her while she was away in America she sat and chatted with Louie.

As they strolled along the Themes river it was a beautiful afternoon.

It would have been even better if Polly had been there they returned to where they'd started as they waited for Carol. 'Do I look ok?' Corey asked 'darling you look great'.

Louie assured her they watched as Carol walked towards them 'tell me that's not your mum' 'it's my mam'.

'She is definitely a MILF' 'Louie!' 'how are you?' she asked 'I'm good' Corey was happy to see her .

'Look how big you are now I've got some things for the baby' 'you shouldn't have' 'I wanted to'.

'I'm happy for you and Polly how is she?' 'good she's in America' 'working' 'yes' 'give me a hug'.

'John's here' 'hello Corey' 'hi John this is Louie my friend' 'hello' the boys appeared as they all greeted each other.

'Dougie' Corey had missed him so much 'when's the baby due?' he asked 'soon I'm five months gone'.

'So you'll have a half-sister soon' 'what are you calling the baby?' 'we haven't decided yet something nice'.

'No weird showbiz names' Louie couldn't get over how good Corey's mum looked 'it's such a nice day'.

'Mind if we take some photos' Carol asked 'no not at all'.

John took out his camera as he took photos Corey was happy she felt like part of a family.

Something she'd never felt growing up Louie looked on happily as she watched Corey's family.

'Our stuffs in the car mind if we go back to your house'.

'No let's go' 'I should go now' Louie said 'I'll just be in the way' 'you won't please stay' Corey said 'ok then'.

'Yes stay don't go on our account' Carol said 'ok then'.

'I'll stay' 'good' they all went back to Corey's house she was happy her family were there.

She and Louie made everyone tea 'Corey you always keep a nice house' 'thanks John' they'd stayed before.

But never with the whole family she didn't mind being kept company while Polly was away.

'You should have said you were pregnant I was here two months ago' 'It's nice you're having another girl'.

'I know Polly's happy' 'I can see the resemblance between you too' Louie said 'oh really' 'I think you look alike'.

John said 'so Louie what do you do?' Carol asked.

'I'm a personal trainer to the stars' 'I thought I'd seen you somewhere' 'I've been on Daybreak and This Morning'.

'You must have to be fit to be a personal trainer' John said 'oh yes very I like it though I've been doing it a while'.

'I do normal people too not just celebrities' 'must be a well paid job' 'oh yes but I love it'.

'The sense of satisfaction helping someone feel good'.

'Do you have a partner?' 'no I'm single just doing the gay scene' 'oh I'm not up on the gay scene' John joked.

'Oh gay clubs are the best you have so much fun'.

'Oh I bet' 'mam runs a record label in Ireland' Corey said 'I like to do my bit to help struggling artists I have a new band a group of lads I'm bringing them over to the UK'.

'You're a proper businesswoman then?' 'oh yes A & R'.

'Well a love of music must run in the family' 'oh I think so I've always loved it like Corey'.

They heard a knock at the door 'hello' Louie answered.

'Darling you're back' 'yeah I'm back not for long' 'give me a hug you look great' Louie said.

'Polly you're back' 'Cor darling I've missed you so much I thought about you everyday' 'me too I feel bad'.

'About not being able to look after you being pregnant'.

'Don't be I'm sure whatever you're working on will be great' 'well I'm back now'.

'Promise you'll take some time off when we have the baby'
'course darling I wouldn't miss the birth'.
'My family's here' 'Carol' 'Polly hello' 'hiya' 'I was just
thinking where's everyone gonna stay' Corey thought.
'Don't worry we'll think of something maybe I could stay
with Stacey Destiny her nanny's away for a week'.
'On holiday so I'm sure it would be ok' Polly offered.
'If it's not too much trouble' Carol said 'no course not'.
'Thanks Polly' 'it's fine really enjoy yourselves while
you're over here' 'thanks' Corey said.
Polly changed into some other clothes as she joined
everyone for tea 'you must work hard'.
'All those long hours on film sets' 'yeah it beats having a
real job the I prefer singing I'll give up acting'.
'At some point I think' 'you must have done a lot of films
by now' 'oh yeah nine I looked on Wikipedia'.
'I love what I do though I love singing more though'.
'You can't beat singing' John agreed 'I know I love it so
much I've been singing since I was a little girl'.
Corey was happy Polly seemed to get on well with John.
Polly rang Stacey to see if it was ok to stay she said yes.
Polly had brought some clothes for Douglas which he
loved everything was good.

She couldn't wait to get all the gossip about Stacey and
Christian she thought they made the perfect couple.
She also had something to talk to Corey about 'Cor listen
you know I spend a lot of time in America'.
'More than half the year there' 'yes I know' 'I was thinking
we could move their permanently'.
'I don't know we've got the apartment in New York for
when you work over there' 'I know that'.
'It's just all the transatlantic flying' 'ok I'll think about it'.
'Really' 'yes' 'imagine waking up sunshine every day'.
'I like the rain' 'well so do I' 'in New York they get all
sorts of seasons but the sunshine makes you feel good'.
'You're not even that good in the heat you've fainted
before' 'I'm alright now I feel really at home in America'.
'You said that about London remember' 'that was when
I was twenty one I like London but I feel I've outgrown it'.
'I just feel it's like my second home please Cor you'd love
it there' 'it's a different culture you know'.
'Just because we speak the same words they call fizzy
drinks soda they call crisps potato chips'.
'So it's fun learning new words' 'you know what I mean
come on in L.A they don't even have taxis'.
'And you don't drive remember' 'so you do you can drive
us places and Malibu beach'.

'And I know I'm not great in the heat we can buy the biggest fans ever' 'I'm not sure' 'come on Cor'.
'It'll be great a fresh start after all the drama of everything over the past few years your mum and dad'.
'They can't bother us out there just us and our kids'.
'I'll think about it' 'is that a yes?' 'maybe' 'oh I'm sorry about Louie I asked him to keep an eye on you'.
'While I was away' 'actually we're friends now' 'you are serious?' 'yes' 'I thought you hated each other'.
'We did we got to know each other I saw dad in prison'.
'But why?' 'he said he was dying of cancer' 'well personally I wouldn't care if the bastard died tomorrow'.
'Neither would I he conned me like he does everyone else he says he's got cancer anyway we had this row'.
'I said I never wanted to see him again he asked me for money can you believe it' 'it doesn't surprise me'
'Anyway Louie was there visiting his brother in prison'.
'He gets out in a few months I was really upset he made sure I was ok took me out for lunch'.
'It took us a while to get along but now I really like him'.
'Well that's great I'm glad he's one of my best friends'.
'He brought us some stuff for the baby' 'that's really nice of him' 'do I hear my name being mentioned'.

'Louie I was just telling Polly you brought some stuff for the baby' 'thanks' 'anytime I wanted to'.

'I'm glad you two are friends' 'so am I darling' Polly was happy no more rows between them.

Things were going to be good with a possible move to America as well as expecting another baby together.

Stacey was excited her mum was coming to see her she also wanted Christian to get to know who she really was.

He knew Kim now he could get to know her mum.

Hopefully he'd like her they'd met at the family dinner months ago.

Stacey didn't know if Christian knew it was her mum now he would the following morning Christian arrived.

As Stacey greeted him happily 'how's things?' he asked.

'Good' 'where's Polly?' he asked 'oh she's just waking up'.

'You know she's not a morning person 'yes I know'

'I'll be down' Polly shouted wearing a baggy T-shirt and jogging trousers 'I can't wait to meet your mum'.

'Do you look alike?' 'kind of I probably look more like dad' 'I hope she likes me' 'oh she'll love you'.

'Did you like my mum?' Christian asked 'oh we only met the once I never had a chance to speak to her much'.

'You did have dinner' 'she seemed nice' Stacey lied she wasn't about to say she couldn't stand her.

'Oh good you'll have to come up to the house again get to know each other' Stacey couldn't think of anything worse. They watched This Morning as they waited for Polly half an hour later she appeared hair and make-up done. 'Susie' 'Stace I'm up and all ready for the day' 'you look great Susie'.

'Should I be nervous about meeting your mum?'

Christian said 'no' 'oh I love you're religious figures are they new?' 'oh their mum's she left them'

'The last time she was here' 'wow is that a black Jesus?'.

'Yes and a white one' 'their a pair' 'can I have a look?' 'yes' Christian picked up the black Jesus as he accidently dropped it he quickly picked it up 'I'm really sorry'.

'It's ok it was an accident' Stacey looked at the figure it's hand was broken 'listen I'm sure mum won't notice'.

Polly said 'you think?' Christian said 'I doubt it' 'it'll be fine trust me' Stacey assured him 'I'll take the blame'.

'I can't let you do that' 'why not?' 'your mum's a chilled out kind of person I wouldn't worry about it'.

Polly assured Christian they heard a knock at the door.

'It'll be mum probably' 'what shall I say?' 'nothing leave it to me' 'no Stace let me' Christian said 'ok if you want'.

Christian answered the door 'hi Marcee' 'Stacey's mum'.

'I think we met at dinner but you didn't know that it was me' 'which dinner?' 'the one with Wendy and Stacey'.
'I've dyed my hair since then that's maybe why you didn't recognise me' 'are you her real mum?' 'yes'.
'I'm her only mum except Sarah her step-mum' 'I'm sorry I didn't mean it like that' 'it's ok we get it all the time'.
'The first time I walked into a record company meeting Stacey was nineteen they thought I was her step-mum'.
'You never know how genes work I'm pleased to meet you properly' 'me too Stacey's told me all about you'.
'I'm really sorry I just broke part of your black Jesus'.
'Really which part?' 'mum' 'Stace' Marcee made her way inside the house 'I'm really sorry'.
Stacey showed Marcee the figure 'oh it's hand'
'I'll look for it' Stacey said sitting on the floor.
'It's fine really Christian' 'it was an accident' 'I feel really bad' 'don't it's ok' Marcee assured him 'found part of it'.
Stacey said getting up from the floor 'keep it and we'll try and glue it back on'.
Christian was glad Stacey's mum wasn't too angry about it 'tea' Stacey asked 'yes please' Marcee sat down.
Christian thought she looked nice Marcee looked good for her age with just below shoulder length curly hair.

Highlighted golden with a slim figure she looked about a size ten despite the difference in skin tone.

She could see where Stacey got her good looks from.

Stacey could tell from the look on Christian's face he was surprised her mum was black.

Yes her mum was mixed but black was black whatever the skin tone maybe she should have told him.

The kettle boiled 'I'll get it' Christian offered 'how do you like it?' 'milky one sugar' 'ok Polly' 'same please' 'ok'.

'Polly are you still working in America?' 'I'm recording music I've got a week off then I'm going back'.

'I feel bad not being there for Corey you know being pregnant' 'well you must be looking forward to the baby'.

'Oh yeah we can't wait' 'do you mind me asking who the father is?' 'an American guy he's a bit older'.

'Blonde hair blue eyes he's an actor' ' I'm sure you'll end up with a lovely looking baby' 'yeah'.

Polly was glad Marcee hadn't enquired further the less people knew the better.

All anyone had to know was that Corey was expecting their baby 'Christian didn't know I was black'.

'You could tell by the look on his face 'he'll get over the shock' Stacey said as they laughed.

He returned with the tea 'thanks Christian' Marcee said.

'I remember that dinner now you asked about my acting'
'yeah you said you were doing King Arthur'.
'Yeah we've finished filming now' 'oh great I can't wait to
see it I love historical stuff and Andy'.
'I'm worried how I'll look on TV' 'I wouldn't worry you're
a good looking young man' 'thanks'.
'I'm really sorry about breaking your Jesus' 'it's fine'.
'There's a religious shop I go to I'll try and fix it if not
I'll get a replacement' 'I really like it and the white Jesus'.
'Oh well I'm mixed race we're a mixed family it represents
the unity of black and white together'.
'Was your mum or dad white?' Christian asked 'my mum's
French from Paris she has red curly hair and pale skin'.
'Stacey looks a lot like her when she was younger only
with dark hair my dad's black from the Caribbean'.
'Then my grandparents on my mother's side are Cuban
and Italian it's a mix my Italian grandmother died'.
'But my granddad Stacey's great-grandfather he lives in
Cuba he's like eighty two'.
'Sounds like a interesting background' 'and I know about
your dad's background German, Irish and Swedish'.
'See no-one's pure British these days' Polly said
'that's so true' Marcee said.
'You said you go to a religious shop are you religious?'.

Christian asked 'yes I go to church when I can either in Lytham with Andy or I go to the gospel church in London'. 'Kim and Stacey come' 'we have fun' Stacey said

'I remember Stacey sang Joy To The World one time and they loved it' 'I thought they wouldn't accept me'. 'Because I looked white but they didn't care they know who my mum is and they accept me'.

'And the music is amazing 'they love Stacey she's a great soul singer' 'thanks mum'.

'You should come some time with us' Marcee suggested. 'I'm white' 'we have white people too' 'I'll come sometime' 'good you'll love it' Marcee said.

Christian decided he liked Marcee she seemed chilled out.

'I know Stacey met your mum' 'yeah' 'they got on well you'll have to meet her again' Christian said.

As Stacey forced a smile 'I met Christian's sister Maria she's really nice' 'that's good'.

'We went backstage at a concert the other week Stacey was great Maria's a big fan of her's' 'oh that was nice'.

Stacey couldn't believe how well her mum and Christian got on even better than they'd expected.

After an hour her mum had to go for a music rehearsal.

'I really wish I could stay longer' she said 'me too'.

Stacey said not wanting her to go.

'It's been nice meeting you' Christian said 'me too'.

'We'll all have to get together as a family' 'that would be good' Stacey said as she kissed her on the cheek.

As they all said goodbye as Marcee left 'I thought that went well' Polly said 'so did I' Stacey agreed.

'Better than...' Polly stopped herself 'better than what?'.

Christian asked 'than when I met Corey's mum Marie'.

'The bitch' Stacey gave Polly a look as they tried not to laugh knowing exactly what she was about to say.

'Well did you like mum?' Stacey asked hoping he'd say yes 'yes she was really nice she looks really good for her age'.

'She's forty six' Stacey informed him 'well she doesn't look it' 'I know' Polly was happy for Stacey.

That everything was going well between her and Christian she deserved to be with someone nice.

Trouble

The next day Stacey spent the day with Christian things were going well and her mum seemed to like him.

It was a beautiful summer afternoon as they sat in the garden 'I had no idea your mum was black'.

'I knew she was Andy's wife I assumed she was a friend of the family' 'things are complicated they were in the past'.

'I didn't meet my mum till I was fourteen I thought Wendy was my mum and my dad was my uncle'.

'What happened?' 'Wendy had my cousin Jonathan he's the same age as me he lives in Dublin'.

'She was in a relationship with this violent man so she had him adopted in Ireland where he was brought up'.

'Later we found out we were cousins and Wendy was his mum she was told she couldn't have anymore kids'.

'Wendy was getting her hair salon started at the time in her early twenties she was with her first husband Adrian'.

'His parents were Italian he had dark curly hair like me so I assumed he was my dad and I always liked him'.

'Then not long before my thirteenth birthday dad told me he wasn't my uncle that he was my dad'.

'We'd always been close I didn't mind then we moved to Ireland we lived together Wendy married your dad'.

'And Polly moved in' 'you don't have an Irish accent'.
'I didn't move there till I was almost thirteen I did a year
at Sylvia Young's stage school they took me out'.
'Because gran thought I was becoming too precocious'.
'I really liked it there and all my family are from Essex'.
'I came back here when I was sixteen' 'you said you met
your mum when you were fourteen' 'yeah and Kim'.
'Andy said my mum was coming to visit I didn't know she
was black until the day before she visited'.
'I didn't care it explained why I had dark curly hair'.
'Brown eyes why everyone else in my family had red hair
and green eyes I got on with Kim straight away'.
'We became close e-mailed each other then when I moved
back to London we started hanging out together'.
'I think I know everything now' 'so you like my mum?'.
'She's nice' 'she really likes you too' that evening
Stacey was happy Christian knew everything about her.
There were no more secrets now he'd met her mum and
they got on well that evening Christian visited a friend.
Stacey watched a DVD episode of Sex And The City with
Destiny as she drank champagne.
She fell asleep after midnight Stacey woke the next
morning around 10am to messages on her answerphone.
One from Steve asking had she read the magazines.

Stacey had breakfast she found something suitable to wear as she went online looking at the showbiz websites.

As she read the headline 'Christian's ex on his bi-sexual past' it talked about how he liked men as well as women.

How he'd never had sex with a woman was he gay? she was confused Stacey read the article.

As she sat on the sofa Laura Christian's ex had sold a story how they'd done everything except have sex.

How he'd been bi-sexual since he was sixteen had a boyfriend Ricky she wasn't sure what the truth was.

Laura was clearly doing it to get back at Christian for dumping her she decided not to let it bother her.

She would ask Christian the truth Stacey went upstairs she chatted to Destiny not mentioning the magazine article.

She heard a knock at the door she opened 'Christian'.

He smiled 'how are you?' 'I'm fine' clearly he'd not seen the article yet 'this morning I woke up'.

'And I had some messages on my answerphone asking if I'd seen any of the celeb magazines'.

Stacey showed Christian the article 'it's Laura she sold a story on you I'm sorry why didn't you tell me'.

'You liked men' 'I didn't know how to tell you I didn't think it mattered'.

'Me not mentioning the fact my mother is black is nothing compared to you lying about the fact your gay'.

'I'm bi-sexual I like women too' 'then why have you never slept with a woman?' 'I've never slept with anyone'.

'A man or a woman' 'why?' 'I don't know I wasn't ready to have sex it's not that I don't want to'.

'I don't have any experience in that department I know that makes me different to some people'

Stacey was surprised Christian was such a good looking man she assumed he would have slept with lots of women.

'I thought you were gay' 'I wanted to be honest with you'.

'I thought you wouldn't like it' 'Polly's a lesbian Louie's gay I'm bi-sexual as well I don't tell many people'.

'See we're a perfect match I don't care if you've never had sex I quite like it actually there's more to relationships'.

'We can get to know each other better' 'you mean it' 'yes'.

'You don't care' 'no I love you besides I have a rampant rabbit' 'you don't mind I fancy men and women?' 'no'.

'I fancy women as well we're compatible it's fate we were meant to be together so that guy we saw at the club'.

'That was Ricky your ex' 'yes' 'he seemed nice' 'you should have said if you want to kiss a man I won't mind'.

'As long as neither of us is sleeping around I love you and I want to be with you' 'I want to be with you too'.

'I would never ask you to deny part of who you are in fact
I quite like it' 'me liking men?' 'yes'.
'As long as we're together' 'Stacey I love you and
I'm committed to our relationship' 'good'.
'We have no secrets now' 'no secrets' Christian smiled.
'I'm half black there's mine and you like men' 'I wish
I met you before' Christian said 'you too'.
'You're the only man I've ever loved imagine if I'd have
met you before I wish I had'.
'Then I wouldn't have had all those bad relationships'.
'I know but then you wouldn't have your little girl' they
kissed Stacey decided the sex didn't matter.
She loved Christian that was all that mattered.
'I was wondering would you come to my twenty first
birthday party' he asked 'I'd love to'.
'Why didn't you tell me it was your birthday' 'I'm sorry'.
'It was a last minute thing I wasn't gonna do anything my
friends insisted' 'course I'll come where is it?'.
'My house' 'the mansion where I went' 'yes there' 'great'.
'Will your mum be there?' 'yes and my brother and sister'.
'Everyone' 'sounds great' 'we'll have fun why don't you
bring Kim' 'I'll ask her Kim loves a good party'.
'That's great we'll have a good night'.

Secretly Stacey couldn't think of anything worse having to go back there again if Kim came maybe it would be ok. She called her she said yes three weeks later it was Christian's birthday party.

That morning Stacey gave him his present she wasn't looking forward to the party but didn't say anything.

That morning Louie came to visit after being on holiday in Spain for two week 'darling tell me all the gossip'.

'Christian is gorgeous and I can't believe he's bi I asked Polly at that house party and she said he wasn't into men'.

'I didn't know until Laura sold that story on him'.

'Don't worry about her she's just jealous trying to split you up' 'well she won't succeed' 'good'.

'Shame about his mother' 'I know and I'm off to his birthday party tonight' 'have a good time' 'I'll try'.

'At least Kim will be with me' 'that's one thing'

'I'm sure it'll be fine maybe his mum was busy'.

'The day we went to his house' 'or maybe she was just a bitch' Louie said.

'Christian said their having a joint birthday party with his mum' 'interesting' 'she's turning forty apparently'.

'You are joking! she looks at least forty seven' 'she looks good for her age' Stacey said 'not that good come on'.

'How old is Christian?' 'twenty one' 'do the maths'.

'How old would that make her?' 'like eighteen nineteen
when she had him do you think?' 'maybe'.
'If she's forty I'm Father Christmas' 'anyway I'll try and
enjoy myself tonight' 'good luck'.
'I suppose there will be free food and drink' 'you should
come' Christian returned he'd gone to get some milk.
From the shops 'Louie's here' 'hi' Louie said smiling 'hi'.
'How are you?' Christian asked 'I'm great' 'I was just
telling Louie about your birthday party tonight'.
'Oh why don't you come' 'I can't I'm sorry I'd love to
I'm busy on my laptop writing details about clients'.
'Boring stuff' 'I understand' 'another time' 'oh yes maybe
we can all go clubbing together again' 'oh I'd love to'.
'Great' 'we'll all go out together' Stacey said 'oh
I wouldn't worry about your ex selling a story'.
'She can't have been a nice person to do that the public
don't like people who kiss and tell'.
'It reflects badly on them' 'thanks Louie I'm trying to
forget about it' 'don't worry you know the saying'.
'Tomorrow's fish and chip paper' 'I never thought she'd
do something like that' 'darling don't worry ok'.
'She's just jealous trying to split you and Stacey up'.
'Well it won't happen' 'you should try and forget it it'll
blow over they'll be a football scandal'.

'Some footballer cheating then it'll be forgotten about'.
'Louie's right let's forget about Laura it's your twenty first birthday you should be having fun' 'Stacey's right '.
'You two go out tonight and have fun' 'we will'.
That afternoon Kim came round as they got ready to go out that evening Kim played it safe with a black dress.
And high heels hair up Stacey wore a black jacket short skirt her hair straight worn up she felt good.
Christian got a friend to drive them to his house Kim couldn't believe how big it was.
The house was already busy when they arrived lots of Christian's friends his sister Maria and his brother Carl.
'Wow! it's massive' Kim said looking around 'it's a mansion' 'even in L.A the houses aren't this big'.
They had a glass of punch as they relaxed a DJ was playing music the latest chart hits 'this is Martin'.
'My friend' Christian said 'hi Martin' 'hi Stacey I've heard so much about you' 'and her sister Kim' 'really sisters?'.
'Yes we're half-sisters same mum different dads' Stacey explained 'right that explains it'.
'I've been waiting for Christian to meet a nice girl for ages' 'I'm Kim' 'Martin'.
'I've never been in a house this big' 'really' 'yeah I grew up in Hackney I'm not posh as you can tell' 'yes'.

'We all come from different backgrounds' Stacey noticed that Kim was trying to make conversation.

But Martin wasn't interested 'I'll see you all later'.

He quickly left them Stacey could sense it would be a long evening they looked over.

As Christian's mum made her entrance walking down the stairs in an emerald green cocktail dress.

And gold earrings 'mum you look great' 'thankyou'.

'Stacey hello again' she looked sour faced as usual 'this is Stacey's sister Kim' 'real sisters?' 'yes'.

'We have the same mum different dads' 'I understand'.

It was the second time she'd had to say that line why did she have to explain her family background.

To a group of strangers 'just in case you're wondering why I'm here it's my fortieth I'm having a joint party'.

'With Christian' 'he told me' 'I'll see you later'.

After seeing her up close she began to suspect Louie was right about her age 'shall we hit the dancefloor?'.

Stacey said 'good idea back soon' Christian said 'he's so nice you're so lucky' Kim said.

'Don't say anything but I don't really like his mum'.

'She didn't seem that friendly' 'she's not'.

'We had dinner with Louie and Polly a few months ago she wasn't nice to them either '.

'She wasn't impressed when I told her about Tally and splitting up with James'.

'You can't help being a single mum' 'it's like she looks down on people I only came because Christian asked me'.

'I'm glad you're here I don't know anyone here their all really posh I know I went to private school'.

'But I'm from a working class family it's just not my world' 'tell me about it you're with Christian not his mum'.

'I'd forget about her and that stupid kiss and tell' 'I'll try to' 'personally I think it's strange having a joint party'.

'Yeah well I doubt she's forty that's what Louie said anyway' 'I agree let's drink eat as much food as we can'.

'Then go at ten thirty' Kim suggested 'sounds like a good idea' Stacey agreed Kim poured them some punch.

'See we'll be so pissed we'll forget what a rubbish time we're having' Stacey drunk her punch.

She was determined to get so tipsy she could forget where she was it soon worked.

As she and Kim danced having a good time 'do you dare me to go up to the DJ booth?' 'Kim' 'it'll be fine Stace'.

'I'll be on my best behaviour' Kim approached the booth. As a good looking light skinned mixed race guy looked in her direction 'hey I'm Kim' 'Gary' 'you don't sound posh'.

'I'm from Hackney' 'like me then' 'I don't usually play these kind of gigs but the money's good' 'I bet'.

'A place like this' 'you know the people here?' 'my sister's going out with Christian' 'Stacey O'Riley'.

'I love your music' 'thanks' 'can we request a record?'. Kim asked 'go ahead' 'can we have two?' 'maybe' 'ok'.

'Goldfrapp Ooh La La and Mariah Get Your Number'.

'Coming right up especially for you' 'I'll go now'.

'Will I see you again?' 'if you want to we're going after ten we'll come back later' 'what's your name again?'

'Kim' 'you look nice' 'thanks listen just Facebook Stacey if you want' 'see you later' 'he was so nice'.

'I'm gonna see him before we leave' Kim said 'he's from Hackney' 'and you never met' 'no'.

'It must be cause I'm in L.A a lot' 'I couldn't do that'.

'Just go up to a DJ and give him my number' 'we're gonna Facebook each other' 'Maria hi' Stacey said.

'Hi I'm glad you're here' 'this is Kim my sister'.

'Your real sister?' 'yes we're half-sisters' 'I always wished I had a sister' 'well we didn't meet till we were fourteen'.

'When I met mum my mum couldn't look after me'.

'Why not?' 'she had me at eighteen and she had alcohol problems but she's fine now and we're all really close'.

'Anyway since me and Kim met each other we've been best friends' 'I don't get on with my brother' 'Christian'. 'No Carl he's a year older than me he's horrible he ignores me Christian I can talk to about anything'.

'You look really pretty' Maria said 'thanks so do you'. Stacey said 'I think you and Christian should get married' 'oh he hasn't asked me to' 'he should'.

'His other girlfriends weren't as nice as you especially Laura I hope you do get married' 'so do I' Kim agreed.

'You make a nice couple and he's good with Tally' 'your daughter?' 'yes I'll show you a photo'.

Stacey took a photo from her purse 'she's pretty just like her mum' 'thanks her dad's black-Italian'.

'In case you were wondering about her skin tone' 'I'm Italian too' Mara said 'everyone looks different in families' Kim said.

'So are you and Christian half-brother and sister you don't look alike?' Kim asked 'no I'm adopted'.

'But Christian's just my brother to me mum adopted me when I was three I've never known anything else'.

'Hello' Christian appeared joining them 'I was just telling Stacey about mum I saw a photo of Stacey's daughter'.

'That's great you two get on so well let's have a dance'.

'Ok' Stacey agreed as they danced to the music.

They were having a good time Kim decided to help herself to crisps, cheese & pineapple on sticks.

And anything else that took her fancy as she sipped wine she could feel herself becoming drunk.

'Don't you think you've had enough' Kim looked up it was Christian's mum 'isn't this supposed to be a party'.

'And this is party food' 'you could leave some for someone else!' Kim gave her a look Stacey looked over.

Kim didn't look very happy 'I don't recall inviting you here! you're not one of Christian's friends'.

'Well you're wrong! I've met Christian twice before he invited me to come with Stacey she's my sister' 'I know'.

'I remember' 'mum what's going on?' Christian asked.

'Maybe next time you could ask me before you invite people to my fortieth birthday party I don't approve of!'.

'Forty you must be joking! you must be pushing fifty!'.

The crowd watched as Stacey decided she had to admire her sister for speaking her mind.

She always said it like it was 'I want you and your sister to leave!' 'mum maybe we could sort this out!'.

'If it's some kind of misunderstanding' 'there's no misunderstanding!'.

'I saw you trying to steal a packet of crisps'.

'It's not like you can't afford to buy more'.

'I'm hardly taking the crown jewels!' 'I want you to go!'.
'Before I call the police!' 'mum don't you think your
overreacting! it's just a packet of crisps' 'stealing is
stealing she's a thief! and a tramp'.

'I saw the way you were flirting with that DJ' 'yeah I did'.
'The only good thing about this party!' 'there's the door!'.
'Right okay!' 'don't worry we're leaving!' Stacey said
angry at Kim being asked to leave.

'Stacey you don't have to leave!' Christian said 'we've got
no choice! you think I want to stay here'.

'The way you're mum just talked to my sister!' 'she didn't
mean it!' 'I meant every word!'.

'Never been in a room with a black girl from Hackney'.
'I bet you wouldn't accuse anyone else in this room of
stealing' 'how dare you accuse me of being a racist!'

'We're going!' Stacey said Kim was drunk as Stacey called
a taxi they stood outside.

Not being able to stand being in the house a moment
longer 'mum why did you have to do that?'.

Christian asked angry 'I didn't do anything!' 'that's my
girlfriend and her sister'.

'Yeah well you should have asked me before you invited
that girl!'. 'Kim' 'yes whoever she is'.

'I don't want to see her in this house ever again!'.

'Well I doubt Stacey will be coming back again thanks a lot!' 'good I'm glad' 'I love Stacey'.

'I want her to feel welcome here how do you think she feels now' 'that's not my problem!' 'I suppose it's mine!'.

'You kicked her out!' 'with good reason this conversation is over I have a party to get back to'.

'Where are you going?' 'to make sure they get home ok!'.

Christian went outside as a taxi pulled up 'Stacey'.

'I'm sorry about mum' 'it's ok it's not your fault Kim's really drunk so maybe it's for the best' 'I'm sorry'.

'I'll make it up to you' 'you don't have to' 'tell Kim I'm sorry I hope she's ok' 'I will' 'I'll phone you' Christian said as he waved goodbye to them.

He felt bad he loved Stacey luckily she seemed ok about being asked to leave.

Christian made his way back inside the house the party was back in full swing but he didn't feel like partying.

'Are you ok?' Maria asked 'I will be' 'what happened?'.

'I heard there was an argument' 'mum asked Kim to leave Stacey went too' 'why?'.

'Mum said Kim took a packet of crisps' 'isn't it a party'.

'Your supposed to eat drink have a good time' 'I know'.

'Kim was a bit drunk she started rowing with mum luckily Stacey was ok about it' 'where are they now?'.

'They called a taxi they've gone home I told Stacey to make sure Kim's ok' 'I really like Stacey' 'so do I'.

'Does this mean she won't come back to the house again?' 'I hope not I'll talk with mum get it sorted'.

'If not you can come see me working in London and maybe we'll go round to Stacey's' 'would she mind'.

'If I visited her house?' 'no she wouldn't mind everything will be ok' 'good I hope you and Stacey get married'.

'So do I'll let you into a secret I was going to propose the other day it wasn't the right time but I will in a few days'.

'Really?' 'yes' 'good tell me what she says' 'oh I will'.

'Can I be bridesmaid if you married?' 'yes I'm sure Stacey wouldn't mind' Maria smiled.

The next morning Stacey woke remembering what a disaster the night before had been.

And wishing she'd never gone to Christian's birthday party 'Stace you're awake' Kim said 'yeah' 'good'.

'I brought you a glass of orange juice' 'thanks I'm sorry about what happened last night' 'Stace it's fine really'.

'It wasn't your fault or Christian it was his mum's the witch how can someone so nice have such a bitch'.

'For a mother' 'I know I never want to go round again'.

'What if you ever got married?' 'Christian's only twenty one a bit younger so I doubt he's ready for that'.

'Maybe it's a good thing imagine having her for a mother in-law' 'I'd rather not think about it' they laughed.

After lunch Marcee came round as they told her all about the night before 'Kim how drunk were you?'.

'I wasn't that bad' 'Kim was really drunk but it wasn't like she was falling on the floor' Stacey said.

'The whole thing sounds ridiculous why would she put food on the table if she didn't want people to eat it'.

Marcee said 'exactly she's a right bitch and a racist'.

'I swear she had a go at me because I'm black' 'Kim you can't go around accusing people of things'.

'Without evidence' 'trust me I know she is' 'are you sure you didn't say anything that would make her angry?' 'no'.

'Mum she had a right soar face on her all night you wouldn't have known it was her birthday party'.

'Kim's right we saw her when we first arrived she didn't seem friendly she's never been nice'.

'When me and Polly went over that time she never made conversation with us or anyone'.

'What did Christian say?' 'he rowed with mum she wouldn't listen' 'you're his girlfriend'.

'How can she make you leave?' 'she did' Stacey said.

'I might just have to pay her a visit'.

'Mum I wouldn't do that' 'no Stace I'm not having her speak to either of you like that tell me where she lives'.

'Really' 'yes I want her address' 'it's just outside London'.

'It's a mansion she was married to a Lord they divorced'.

'She renounced her title for the house she's originally from Yorkshire but it's like she's forgotten her roots'.

'Like she's Lady of the manor' 'oh I know the type trying to forget their roots who she is'.

'So she can fit in with the posh set' 'what's so ridiculous is she's as working class as we are' 'don't worry'.

'I'll sort it tomorrow you can come with me and we'll pay her a visit' 'you don't want me there' 'Kim'.

'Please don't take it the wrong way but you do sometimes say the wrong thing at the wrong time'.

'And I don't want you getting into a row with her' 'you don't really want to go back there again' Stacey said 'no'.

'Not really I guess if we all went she'd be really angry'.

'You think she'll apologise?' Kim asked 'I doubt it'

Stacey said 'I won't have her speaking to you the way she did I'll sort it' 'thanks mum'.

Stacey didn't know if it would do any good having her mum going there to pay Christian's mum a visit.

But if it sorted things out the next day at 10am the two of them set off to Christian's house 'what if he's home?'

Stacey asked 'you said yourself he wasn't happy about it'.
'I'm sure he'd understand' they parked outside the house
they walked together as they stood at the gates
There was an intercom 'hello' Marcee said 'who is it?'.
'Stacey's mum' 'just a minute' they waited until the voice
spoke again 'the gates are opening'.
'You may come in' they stood back as the gates opened as
they walked down the path 'talk about security'.
Marcee said 'I bet they've got cameras everywhere'.
'Now I think about it I bet they were filming us at the
party that's why she went off for a bit only guessing'.
They finally arrived at the house as they saw another
intercom 'hello' 'just a minute I'll let you in'.
A stern voice answered 'it sounds like her' Stacey said the
door opened as Christian's mother answered.
A look of surprise on her face 'Stacey this isn't...' 'yes'.
'My mum' 'you didn't tell me you were mixed that your
mum was...' 'black'.
Stacey was aware she was finishing off sentences 'genes
work in a funny way' 'I'm Marcee Stacey's mum'.
'Jean or Mrs Bell' 'I'm not happy about the way you spoke
to my daughters the other night I know Kim was drunk'.
'And I'm not making excuses but to be forced to get a taxi
home when you're stuck in the middle of nowhere'.

'That's not my problem she was stealing' 'a packet of crisps you can get a six pack in Iceland'.

'I don't find it funny!' 'how do you know anyway?' 'I have proof' 'CCTV I can imagine the whole house right'.

'We're probably being filmed now' 'what is this all about?'

'I've told you Kim was pretty angry at being asked to leave like that' 'she shouldn't have been so drunk'.

'And behaved like a tart chatting up the DJ' 'isn't that what you did when you were younger' 'I did not!'.

'I'd never embarrass myself like that' 'how is it embarrassing he was from Hackney like Kim'.

'Better be careful who you hire next time wouldn't want to bring down your standards' 'how dare you!'.

'I don't know you but you've got no right! to come here and insult me in my own home!'.

'But it's ok for you to insult my daughters!' 'I told you she was drunk and stealing a packet of crisps!'.

'What's your excuse for the way you spoke to Stacey!'.

'I don't know what you mean' 'Stacey is Christian's girlfriend that is so out of order!' 'I was referring to Kim'.

'And me why don't you just admit you don't like me or my friends or my sister too working class for you are we'.

'Don't be ridiculous!' 'it's the truth! oh and are you forgetting your working class too' Stacey said.

'You know nothing about me!' 'I'm a millionaire too!'.
'But my money comes from hard work not rich
ex-husbands!' 'your just a singer!' 'a successful one!'.
'I don't know what Christian see's in you!' 'that's easy'.
Marcee said 'Stacey's pretty intelligent a nice person good
career' 'you won't be around'.
'When he gets back with Laura' 'he loves me that's over'.
'We'll see won't we!' 'I get it now you're jealous of
Stacey'.
'Because you think she's taking your son away from you'.
'As if Marcee! as if I'd be jealous of you!' 'why else would
you hate Stacey so much!' 'did I say I hated her'.
'You haven't exactly made her feel welcome!' 'I have!'.
'It's because I'm a single mum because half my family are
black' 'I'm not a racist' 'really' 'yes'.
'I want you and you're mum to leave this house! the only
reason I let you into the house is because I was curious'.
'To hear what your mum had to say' 'no apologises then'.
Marcce said 'should there be' 'you know the answer to
that one! come on Stace let's go'.
'It's obvious we're wasting our time talking to you if you
think Stacey's not good enough for Christian'.
'The truth hurts does it!' 'the truth is you're a nasty piece
of work!'.

'Luckily Christian takes after his dad and not you!'
'get out both of you!' 'with pleasure!'.

Jean pressed a button as the gates opened they walked out as quickly as they could as they reached the car.

Glad to be out of there 'there's no point arguing with someone like that' Marcee said angry.

'You tried to get her to apologise' 'I know no chance'.

'I just won't go round there anymore it taught me something that I'm really lucky'.

'To have such a nice family' 'just don't ever marry him ok his mother she'd be the mother in-law from hell'.

'That's what Louie said' 'he's right' 'but if Christian did ever propose I'd still say yes'.

'I'll just make sure I don't go round his house I'll just say we don't get on he'll understand' 'yeah he would'.

'I'm really glad you found someone nice shame about his mum' 'everything will be ok'.

When Stacey got home she couldn't stop thinking about her row with Jean.

She decided the best thing would be to avoid her completely since she was obviously not a nice person.

Hopefully Christian would understand knowing her she would already be on the phone.

Telling Christian about their row.

There was nothing she could do other than forget about her that evening Stacey received a phone call.

From Christian about her row with his mum she explained that her mum had said they go round sort things out.

How Jean had criticised Kim suggested that he might like to get back with his ex-Laura.

Not exactly what Stacey wanted to hear on reflection her mum's suggestion to turn up at Christian's house.

Unannounced demanding an apology for being asked to leave the party wasn't the best idea.

However Jean had shown her true colours shown what she was really like Christian was understanding.

Listening to her side of the story promising to sort things out Stacey vowed not to go to his house.

Unless she really had to a few days later Christian came round to see her they talked.

He promised there would be no more rows she didn't believe him clearly Jean had a problem with her.

Maybe her mum was right maybe she was jealous Stacey probably knew it was only so long before he moved out.

That evening they arranged to go out for a romantic meal. Stacey was looking forward to spending time with Christian it would make her feel better.

True romance

Take her mind off things as they arrived at the restaurant .
Someone took her coat they sat down and ordered.
'This is nice' Stacey said 'yeah we should do this more
often' Christian said 'I'd love to if we had the time'.
'We can make time' 'yeah we should I love you'
'love you too' he said 'good let's have a toast'.
Stacey suggested 'to us' Christian said 'listen I have
something to ask you' 'what is it? go on' Stacey asked.
Christian pulled out a blue velvet box going down on one
knee 'will you marry me?' he asked Stacey was in shock.
Of course she'd hoped they'd get engaged but she hadn't
expected it 'yes I will' people clapped.
As Christian got up sitting down again 'I didn't know you
were going to propose' 'really you had no idea?' 'no'.
'I thought because you're a few years younger than me'.
'That you would want to wait a while that you weren't
ready to settle down' 'I am I know I'm only twenty one'.
'But I don't want to date lots of different people I'm not
that type of person' 'I'm glad neither am I'.
'When shall we get married?' Stacey asked 'whenever you
want to' 'we'll have to plan it I want to do it properly'.
'We will ok we'll do it properly a big white wedding'.

Christian said 'I can't wait for us to get married'
Stacey said 'me either I'd love us to get married soon'.
'If you want' 'that would be fantastic I can't wait to tell
Polly she'll be so happy for us'.
'I know Maria will be happy I told her I was going to
propose' 'what did she say?' 'to tell her everything'.
'All the gossip now I can tell her that you said yes'.
'Maybe she can be bridesmaid' 'she'd love that'
'and Polly and Corey' 'that would be great'.
'See we've planned some of it already' Christian said.
'We have we'll plan it together can we get married in a
church?' Stacey asked 'of course we can'.
'I know how important your faith is to you and we'll have
the honeymoon somewhere nice wherever you want'
'Paris' 'sounds great' 'or maybe Italy Venice' 'great'.
'I love Europe' Stacey was on cloud nine Christian had
just proposed to her they were in love.
And she couldn't wait for them to get married dating the
wrong men had been worth it to find her prince charming.
That evening she texted Kim, Corey, Polly and anyone else
she could think of.
The next day she spoke to Polly who was happy for her.
Somehow she'd have to find a way of dealing with Jean.
No-one would stop her being happy.

Marrying the man of her dreams Stacey decided she wanted to get married in November.

Have a winter wedding it would be really magical with snow she'd have the best reception ever.

She couldn't wait to marry Christian Stacey decided to go round Corey's house chat about her good news 'hi Cor'.

'You get bigger every time I see you' 'thanks I can't move at the moment do you remember what it was like'.

'To be pregnant?' 'yeah a bit I was really lucky I didn't get big not till the last few weeks' 'you're so lucky'.

'Think of pregnancy as the best excuse to eat what you want be lazy and get people to do things for you'.

Corey laughed 'maybe just think ten years ago lesbians couldn't get pregnant' 'what did the father say?'.

'I sent an e-mail about three months ago I'm still waiting for a reply' 'if he doesn't get back to you he's not worth it'.

'Thanks' 'you know what men are like' 'except Christian'.

'Congratulations' 'thanks' 'I'm glad you found someone nice' 'so am I it took me ten years after leaving school'.

'To find the one' 'well it'll be nice when you get married'.

'I know I'm doing it properly a big white wedding' 'oh do you want to be bridesmaid with Polly?' 'I wish'.

'I can't not while I'm pregnant' 'you can because I'm getting married in November a nice winter wedding'.

'In that case I'd love to' 'great Maria Christian's sister is going to be bridesmaid as well she's fourteen'.

'She's really sweet' 'sounds like it's sorted' 'yeah and we're having our honeymoon in Paris or Italy' 'sounds nice'.

'I can't wait it's going to be the best day of my life you know I thought I'd be married'.

'By the time I was like twenty two but I'm really glad I waited' 'you found the right person' 'I know'.

'It only took like ten years after leaving school you were lucky with Polly she loves you so much' 'I love her too'.

'Yeah' 'I can't believe you were ever an escort girl'.

'Neither can I I worked at this Art Gallery in the café dad found out and he didn't want me working there'.

'And anyway I needed some money' 'did you like it?'.

'Being an escort girl?' 'it was good money I got to sleep with lots of women' 'I'm interested I left school'.

'A year and a half performing and doing demos you went to Art College worked as an escort girl'.

'It's not that glamorous' 'it sounds like it to me' 'some women were attractive some weren't a lot were older'.

'In their thirties and forties I usually met them in hotels'.

'I had a fake name Carol sometimes I would stay with the clients in five star hotels in Dublin'.

'You always had to be discreet it was to get money'.

'For rent and demos sometimes I even went to Paris' 'how did you get into it?' 'I was seventeen'.

'At Art College I met this friend Michelle a real party girl we had fun she'd just moved from Yorkshire'.

'She used to wear all the latest things the coolest clothes'.

'I asked her how she got her money at first she wouldn't tell me then finally she did'.

'Michelle was a few years older nearly twenty we went out most nights unless we had to be up early for College'.

'Or had coursework to do in between College I sang in pubs around Dublin sometimes alone'.

'Sometimes with bands I wanted a proper band not to keep going through different people'.

'I was also doing demos they cost a lot of money a few hundred pounds a time I was a struggling Art student'.

'I'd left my old waitressing job Michelle had a good job'.

'I could tell all the nice things she wore no early mornings hours get up whenever she wanted'.

'It sounded too good to be true I wanted to be able to buy nice things without struggling'.

'Michelle said she'd done it for six months back in Yorkshire that she could but shoes jewellery'.

'That she didn't have to worry about paying the rent she asked me if I wanted to do it I texted Michelle'.

'To say she I was interested the next day she arranged for me to meet the woman who ran the agency'.

'We went to an office just off the High Street you wouldn't have known it was there which was probably deliberate'.

'They pretended they were a temp agency the woman Mary was older late forties blonde hair'.

'She told me some clients were straight but they wanted a night of passion to fufill a fantasy sex with a woman '.

'On the side then some women knew they were lesbians'.

'But were married she asked me how many women I'd slept with I said three or four'.

'It was only Polly and my ex-Amy Mary told me I was pretty and I wouldn't have problems getting work'.

'She told me to say I was a year older that I was eighteen she told me how it all worked'.

'She said I didn't have to have sex with them they might not request it but most of the time they did'.

'That I should give them a romantic bath as it puts them in the mood relaxes them usually you go out to dinner'.

'That it was about getting to know the client putting them at ease she said the agency had a reputation to uphold'.

'Mary said I had to show them a good time wear nice clothes a bit of make-up'.

'And that you make them feel good special wanted'.

'Sometimes it would go great other times you had to cut the date short we usually met at a hotel or a pub or bar'

'Mary said to demand the money up front and not to wear too much jewellery some nice earrings and a bracelet'.

'What did you earn?' 'three hours three hundred euros going up to five hundred for all night staying over'.

'Did your parents know?' 'no I didn't tell dad I even lied to my ex Amy about what she was up to'.

'I was falling in love with her I kept it a secret I lied about her age to clients saying I was nineteen '.

'They seemed to believe me my favourite client was Violet she was thirty seven blonde slim'.

'And attractive for her age a lingerie businesswoman if all the other clients had been like her it would be great'.

'She brought me lingerie then she a requested me again we soon built up a relationship she would buy me gifts'.

'Jewellery I lied to Amy saying they were from my mam or aunty it was a friendship Violet was my sugar mummy'.

'She insisted on taking me on a weekend to Paris I lied to dad and said it was a College trip'.

'I even took my Art tools I loved it we went to the Moulin Rouge to all the best shops and a boat trip'.

'When we got back dad found out I came back from College one day he said he rang up the College'.

'He found out there was no trip to Paris I said did go to Paris not with College a friend'.

'Dad printed out my profile on the agency website his friend used bi-sexual websites'.

'I explained it was just for a few months to get some money saved up to do some demos'.

'A few weeks later I had enough money saved up to buy Amy an engagement ring the best money could buy'.

'White gold with a diamond she said yes although we split up later on' 'so what happened next?' Stacey asked.

'A year later I moved to London with Mike I had a waitressing job but the demos we made'.

'We wanted them to sound good so I joined an agency'.

'I tried to do some more escort work on the side but they wanted me to sleep with men and I couldn't do it'.

'I did some dominatrix work for a bit you know S & M no sex I never told the band I think they were grateful'.

'I had money to pay for our recordings' 'they know now'.

Stacey said 'yes' 'what did they say?' 'not much they were shocked they had no idea I still did my waitressing job'.

'So no-one would know what I was up to now you know everything about me'

'What did Polly say when she found out you'd been an escort girl?' 'she was she ok about it?' I never told Polly'.

'It wasn't until Romina sold a story on me she found out everything maybe she did me a favour' 'it was still low'.
'She was supposed to be our friend what happened to her? I mean I know she could be annoying but to sell a story'.
'On you even if I was really poor I wouldn't do it I'd get a job in a supermarket' Stacey said.
'I don't know what happened I don't really want anything to do with her' Corey said 'me either'.
'I don't really care what she's up to' 'last time I saw her was three months ago in the Kings Arms baggy clothes'.
'She didn't look her best she'd been made homeless' 'you talked to her' 'yes she lost her job'.
'As an assistant manager at the florists she lost her flat'.
'She was out on the streets I saw her before in Brighton with Polly then again on my own'.

Dreams can come true

'I couldn't forgive her twice she sold a story on me I gave her a hundred pounds' 'what! why?'.

'I wouldn't have given her anything she's a bitch!'

'I know ok what if things had happened to her'.

'If she'd have dropped down dead in the gutter somewhere I thought she could do the right thing go home to Wales'.

'On the train she fell out with her mum' 'was she there for you when you had Douglas taken away from you'.

'Or when you had problems with your mum' 'no' 'exactly'.

'And if she ends up in the gutter somewhere that's her fault not yours if she got sacked from her job'.

'It's probably because she's a bitch there's thousands of people out there out of work do they all get handouts'.

'She has a mum in Wales Romina chose to move to London without having the money to fund a lifestyle'.

'Everyone knows how expensive it is to live here it's not like she's a singer or an actress'.

'I don't even know why she moved here' 'because of Polly'. Corey said 'yeah well that plan backfired when Polly told her she didn't want to see her anymore'.

'I know you're right ok maybe I shouldn't have given her the money let's forget about her'.

'Think she'll come back here?' Stacey wondered 'probably not' 'she probably used the money to buy drugs'.

'It's true the few times I saw her she looked awful not at all how I remembered her from school'.

'Anyway I don't like her' Stacey said 'well neither do I'. Corey agreed 'I can't believe Susie stayed friends with her for so long' 'I tried to warn her she wouldn't listen'.

'She almost ruined our relationship' 'at least she's out of your life now' 'I know Polly wants to move to America'.

'What did you say?' 'I don't know I did love New York'.

'But to move their permanently' 'think of the good weather except in winter I lived there for a few months'.

'When I was with James it's ok New York it's busy Central Park's nice and there's Broadway for shows'.

'Christian seems really nice' 'he is it's just his mum she hates me and Kim we're engaged now'.

'I don't care if she hates me we're getting married I'll just have to stay out of her way' 'well I can't wait'.

'Neither can I there's so much planning to do' 'if you need any help' 'thanks' 'I mean I am six months pregnant'.

'How's the script going?' Stacey asked they were both going to starring in the same film a british drama.

'Oh great it keeps me occupied while I'm pregnant'.

'We can go over it together' 'that's a great idea'.

Corey agreed 'I know I can't wait to start have you thought anymore about having a baby shower'.

'Not really I don't have one planned' 'why not? you have to' 'maybe I don't know'.

'If you do you better make it quick else you'll be giving birth by the time you have one' 'I know I'll do something'.

'How about a picnic?' Stacey suggested 'great idea'.

Corey agreed 'I mean it's summer I would have suggested bowling but I know you can't lift heavy objects'.

'A picnic sounds nice' 'great how about in like two weeks' 'it's a deal' Stacey noticed Corey had seemed happier.

She'd make sure she had a good time that evening after Stacey had gone home Daniel came round to see her.

He was in London with his band 'hey how's things?' he asked 'great Stacey came round' 'good'.

'You know it's a shame you two never got together she's with Christian now'.

'Well everything happens for a reason actually I just had a date' 'really anyone I know?' Corey asked curious 'yes'.

'Actually it's Kitty' 'not my friend band mate Kitty' 'yes'.

'Do you mind?' 'course not I want you to meet someone nice you should've said'.

'She had a few not too good boyfriends now I think about it you'd be perfect together' 'it's just a date' 'I know that'.

'It could lead to something else' 'maybe she's really nice'.
'She's a great person' 'how are you feeling?' Daniel asked
'great no sickness just really bad back pain'.
'It'll be worth it' 'it's ok you're not the one who has to
carry the baby for nine months'.
'I can't wait to get my body back I have to get back in
shape after I have the baby'.
'When the band release a new album and we're touring'.
'How's it going with your band?' 'it's been five years still
no record deal' 'you're still young' 'I'm twenty seven'.
'You've got a publishing deal to write for other artists'.
'I know but I always had this fantasy of playing guitar on
stage I know I do but I mean you're in a successful band'.
'Not a local level' 'you were great on our last tour when
you played with us we could do with someone else'.
'I mean if there's a song where me and Kitty want to dance
just sing and you're a good singer' 'thanks'.
'Imagine me and you on stage together' 'it would be
great' 'well do you want to join the group permanently?'.
'Really Mike said something a while ago I'd love to if it's
ok with everyone else' 'course it is'.
'You're a great musician we'll have fun together on stage'
'can I ask you a question?' Daniel asked.

'Go on' 'who the father of the baby is' 'you can't tell
anyone' 'why not? I thought you wouldn't care'.
'You used a surrogate father' 'we didn't' 'what?'
'I had sex with a man' 'I thought you hated the idea'.
'Of sex with a man' 'I do I was drunk when we did it it was
Steve my co-star in I Love New York' 'you are joking!'.
'No' 'he agreed to be the father of your baby' 'no he said
he liked me I said I was a lesbian and married'.
'Then one night we ended up having sex I don't know how
it happened' 'he's the father' 'yes'.
'Hang on what do you mean?' 'it was a mistake
I'm a lesbian nothing's changed' 'what did Polly say?'.
'She wasn't happy it was all my fault we could've split up
because of it she doesn't know who the father is'.
'You are going to tell her?' 'I haven't decided does it
matter?' 'no but she is your wife' 'I might ok'.
'I e-mailed him no reply yet' 'I wouldn't worry you've got
me Polly Stacey if he doesn't want to be involved'.
'It's his problem' 'we were friends' 'he's a Hollywood actor
you know what their like'.
'I doubt he'd want the scandal of a lesbian singer getting
pregnant with a baby on his conscious'.
'You're right' secretly Corey was still hurt she'd hoped for
a reply.

One way or the other she'd thought of Steve as a good friend how could her brother understand?.

Now their friendship was probably over 'I'm still getting over the fact you slept with a man' 'so am I ok'.

'It doesn't change my sexuality it's not the first time I've kissed a man' 'oh really are we talking about Colin?'.

'Maybe maybe not' 'tell me' 'I did it as a favour to a friend' 'which friend?' 'Mike' 'you are joking'.

'No he said he'd always been in love with me had a crush on me I was surprised we were drunk'.

'I didn't know I was pregnant at the time so I made his fantasies come true' 'when was this?' 'a few months ago'.

'When we did some gigs it didn't mean anything don't tell Polly and for the record I still love women'.

'You do know Mike's your cousin' 'what? since when'.

'Well I found out your mam Carol her sister's his mam'.

'How?' 'Carol told me the other day' 'she never told me'.

'Maybe she never got round to it' 'we'll have to ask her'.

Corey said surprised 'well it's true' 'that's great news I'll have to talk to Mike' 'you should'.

'You must miss Polly being away in the States' 'yeah'.

'What should I do? about moving to America?' 'I think you should I mean the amount of time you're spending apart'.

'I'm surprised you're still married' 'I'm not sure'.

'It's my kind of place' 'maybe you should give it a chance'.
'Maybe I could' 'also for us writing songs together and
you getting into producing think of the opportunities'.
'The contacts in the music industry' 'I have contacts'.
'This is America you'd be in a place where you could
really do well get respect as a songwriter' 'maybe'.
'You're right' 'I know I am and the good weather movie
opportunities' 'you're making it sound really good now'.
'If you don't go you'll look back in ten years time and
regret it' 'I know you're right' 'I know I am'.
'And you and Polly will be together with the new baby
it'll be great' 'I could give it a try I just want to be happy'.
'You will be' Corey decided Daniel was right the musical
opportunities would be endless.
Wasn't life about trying new things that evening she sent
an e-mail to Polly telling her she would move to America.
Corey knew she would be happy as she checked her inbox
she was surprised to see an e-mail from Steve.
She almost didn't want to open it scared of what it might
say.
'To Corey'.
'Sorry I've taken so long to reply I've been busy
working on several films'.

'For the last few months when you told me you were pregnant I was shocked but once I got used to the idea I was happy about being a father'.

'I would like to be part of the child's life if you will let me I would certainly like to contribute financially'.

'I hope this doesn't affect our friendship I like you a lot and would like to see you again soon if you want to'.

'I can't wait to see you again soon love Steve xxx

Corey was happy he'd replied which she was happy about at least Steve didn't hate her.

And wanted to be involved in the baby's life the next day Corey decided to plan her baby shower.

It would be a small get together two weeks later along with Stacey, Kim and some of her friends.

They went to Hyde Park for their picnic it was a beautiful sunny autumn day.

Corey was trying to enjoy the last few weeks of her pregnancy she decided to enjoy herself she felt relaxed.

And decided having a picnic was a good idea Corey enjoyed her friends company.

Stacey gave her a designer rattle and baby clothes Kim a baby blanket it was a nice day.

The good weather made her feel even better.

Corey knew when she moved to America she would have more sunshine.

After their picnic they went on a river cruise then a film it had been a good day.

Corey only wished Polly could have been there but she knew she'd see her soon.

She would make sure the house was nice for when Polly arrived she didn't have a nursery.

As they were moving to L.A Polly promised her a fantastic surprise when she moved there.

Corey couldn't wait to see what she'd done Polly had always had an interest in interior design .

How to make things look good even though she had doubts about moving to America.

Corey was sure once she got there she'd feel at home that Friday Polly returned home.

As soon as she saw Polly she was happy to have her home she hugged Corey 'let's see how big you are'.

'You still look good I'm gonna have a cup of tea then we'll have a chat so any gossip?' 'not really'.

'I didn't have a proper baby shower I had a nice picnic with Stacey and Kim' 'that's good don't worry'.

'After the baby's born we can have a christening party'.

'Good idea' Corey agreed 'thought of any names?'.
Polly asked 'no what about you?' 'I was thinking'.
'You can say no if you want to what about my name?'.
'Polly' 'no Susan my real name' 'I like it' 'really?' 'yes'.
'Let's call our daughter Susan' 'alright then' Polly was
happy Corey liked her name for the baby.
'What do you think about Stacey getting married?'.
'I can't wait I'm happy for her and Christian' 'me too'.
'Stacey says we can be bridesmaids' 'great a winter
wedding' 'I know it'll be grand I've missed you so much'.
'From now on it'll be just the two of us together'
Polly said 'I can't wait' 'I love New York' 'you'll love L.A'.
Corey wasn't sure she had nothing to lose by moving there
she might like it good weather make some music contacts.
Stacey decided to start planning her wedding early as she
was due to start her new film in the middle of October.
She was busy learning her script she wanted to make sure
everything was perfect.
She knew she could have got a wedding planner but she
wanted to do it with Christian together the two of them.
It would be good they'd already decided they wanted ivory
paper with a gold trim with two gold wedding rings.
On their wedding invitations a nice hotel for the reception
with purple lights in a mint green marque.

And she knew she wanted to wear an ivory dress and a tiara crème wedding shoes.

With a three inch heel everything was almost planned Stacey knew her wedding would be perfect.

If it wasn't for Jean interfering in their plans one day she came to Stacey's house with Christian.

She was slightly annoyed Christian hadn't said she was coming round but she decided to remain calm.

Despite the fact she couldn't stand her 'Stacey' she smiled 'hi' 'listen I'm sorry about what happened that night'.

'At the house I don't have a problem with you it's your sister Kim the way she acted I wasn't happy about it' Stacey couldn't believe what she was hearing Jean obviously had a short memory.

And had forgotten about the fact she'd said she wasn't good enough for Christian.

And would be better off with his ex Laura and the fact that she'd been nasty to her mum Stacey decided to stay quiet.

She didn't want another row after tea and saying how nice the August weather was they sat down and chatted.

'Stacey listen I've been thinking about the wedding why don't you get married at our house' 'your house'.

'Yes we have so much room nice gardens and a massive hall we could have the congregation in there'.

'What do you think?' 'I was thinking about a castle maybe in Ireland' 'why go all the way there make people travel'. 'It would be so much easier if you had the wedding at our house' 'mum's right I think it's a good idea think about it'. 'I suppose it would save costs' 'exactly it makes sense we'll do it up really nice' Jean said.

Stacey couldn't understand why she was being so nice to her 'what about the reception?' Stacey asked.

'We'll have it there too' Christian smiled inside she felt a bit annoyed maybe they could have the wedding there. But not the reception suddenly Stacey had flashbacks to Christian's birthday party.

'We can still have what you want' 'Stacey wants purple and pink lights and a mint green marque and gold seats'. 'We can do any colour scheme you want' 'ok sounds good' Stacey still felt angry 'see it'll be great' Christian said. As she smiled 'have you chosen a dress?' Jean asked 'not yet I just know I want it to be ivory with a veil'. 'I have something you might like' 'what do you mean?'. 'Christian's grandmother my mum when she died she has a beautiful dress you'll love it' 'what style?'. 'It's classic vintage she was about the same height as you'. 'You'll like it suits any age' Stacey's heart sank she wanted to choose her own wedding dress.

But didn't want a row with Jean in front of Christian.

'I suppose I could see what it's like' 'great you come over and I'll show you there's matching wedding shoes'.

'Well I can't wait to see it' 'you don't have to wear it but just see you might like it' Christian said.

'I know our local vicar really well so you don't have to worry about the religious side of it and a choir'.

'They can sing as you go down the aisle' now Jean was going too far.

It was bad enough having to get married at her house possibly wear Christian's grandmother's dress.

Now she was choosing the music 'looks like we'll get this wedding planned really quickly' Christian said 'I know'.

'It's great and I'm so busy with the film' exactly it's easier this way' Jean said 'have you chosen bridesmaids?' 'yes'.

'I thought Maria' 'oh she'll love that' Jean said an excited tone to her voice 'Corey she'll have had the baby'.

'Then Polly' 'three's a nice number' 'I was thinking Kim'.

'She is my sister' 'we'll have to talk about that' Jean said.

Sounding stern 'why? I promise they'll be no more trouble' 'how can you say that'.

'What if she decides to steal one of my valuable ornaments' 'she won't ok I'll have a word sort it'.

'As long as you do' 'I will I promise' 'good then'.

'Everything will be ok' 'I think it's gonna be a great wedding' Christian said 'I'm excited'.

'The first of my children to go up the aisle' 'we can't wait' Stacey said 'I'm really excited' Christian said.

'Not long to go now then' Jean said the next day Stacey told Kim all about the plans for the wedding.

How she was angry Jean had taken over as they strolled around town.

'I can't believe it making you get married at her mansion'.

'I know ok maybe it's not such a bad idea if it makes Christian happy' 'what about making you happy'.

'You always said whenever we discussed our dream wedding that you wanted to get married in a castle'.

'In Ireland with a traditional Irish band and a black gospel choir at the wedding' 'I know alright'.

'Maybe it's better this way I mean then people don't have to travel to get to the wedding' 'Stace it's Ireland'.

'We're talking about not the other side of the world how hard is it to get a ferry'.

'And making you wear his grandmother's dress that's so low I bet it's really awful' 'I haven't seen it'.

'It comes with wedding shoes apparently she knows a local vicar and a choir' 'this gets worse'.

'What about what you want' 'I'll talk to Christian'.

'You better sounds like she's trying to take over the wedding' 'it's his mum I know she's a bitch'.
'But if I have a go at her we'll row and then the wedding won't happen' 'are you sure it's what you want'.
'Marrying Christian I know he's really nice' 'listen Kim'.
'You don't get it it's like a psychological game she's playing she's testing me trying to split us up'.
'But it won't happen I'm gonna marry Christian'.
'And it will be my dress' 'good' 'oh listen you're gonna be a bridesmaid but you have to be on your best behaviour'.
'Stacey' 'no listen I know she's a bitch but if you start a row that'll be it and I really want you to be bridesmaid'.
'I'm not sucking up to her' 'I'm not asking you to I just don't want any rows just a really nice day'.
'Ok I promise I'll be on my best behaviour so what colour are the bridesmaids dresses gonna be' 'I haven't decided'.
'I'm wearing ivory maybe berry coloured' 'I'm excited for you I just feel bad that she's your mother-in-law'.
'Tell me about it hopefully once we're married she'll leave us alone' 'yeah well she better'.
'Else she'll have me and mum to deal with' 'you should have been there that time they rowed' 'wish I had been'.
'I've just thought what if she tries to stop mum coming'.
Stacey wondered 'she won't ok we're a family'.

'How's Corey?' 'good the size of a house she's just waiting to give birth I'm sure you won't have to wait long'.

'To have a baby' 'I know put it this way I want a baby by two years time I just need to find the right man' 'you will'.

Stacey loved hanging out with Kim they weren't just sisters they were best friends.

They had clicked from the moment they had met as teenagers.

Stacey was sure when they were together people thought they were friends rather than sisters but she didn't care.

What people thought a few days later Stacey was forced to visit the mansion again.

As Jean wanted her to try on the wedding dress she wasn't looking forward to it she would just have to smile.

And pretend everything was ok as she arrived Jean was there ready to greet her 'Stacey'.

'We'll have some refreshments then you can see the dress' 'great' Stacey drank lemonade ate and fairy cakes.

Before going upstairs to see the dress Jean opened up a wooden mahogany wardrobe.

The moment she was dreading had come 'here it is' Stacey looked at the dress long sleeved ivory & silver.

Almost Elizabethan in style with a long skirt and ivory wedding shoes one and a half inches.

'What size is the dress?' 'a ten but we could take it in'.
'I know you're an eight' the dress wasn't as bad as she
imagined it was vintage beautiful 'please try it on'.
'We'll leave you a minute' 'ok' Christian and Jean went
outside she was almost scared to try it on.
It was obviously an old family heir loom as Stacey tried it
on it was obviously a size too big but still looked nice.
She felt like a princess however nice the dress was it
wasn't right for her wedding she tried on the shoes.
They were silver not even two inches high but still felt nice
'finished yet?' Jean asked 'yes'.
They came back in the room 'wow! it looks great very
classic' Christian said 'it's a really nice dress'.
'So you think you might wear it?' Jean asked 'mum it's too
big for Stacey' 'we can take it in' 'I know'.
'But it's up to Stacey what dress she wears' 'I know that'.
'Let Stacey decide' 'well the offers there if you want it'.
'Thanks' Stacey felt bad the dress was beautiful just not
her style Jean left the room as Christian talked to Stacey.
'Tell me what you think?' 'it's gorgeous but it's too big and
not really my style' 'I thought so'.
'You know I could really see Polly wearing something like
this but not me' 'I understand'.
'I don't want to sound ungrateful' 'you're not'.

'I'll tell mum you won't be wearing the dress' 'thanks will she be angry?' 'no course not we'll explain everything'.

'That you like it but it's not your style' 'thanks maybe Maria could wear it when she gets married' 'great idea'.

Stacey was happy Christian was ok about her not wearing the dress maybe everything would be ok.

Maybe she could have her dream wedding after all it was nearly the end of November.

Corey was now staying in most days she could have gone out but it was easier to stay inside.

That way no-one would stare at her she enjoyed watching some films she was hoping she would have the baby soon.

Luckily she'd been given a great part in her new film learning the script kept her going during her pregnancy Polly had gone out to a business meeting about her new lingerie range Corey was sat outside reading a magazine.

She realised the pain she felt meant she going into labour. Corey tried to call Polly's mobile no answer it just rang she left a message she called her midwife June .

Who luckily only lived a few doors away she quickly came round she felt better now she wasn't alone 'Corey '.

'I came as quickly as I could' 'it's ok I'm just pissed off Polly's not answering her mobile' 'I'm sure she will'.

'I should have been prepared I mean I'm eight months gone' 'it's fine we'll get everything ready'.

'The contractions have just started' Corey had planned to have a water birth she had a pool set up.

She also planned to light candles and incense she was very much a spiritualist.

She'd had two children in hospital and hated every minute this time it would be different calmer.

As calm as giving birth could be 'shall I get your cd's?'.

June asked 'yes' Corey had a selection of five cd's of world music African rhythms. rainforest, tropical island.

And Irish Celtic long enough for the birth Corey despite the pain she couldn't wait to meet her baby.

She hoped Polly's meeting would finish soon Corey sipped orange juice in between contractions.

Trying to remain calm taking deep breaths June tried Polly's phone again still no answer .

She decided to call Stacey who came over 'have you had the baby?' Stacey asked 'not yet very soon'.

'This is so cool incense candles why didn't I think of that'.

'Let me know if there's anything I can do' 'thanks'

Corey was grateful Stacey was there she noticed Corey seemed calm despite knowing what was ahead.

She had to be there especially since Polly was in a business meeting.

Stacey was sure she would be on her way soon two hours later Corey gave birth Stacey thought it was quick.

The baby was fine though it was hard to tell if she looked like Corey 'congratulations' Stacey said 'thanks'.

'You seemed so calm' 'I enjoyed it in a weird way' Stacey was happy for Corey finally Polly turned up.

'Did I miss anything?' 'yes but I forgive you' 'I'm sorry'.

'My phone was off I went out for a drink with Louie'

'It's ok you're here now' 'how is she?' 'grand' Polly looked at the baby 'I'm sorry I wasn't there I feel really bad'.

'It's fine June and Stacey were with me they kept me calm'

'I am sorry I wasn't there' 'really it's ok' Corey said

'am I forgiven?' 'yes' 'thanks she's beautiful' 'she is'.

'I really like the name Susan' Polly smiled she was glad Corey wasn't too angry at her .

She was happy she'd gotten pregnant yes she'd been hurt and angry over her fling with Steve.

But now she thought everything happened for a reason now Corey was moving with her to America.

Everything would be perfect they would be together like a proper family 'I can't wait to see the nursery in L.A'.

'Oh darling you'll love it' they kissed.

The next day Louie came round to see baby Susan as he held her in his arms 'she's gorgeous like her mum'.

'Thanks you're good with her' Corey said 'I don't know'.

'I bet I'd be terrible changing nappies' 'you never know'.

'Think you'll have kids?' 'I hope so I'm almost getting too old' 'Louie thirty two is not old' 'it is not'.

'I guess anyway I need to find a stable partner first' 'you will' 'thanks ragdoll oh I brought a present'.

'For you and the baby' Louie pulled out a giant teddy bear from his bag 'wow! thanks it's really nice'.

'Only the best for you I got something else for you' 'me'.

'Yes maybe you won't like it...I just thought of you' 'whatever it is I'm sure I'll like it' Louie pulled out a doll.

From his bag followed by another two 'I know you said you weren't allowed to play with dolls as a child'.

'Louie that's so sweet' 'you like them?' 'yes their really nice' 'one's porcine' Corey looked at the doll.

Wearing a satin checked tartan dress brown curly hair a red ribbon in her hair.

The kind of doll she would love to have owned as a child.

'She's lovely' 'the other one's a ragdoll' Corey laughed the other doll was wearing a blue dress.

Her golden hair in pigtails 'I love her it's me when I was thirteen' Corey joked 'I think she's my favourite'.

'I thought you might think it was a stupid idea'
'the dolls no I love them I wasn't allowed dolls as a child'.
'Now you can have some dolls of your own' 'thanks Louie'
they hugged 'how was the birth?' 'not too bad actually'.
'Good Louie you are going to be godfather' 'yes I'd love
to' 'Stacey and Jane my old friend from College'.
'Are godmothers' 'that's great she's gorgeous'
Louie opened some champagne as they toasted.
To baby Susan and the future Corey was happy she was
going to America for a new start.
Maybe make some music contacts Stacey had also landed
another film role in Hollywood.
Playing Lila in a film version of Sweet Valley High.
Since her performance in a re-make of 'Imitation Of Life'
casting directors in Hollywood were interested in her.
She'd always wanted a successful film career as well as a
music career Stacey was excited about the wedding.
She had decided to have it at Christian's house it wasn't
her first choice but it made sense.
It was just outside London and easier for people to get to
she had also chosen a beautiful ivory wedding dress.
A simple design with a silver tiara and three inch high
heeled wedding shoes she was only 5ft 2ins.
Where as Christian was 5ft 8ins.

She'd also chosen a bouquet of red roses her favourites.
Everything would be perfect she would be marrying the
man of her dreams.

She'd planned to have a black gospel choir from the
church she'd been going to since she was seventeen.

She was gutted when Jean told her it wasn't possible since
she'd already arranged a choir.

Stacey hoped they were good something her mum wasn't
happy about 'Stace she's trying to control the wedding'.

Marcce said one evening as they chatted in her house.

Stacey had come home from a hard day's recording in
central London of her album 'listen I'm really busy'.

'With the film maybe she'd done me a favour' 'you think
so' 'well all I've had to do is get a dress flowers'.

'And we did the invitations ages ok so it's all sorted and
getting married at their house'.

'It saves people having to travel out of the UK'

'I suppose you're right you always said you're dream
wedding was either a Scottish or Irish castle'.

'And a black gospel choir you said that was what you
always wanted' 'I did ok'.

'But if someone's organised a choir I can't turn round and
say no' 'why not it's your wedding'.

'I don't want any rows' 'are you sure you're doing the right thing?' 'what do you mean?' 'marrying Christian'.

'It's not him Christian's lovely it's his mum I don't want her causing any problems for you later on' 'she won't'.

'What if she does?' 'I don't like her but I love Christian'.

'I'm willing to put up with her just about oh and I am having a traditional Irish band at the reception'.

'We made a compromise' 'at least that's something'.

'It'll be a really good wedding' 'I can't wait I bet you're excited walking down the aisle' 'yeah I am'.

'I bet your dad's really excited too' 'yeah' 'what does he think of Jean?' 'he hasn't met her yet'.

'But he's heard all the gossip' 'tell him from me he doesn't want to meet her' 'that's what Sarah said'.

'Anyway I hope it's a good day' 'thanks so do I is Aunt Vee looking forward to it?'.

'Oh yes any excuse for a good day out' Stacey had visited Veronica a few times and really liked her.

She felt just as in touch with the black side of her family as the white which was good.

She only wished she'd met her mum and sister sooner but now she felt really close to them.

A month later it was time for the wedding Stacey couldn't wait to get married.

As Stacey put on her wedding dress and tiara she felt like
a princess her hair was naturally dark brown.
Straight at the front curly at the back a berry coloured
lipstick silver eyeshadow she loved her dress.
She wished she'd just worn her hair straight though as the
curly bit at the back didn't quite look right with the tiara.
It was too late now Stacey had her bouquet as she waited
for the other bridesmaids.
Kim, Polly, Maria & Corey who all looked pretty in berry
coloured satin dresses the colour didn't quite suit Polly.
Who looked better in gold like the dresses they'd worn to
her mum Sarah's wedding but they all looked nice.
People had started arriving in the big hall where the
wedding was being held Polly caught a glimpse of Wendy.
Who looked gorgeous in a crème suit & skirt with a big
wedding hat her mum was sat near the front with Kaleigh.
She was wearing black and white with a wedding hat from
BHS Kaleigh wore a crème dress they both looked great.
Christian wore a navy suit which went well with his
blonde hair Polly saw Marcee come in with Veronica.
And her friend they looked around unable to find a seat
suddenly Sarah realised there were no free seats
'Christian I think you've got a problem' Sarah said.
'What's wrong?' he asked 'oh not enough seats'.

'How could this happen?' 'just one of those things'
Jean said appearing in a pale pink suit smiling.
'Listen I'll sort it I'll go get some seats' 'Christian'.
'The service is about to start' 'I'm sure they can hold on
five minutes!' Polly noticed Jean looked angry.
Polly suspected the lack of seats had been deliberate.
Stacey had told her about the row with Jean and her mum
Polly had never gotten on with Marcee.
But she actually felt sorry for her as Christian brought
over three gold chairs 'thanks Christian' Marcee said.
'Anytime' he smiled Jean walked off 'he's so nice'
Veronica said 'I know he's lovely' Marcee said 'not keen
on his mum though she has an attitude problem'.
Veronica said 'you don't know the half of it' Marcee wasn't
happy even though she liked Christian.
She was worried Stacey was making a mistake she would
be marrying into his family whether she liked it or not.
Jean wasn't the nicest of people soon it was time for the
service to begin as everyone stood up.
Stacey waited for the service to begin she'd planned to
walk down the aisle to Abba's I do I do I do.
It was a fun song that no-one would expect as the music
started Stacey was confused.
As Pachbel's no5 played a beautiful piece of music.

But not the song she wanted she realised the music had been switched Stacey knew she couldn't just stand there.

As she began walking down the aisle she didn't feel emotional at all she felt angry.

Jean had obviously switched the music deliberately Stacey tried not to show how angry she felt.

As she saw all eyes watching her she began to wish she'd gone for a more intimate wedding.

Off stage she was a quiet person she felt like she was on show as she got to the front of the hall.

Stacey relaxed she saw how gorgeous Christian looked yes Jean was a bitch but it was worth it.

To marry the man of her dreams she said her vows wanting to get through it as quickly as possible.

'Do you Stacey-Marie Jane O'Riley take Christian John Bell to be your lawful wedded husband?' 'I do'.

'And do you take Stacey to be your wife?' 'I do' 'you may exchange rings'

Stacey's wedding ring was a white gold ring engraved with each other's name on she liked it.

'Now you may kiss the bride' Christian lifted up her veil as they kissed she was happy.

Now they were husband and wife everyone clapped as they went to get changed into some other clothes.

For the reception Stacey was glad it was over now she could enjoy herself Polly looked over.

Marcee looked happy that the wedding was over she decided to say something 'I thought it was low'.

'What she did I mean your mother of the bride' 'thanks Polly it's fine' 'Polly's right' Sarah said joining them.

'She seems like a right bitch to me still Stacey's marrying Christian not his mum' 'well she may as well be'.

Polly said 'it's Stacey's choice I suppose they both looked gorgeous' Marcee said 'enjoying the wedding?'.

Jean asked 'immensely' Marcee replied 'well I'll see everyone at the reception in the marquee in half an hour'.

Jean walked off 'it's Christian I feel sorry for' Sarah said. 'Being raised by that cow! who does she think she is lady of the manor!'.

'Couldn't have put it better myself' Marcee said half an hour later they went to the Marquee which was crème.

Apparently they couldn't get mint green Stacey didn't mind it seemed nice enough everyone went to their seats.

To enjoy their meal as Marcee and Veronica went to their table they couldn't believe they'd been sat separately.

Marcee was convinced it was deliberate she saw Jean she was angry.

'I'd like to know why we've been sat separately'.

'I don't know' 'this is my sister Veronica she doesn't know anyone here so you better sort it out!' 'fine!'.
'Come with me I'll find you a table! and another thing'.
'If I had it my way I'd have you and your daughter banned from this wedding!' 'how are you gonna do that'.
'I'm Stacey's mum!' 'quite easily this is my house!'
'actually it was your ex-husbands house'.
'You're on thin ice one more move I'll have you escorted off the property!' 'what would Christian say about that!'.
'Don't worry we won't stay long' 'enjoy your meal'
'we'll try' Stacey came over to see them 'hi Stace'.
'How's everything?' 'fine Jean says another wrong move we'll be kicked out for asking to move tables'.
'She can't do that don't worry she hates me too she swapped my music' 'I noticed that'.
'How bad was the choir' Marcee said 'Jean's idea'.
'Now I know why she was being so nice to me before the wedding so she could control everything'.
'We won't be staying much longer' 'please mum I can't do this without you' 'Stacey listen to me this is your wedding'
'You made a big mistake having it here' 'I know it's too late now at least I'm married to Christian'.
'That's one good thing' 'where's Andy?' Stacey asked.
'Over there' Marcee said pointing to another table.

Across the room 'you are joking why aren't you seated together he's your husband?' 'she's one sly bitch'.
'She even tried to separate me and Vee I told her she doesn't know anyone listen we'll stay'.
'Till after the speeches a bit of dancing and that's it' 'thanks' Stacey was grateful her mum would stay a bit. As Polly walked around trying to get some food and champagne she heard a conversation between Jean. And a male friend 'who are they?' he said pointing to Marcee and Veronica 'the black people friends of yours?'. 'No Stacey's family that's her mum' 'she's mixed race'. 'Yes that's her dad' Jean said pointing to Paul 'does that mean any grandchildren you might have might be...' 'no'. 'Stacey looks white and Christian's fair haired with green eyes the father is nearly always the dominant gene'. 'The kids will look white let's get ready for the speeches'. Jean said as they walked away Polly couldn't believe it even though Jean hadn't made it obvious.
Polly suspected she was a secret racist.
She couldn't believe someone as nice as Christian had such a bitch for a mother she decided to get tipsy.
As she drank champagne soon it time for the speeches. Christian stood up 'I just wanted to thank everyone for coming to our wedding I'm really happy'.

'To be married to the girl of my dreams I'm glad we had the wedding here so everyone could travel here'.

'All our friends and family I want to thank everyone who helped to organise the wedding'.

'I couldn't have done it without mum and my family and friends I'm really glad I found Stacey'.

'I know I'm only twenty one but I feel in my heart she's the right person who I love'.

'That I want to spend the rest of my life with thanks everyone' they clapped.

Christian's best man also made a speech as well as another friend who was a stand up comedian.

Only he wasn't as funny as he thought he was Polly got bored as she drank glass after glass of champagne.

It was a wedding after all 'Susie' 'mum' 'careful' 'it's a wedding' 'you'll make yourself ill'.

'You're doing a speech in a minute' 'I'll be fine I'm just tipsy' 'Susie you look more than tipsy'.

'How many have you had?' 'only four maybe five' 'well you've had enough!' 'it's fine mum' 'I wouldn't ok!'.

'It's fine I just thought you know what I'm just gonna enjoy myself get drunk' 'you'll make a fool of yourself'.

'Susie you'll get us thrown out!' 'hardly it's Stacey's wedding' 'yeah well'.

'Jean's already threatened to ask Marcee to leave'.
'so what Jean's a bitch! she throws me out I'll have something to say about it!' 'you're up next' 'what?'.
'Your speech if you can remember it' 'I never wrote one down all from memory'.

Christian got ready to introduce Polly to everyone 'and now someone very special to me my lovely sister Polly'.
'Is gonna make a speech' Polly made her way to his table Sarah could see she was unsteady.

She was worried what she'd say 'hi everyone I'm a bit drunk but I'll try my best I just wanted to say I love you'.
'Both of you' Sarah noticed she was stuttering over her words 'I'm glad to be here I mean Stace I love you'.
'But you did make some bad choices when it comes to men but it's fine now you found each other at last'.
'Sarah noticed people seemed to like her speech despite the fact she was obviously drunk 'I'm drunk...I'm sorry'.
Jean looked pissed off Marcce noticed as Polly continued talking 'listen words can't describe how happy I am'.
'For you both best couple ever' Stacey laughed 'the best couple in the universe in the solar system'.
'You deserve to be happy' yes Polly was drunk but she still found her speech funny Jean stood up.

'Is this actually going anywhere! if not let someone else speak!' 'I don't care that Polly's drunk'.

'I want her to finish her speech' Stacey said Jean reluctantly sat down 'I knew when I saw you two'.

'You were meant to be together you're perfect together like fish and chips strawberries and crème'.

'Night and day Ant and Dec' 'alright! point made!'.

Jean said getting angrier by the minute 'like summer and ice-creams' 'there she goes again!'.

'I have to say I can't wait for you to have a baby together I love you so much my brother and my step-sister'.

'I don't know what I'd do without you in my life everyone have a toast to the happy couple' everyone did.

As they clapped Marcce noticed how angry Jean was at her speech 'Polly and drink don't mix' Sarah said.

'Wait here' she said to Kaleigh as she went to find Polly. Knowing Jean wouldn't be happy 'hey' 'Marcee' 'I loved the speech' 'Polly can't take her drink'.

'I'm off to find her now before she causes more trouble'.

'Are you Polly's mum?' 'yes' 'well you can tell your daughter I want her off my property!' 'listen'.

'I know she's drunk and the speech didn't go as planned but you can't do that she's Christian's sister!'.

'I can do what I like it's my house!'.

'Not that rubbish again!' Marcee said 'still hanging around unwanted! I told you to leave'.

'You said you were going!' 'we are!' 'hang on let me get this straight you want me to go Polly Marcee'.

'Who's is Stacey's mum her sister anyone else how about Kaleigh my husband Paul Andy who else is there!'.

'Wendy maybe?' 'don't be ridiculous!' 'you're ridiculous!'.

'Everyone knows you never wanted Stacey to marry Christian!' Sarah said angry.

'Here's why you're jealous you can't bear to see Christian happy! let's hope he see's sense moves out'.

'And goes to live with Stacey away from you!' 'how dare you! your daughter is a drunk who showed Christian up!'.

'At his own wedding!' 'what's going on?' Christian asked.

'Not much! these people are leaving!' 'these people I'm Stacey's step-mum!' 'I don't care who you are!'.

'Mum!' 'no Christian I want them to go now!' 'you can't do this!' 'I can do what I want!' 'this is our wedding day!'.

'You can't ask Sarah to leave!' 'I can do what I want just watch me!'.

They watched as Jean picked up a nearby megaphone.

'What is she doing?' Sarah asked 'I have no idea'

Marcee said 'would the following people please leave the premises before I call the police'.

'Marcee her sister Veronica, Sarah and her daughter Kaleigh' Sarah was angry.

'Mum what have I done wrong?' Kaleigh asked 'nothing'.

'She's a bitch' 'she has seriously lost the plot' Marcee said 'well are you going!' 'yes give us a minute'.

'And we'll be off' Sarah said as they walked past tables as everyone looked in their direction 'what is going on?'.

Andy asked 'she's off her head! back soon' Sarah said as she walked towards the stage.

Where a traditional Irish band had been playing until Jean asked them to leave.

As Sarah picked up the megaphone 'would the following people please listen to what I have to say'.

'Jean your mental and for the record no-one f**k's with Stacey's family if you want us to leave'.

'You'll have to have us physically removed oh another thing we shall not be moved' Stacey laughed.

'Mum has seriously lost it' Christian said 'what shall we do?' Stacey asked 'I don't know'.

'I could try and get mum to calm down' they couldn't believe it minutes later when a police car arrived outside.

'That better not be for us she can't arrest all of us' Marcee said 'are you aware this is private property'.

'Alright we're going!' Sarah said 'you can't leave!'

Stacey said 'it's alright this isn't your fault' Sarah said.

Stacey felt out of control at her own wedding how could Jean force her mum and step-mum to leave.

At her own wedding 'she can't do this!' 'I can and I will'.

'Pathetic bitch! well done for ruining Stacey's big day!'.

Marcee said angry at Jean 'mum you've gone too far!'

Christian said trying to make it ok between them.

'Listen we're all going' 'you don't have to!' Christian said 'get off my property!' 'mum's not usually like this'.

'It's the divorce the last two years she hasn't been the same' 'Christian you're a lovely lad'.

'But your mum's a psycho!' Sarah said 'I'm sorry'.

'It's fine really have a nice honeymoon' 'thanks' as they walked away Christian felt bad.

What was his mum playing at? 'thank god the rabbles gone!' 'you are joking! how could you do that!'.

'Do what?' 'it's Stacey's mum and step-mum' 'I don't want them here!' 'what about Stacey? it's her family'.

'I don't care that's not my problem!' Jean walked away as Christian looked on in disbelief.

Stacey wished she'd have got married in a fairytale castle 'I'm so sorry' 'Christian it's ok it's not your fault'.

'I feel like it is' 'it's not it's your mum's fault'.

'Which makes it worse!' 'come on let's go find Polly'
Stacey suggested 'now we have to explain things'.
'She'll be fine about it' they looked around they spied
Andy 'what happened?' 'they've all gone'.
'Jean kicked them out' Stacey explained 'mum's lost it'.
'I'll phone Marcee I thought I'd stay' 'thanks I don't know
what I'd do without you' Stacey said.
'Your my favourite niece' 'have you seen Polly?' 'yes'.
'She had a sit down she's not feeling well' 'the drink?'
'Stacey asked probably' 'I hope she's ok' 'she will be'.
'Where's Kim?' 'around trying to keep a low profile in
case Jean kicks her out' 'she's ruined everything'.
Stacey said as Christian went to get a drink 'I hate to say
I told you so' 'I wish I'd never got married here'.
'I'm sorry it makes two of us' 'she ruined my wedding!'.
'I thought it would be ok I didn't know she'd ruin
everything' 'I could have told you that'.
'I wasn't impressed with the way she treated Marcee'.
'She even switched my music' 'I know I wouldn't put
anything past her' 'I feel sorry'.
'That you'll never get this day back' 'it's my fault' 'why?'.
'For thinking it would work out ok' 'listen maybe in a
while you could get married again' 'maybe'.
'At least I got to pick my own dress' 'I guess'.

'At least that's something I'll never forgive that woman for ruining your day' Christian returned 'I saw Polly'.

'She's ok trying to get sober drinking water she says she's spent the last half an hour on the toilet' Stacey laughed.

At least Polly had provided the entertainment Stacey picked up a glass of champagne 'to us' 'can I join in?'.

'Kim' she poured herself a glass as they toasted 'the bitch is coming!' Kim said 'I want you to leave!'.

'I think you've had enough!' 'you're talking to me!'

'who else would I be talking to!' 'mum!' 'Christian'.

'Stay out of this!' 'you want me to go! ok I'll go!'

Kim poured a glass of champagne over Jean 'you bitch!'.

'You're the bitch! I am so over this wedding I feel sorry for my sister!' Kim walked off as Jean followed her.

'Mum leave her alone!' 'I don't want to see that girl round here again!' 'I doubt anyone wants to come round here'.

'The way you've behaved!' 'I never wanted her here or her mum!' 'Marcee is Stacey's mum and Kim is her sister'.

'You don't like them fine! but you don't need to cause trouble for the sake of it!' 'I'm not!' 'you are!'.

'I think you should calm down!' 'I am calm!' 'oh really'.

'What must people think' 'I don't care what people think!'.

'I don't want them here!' 'this is a wedding! my wedding our wedding you've tried to ruin!' 'I haven't ruined it!'.

'You have!' Stacey was happy finally Christian was sticking up for himself 'your family Stacey...'.

'My family are kind decent people whatever you say!'.

'You wanna start something I can!' Andy said 'the way you've behaved is a disgrace!'.

'You've ruined Stacey's big day! and she'll never get it back she doesn't deserve to be treated like that by you!'.

'Andy's right' Christian said 'I still want your sister gone!' Stacey was angry as she walked up to the stage.

As she picked up the megaphone 'everyone thankyou for coming to my own wedding'.

'But this isn't the day I planned a big thankyou to Jean for ruining my wedding getting rid of my family'.

'Looks like you got your wish this is me signing off from my own wedding!' 'Stace listen I'll sort it' Christian said.

'You can't sort it everything's ruined! your mum has ruined our wedding our perfect day'.

'I need to get out of this house' 'what about our wedding night?' 'it's ok you can come to mine'.

'I can't leave this house it's our wedding reception it's not a wedding to me if my family aren't here!'.

'It's not even six o clock' 'I can't stay here I'm sorry'.

'Alright please stay half an hour we'll have a few drinks'.

'Twenty minutes listen I'll go home'.

'You can meet me later' 'I won't go without you you're my wife I'm sorry for everything'.

'I had no idea mum would behave like that' 'alright let me find Kim and we can go together'.

Christian went to tell his friends that he was leaving Andy said he would drive them all back to her house.

Stacey didn't feel guilty about leaving the wedding after all it wasn't really her wedding it was Jean's.

Who had deliberately sabotaged it and succeeded at least she hadn't done a magazine deal.

She could imagine what the headlines would have been in the magazines.

Stacey vowed one day in a few years time she would have her dream wedding and it would be perfect.

How she wished she'd listened to her mum and Kim it was too late now she hoped the honeymoon would go better.

They had planned a trip to Paris & Italy and couldn't wait the next day she woke happy.

The wedding from hell was over Polly and Kim had stayed over now she was ready to start her new life.

With Christian 'how are you feeling Susie?' Stacey asked Polly as she sipped tea 'good'.

'Did you enjoy the wedding?' Polly asked 'no Jean ruined it for me' 'I can't remember the reception'.

'I was drunk I just remember the service your mum and Aunt not having anywhere to sit'.

'It was Jean's fault acting innocent' Kim said joining them 'I should've listened to you'.

'I should've had my dream wedding' 'I told you'

'I thought it would be ok' 'with that witch! it's ok'.

'You're married to Christian now and he's gorgeous'.

'I know I am happy even if the wedding didn't go to plan'

'I'm so jealous' 'why?' 'I wanna get married' 'you'll find someone' Stacey assured Kim.

'I have started dating someone' 'you never told me'

'he's divorced he's really nice he's called John'.

'He's a lawyer thirty four' 'older man' 'yes he has an eight year old daughter' 'he sounds really nice' 'he is'.

'You'll love him' 'I hope it goes well' 'me too maybe you can meet him' Stacey noticed Kim seemed happy.

Maybe now they could have better luck with men and their lives 'looks like everyone's happy' Polly said.

'I know Susie and now Corey's moving to America with you you can be together' 'yeah I can't wait'.

'Don't worry about Jean don't let her ruin your happiness you've got a honeymoon to look forward to as well'.

'I won't let her ruin my life when Christian moves in a few weeks time I won't have to worry'.

'About going back to that house again' 'I'm happy for you Stace' 'thanks Susie'.

'All you need now is a brother or sister for Tally' 'not yet'. 'I'm focusing on films this year and I'm recording a new album we've decided in two years'.

'Give us enough time to get to know each other' 'sounds like a good idea' Polly agreed

'I want a baby so bad but then I love being with the group but I like my freedom' Kim said.

'You should do it when your ready get to know John first see what happens' 'good idea Stace'.

'You're the best at giving advice' Kim poured some orange juice 'let's have a toast to the future' 'to us'.

They toasted their glasses the next day Stacey and Christian took the Eurostar to Paris.

To begin what turned out to be a fantastic honeymoon they went up the Eiffel Tower did some shopping.

Before going to Italy as they took a boat ride together in Venice they could only stay five days.

As Stacey had to get back to filming in London of her new film she didn't mind.

Her career seemed to be going better than ever screw Jean she thought nothing was going to ruin her happiness.

Corey was moving to L.A with Polly as she expected the nursery looked amazing with baby blue and crème.

With a stars and moon border with a lovely cot a mobile and a device that made different noises.

Water, rainforest and waterfalls Corey loved it she decided she'd done the right thing by moving to America.

She was now the one doing the transatlantic flying as she tried to finish the film in London.

And do a good performance she enjoyed it Corey loved doing the film and her character.

When she finished the band would be going on tour and releasing a new album.

Before they knew it Christmas was approaching they had decided to go to New York to Polly's apartment.

Everything seemed to be working out well Corey had spoken to Steve on the phone.

He said he couldn't wait to meet baby Susan she decided to invite him round one day so they could talk properly.

And Steve could meet his new daughter he sounded excited on the phone which was a good sign.

Corey couldn't wait to see him again she hoped everything would go well as he rang the doorbell.

That Friday afternoon Corey felt slightly nervous she hoped he'd be ok about the baby.

Despite what he'd said in his e-mails and on the phone she was still worried that he might reject her and the baby.

As she opened the door wearing a berry coloured polo neck jumper small silver hoop earrings Steve smiled.

'How are you?' he asked 'fine' he hugged her he seemed happy to see her 'you look fantastic' 'me?'.

'I mean for just having had a baby' 'thanks you think so?' 'yes you look great it's good to see you' 'you too'.

'I thought you might hate me' Corey said 'what for?'.

'Getting pregnant' 'don't worry these things happen now I have a daughter you made me so happy come here'.

They hugged it felt nice she was happy he wasn't mad at her 'Steve would you like to see the baby?' 'I'd love to'.

'She's almost a month old she's a beautiful baby I think you'll fall in love with her' 'I'm sure I will'.

'I can't wait to see her' 'Polly did the nursery really nice in L.A and he's done a room for the baby here'.

Steve followed Corey to the baby's room 'she's beautiful' they watched her sleeping 'do you want to hold her?'.

'I don't want to wake her I can't wait to hold her she looks perfect to meI wish I don't regret our one night stand'.

'I can't believe I'm a father again I can't wait for her to meet her two older brothers'.

'I registered your name on the birth certificate'.

'I hope you don't mind' 'course not I'm proud to be her father' 'I put nationality American occupation Actor'.

'Since your Irish I guess she'll be Irish-American'.

'Looks like it my grandparents on my mother's side are Russian and Czech'.

'So she'll have eastern European heritage as well' 'she'll be multinational my mother's Jewish' Steve said.

'She wasn't born Jewish she married my dad converted to Judaism' 'well I'm Catholic'.

'But she can choose whatever religion she wants' 'well she's gorgeous like you' 'thanks we had her christened'.

'I hope your mother's ok about it' 'she'll be fine I haven't told her about the baby yet'.

'I wanted to get to know her first' 'I understand well tell her she can visit the baby if she wants' 'she'd love that'.

'My brother has four kids' 'well you can tell her she has another grandchild' 'I will she'll be so happy'.

'I'm so happy everything's ok between us' 'so am I you're a really good friend to me I never want that to change'.

'It never will' Corey assured him Steve kissed her on the cheek she was so happy Steve loved baby Susan.

And he was a good friend to her.

A week later after a fantastic Christmas Polly decided to have a New Year's Eve party at their apartment.

She invited Stacey and Christian and some close friends
Polly had made in America she loved playing hostess.
As she served champagne and cocktails quiches sausages
& pineapples on sticks.
Everyone seemed to be enjoying themselves Christian was
enjoying his first time in New York Stacey loved it there.
It was like their second honeymoon Corey was finally able
to enjoy herself after spending the last year pregnant.
She liked being able to dance around play her electric
guitar she was back with Polly after being separated.
Due to her film career things were going well Corey
couldn't wait to tour with the band.
Stacey was also feeling great after marrying the man of
her dreams she couldn't wait to have children.
with Christian when the time was right Polly was also
enjoying her business ventures launching a new perfume.
Producing films as well as opening the gay club with her
uncle Sam Adrian had been caught trying to break in.
Of course she had him arrested and vowed not to have
anything to do with him again 'hey more champagne?'.
'Thanks Susie' Stacey never drank much but it was
New Year's Eve after all 'cheers darling' 'cheers Susie'.
'It's such a nice apartment' 'I know Stace I love New York
I feel really at home here' 'that's good I love it too'.

'I'm happy in London for now though' 'well if you ever change your mind we could hang out together'.

'Well I'm doing my new movie really soon' 'it's a great party' 'thanks Stace I try my best' 'you're a great hostess'.

'I'm glad you could come' 'so am I Christian likes it too especially since it's his first time here'.

'Well I'm happy to help on your travels you make a great couple' 'I'm really in love for the first time ever'.

'That's great you picked really well Christian's lovely'.

'Is it ok Susie? I married my cousin' 'you said yourself your not blood related so it's ok' 'I guess'.

'Besides if my cousin looked as gorgeous as Christian don't worry what people say as long as your happy'.

'We are' 'hey Cor I was just saying to Stacey what a great couple you and Christian make' 'the best'.

'This champagne is lovely I'm so glad I can drink again'.

'Only the best for everyone' 'this is a great party and a great view of NYC' Christian said joining them.

'It's great you could be here' Polly said 'I wouldn't have missed it' everyone was having a great time that night.

Polly was sure they would be many more parties and good times ahead.

To be continued...

English Girl Irish Heart

Polly has grown up in Liverpool without her parents one day when she is thirteen she is rescued from a life in care. And sent to live in Ireland for a better life.
After her mysterious uncle Craig pays for her to go to an all-girls private school outside Dublin Angelsfields.
There she meets best friends Stacey and Romina.
Together they navigate their way through school, relationships and life.

Glamour Girl

Polly is seventeen and is training to be a hairdresser when she is spotted on Oxford Street in London .
As a glamour model as she becomes a celebrity it changes her life forever.
But life in showbiz is not all she thought it would be.
When manager Adrian tries to control her career music boss Steve offers her the chance to manage her.
Polly must decide if she still wants to be a star.

Spotlight

Polly has a successful career as a glamour model.
When she gets a role in a hit movie it takes her career to
another level and she becomes a Hollywood star.
Unhappy in her marriage she leaves her husband for close
friend Corey she must start another chapter in her life.
With Corey's parents refusing to accept her sexuality and
secrets from her past about to be revealed.
Can they have the happy ever after they deserve?

Out now in paperback & PDF